DRAWING FROM THE ARCHIVES

Following Art Spiegelman's declaration that "the future of comics is in the past," this book considers comics memory in the contemporary North American graphic novel. Cartoonists such as Chris Ware, Seth, Charles Burns, Daniel Clowes, and others have not only produced some of the most important graphic novels, they have also turned to the history of comics as a common visual heritage to pass on to new readers. This book is a full-length study of contemporary cartoonists when they are at work as historians: it offers a detailed description of how they draw from the archives of comics history, examining the different gestures of collecting, curating, reprinting, forging, swiping, and undrawing that give shape to their engagement with the past. In recognizing these different acts of transmission, this book argues for a material and vernacular history of how comics are remembered, shared, and recirculated over time.

Benoît Crucifix is Assistant Professor of Cultural Studies at KU Leuven and researcher at the Royal Library of Belgium (KBR), working on the FED-tWIN project "Pop Heritage". He coedited *Comics Memory: Archives and Styles* (2018) and *Abstraction and Comics* (2019). He is a member of ACME and a coeditor for the journal *Comicalités*.

CAMBRIDGE STUDIES IN GRAPHIC NARRATIVES

Editor

Jan Baetens, *Katholieke Universiteit Leuven*
Hugo Frey, *University of Chichester*
Martha Kuhlman, *Bryant University*

This series has been established to give readers access to the latest ground breaking research on graphic narratives. Combining meticulously researched historical studies with new theoretically rich critical engagements, it will publish the leading scholars at work today. Graphic narrative – the study of both comics and graphic novels, as well as other associated text-image materials – is a deliberately open approach that invites a move away from sterile, and too insider, discussions on the definition of forms. Works published in the series will be focussed on Anglophone and North American graphic narrative but will also explore where that milieu is central to the developments of 'world' graphic narrative. The series will upgrade notions of where graphic narrative has come from and where it is going next. It will provide original re-interpretation of classic works and bring to new attention missing masterpieces now ripe for re-evaluation. It opens a new conversation on how text and image combine to tell powerful stories that really matter. In a period of significant change in how texts and images are consumed via digital platforms, the series is intended to be a research landmark that will shape scholarly thinking and teaching through the 2020s.

DRAWING FROM THE ARCHIVES

Comics Memory in the Contemporary Graphic Novel

Benoît Crucifix

KU Leuven & Royal Library of Belgium

CAMBRIDGE
UNIVERSITY PRESS

CAMBRIDGE
UNIVERSITY PRESS

Shaftesbury Road, Cambridge CB2 8EA, United Kingdom

One Liberty Plaza, 20th Floor, New York, NY 10006, USA

477 Williamstown Road, Port Melbourne, VIC 3207, Australia

314–321, 3rd Floor, Plot 3, Splendor Forum, Jasola District Centre, New Delhi – 110025, India

103 Penang Road, #05–06/07, Visioncrest Commercial, Singapore 238467

Cambridge University Press is part of Cambridge University Press & Assessment, a department of the University of Cambridge.

We share the University's mission to contribute to society through the pursuit of education, learning and research at the highest international levels of excellence.

www.cambridge.org
Information on this title: www.cambridge.org/9781009250931

DOI: 10.1017/9781009250955

First published 2023

A catalogue record for this publication is available from the British Library.

A Cataloging-in-Publication data record for this book is available from the Library of Congress.

ISBN 978-1-009-25093-1 Hardback

The comics medium is a survivor.
              – Paul Karasik and Mark Newgarden

Contents

Figures

Acknowledgments

This book was written in quite a few places and different circumstances and owes thanks to many different people – any such list cannot but fail to account for everyone who helped in a big or small way; hence, the first persons I want to thank are the ones that I will have forgotten to remember here.

I am particularly grateful to the series editors Jan Baetens, Hugo Frey, and Martha Kuhlman for their encouragement and confidence in this work; and to the anonymous reviewers of this book for their eagle-eyed comments and their extremely thoughtful reading and challenging suggestions. The research behind this book would not have started without the support of a doctoral fellowship from the Fund for Scientific Research (F.R.S.–FNRS) in Belgium and could not have been completed without the stability of a postdoctoral contract at Ghent University, as part of the COMICS project funded by the European Research Council (ERC) under the European Union's Horizon 2020 research and innovation program (grant agreement no. 758502). In these contexts, I want to thank my advisors Björn-Olav Dozo and Véronique Bragard for their unflagging support, as well as the jury members Jan Baetens, Jared Gardner, Maud Hagelstein, and Fabrice Preyat for being such alert and attentive readers. A big thanks to Maaheen Ahmed for having shared so many thoughts and conversations about comics memory; and to my colleagues and friends at Ghent University for their caring support. At Ohio State University and at the Billy Ireland Cartoon Library & Museum (which I was able to visit thanks to the support of a travel grant from the Wallonia-Brussels Federation), many thanks to Project Narrative and to the incredible archivists and librarians Susan Liberator, Caitlin McGurk, and Jenny Robb.

I also want to thank the comics communities that have made my research feel worth continuing, always rekindling my curiosity, and the research networks and collectives like ACME and La Brèche that make those conversations possible. Special thanks to Julien Baudry, Philippe Capart, Sébastien Conard, Brian Cremins, Erwin Dejasse, Christophe Dony, Margaret Flinn, Jean-Paul Gabilliet, Simon Grennan, Jessica Kohn, Shiamin Kwa, Nicolas Labarre, Sylvain Lesage, Isabelle Licari-Guillaume, Ilan Manouach, Côme Martin, Gert Meesters, Jean-Matthieu Méon, Rachel Miller, Pedro Moura, Stéphane Noël, Christopher Pizzino, Noah Van Sciver, and Daniel Worden. Beyond the comics universe, thanks to Dennis, Lieven, and Serge, for the good times; David, Ida, Julie, Marie, and Clea, for making a home, where this book was finished; my parents, for their indispensable support; and Celien, for her lovely support and enthusiastic cheering.

Working on cartoonists' gestures of reframing, reusing, and redrawing other images sometimes led me down convoluted paths and toward nebulous copyright issues, reminding me each time of the multiple layers of mediation and actors when it comes to the transmission of past comics and maintenance of heritage. I am all the more grateful to the cartoonists, editors, permissions managers, and copyright holders who facilitated my obtaining permissions for the images used in this book – and, conversely, ungrateful for the barriers that made it impossible to reproduce other images. Some parts of this book have seen print in a previous version elsewhere, for which I am vastly indebted to the generous guidance and level of care and attention offered by the editors, as well as the constructive and detailed comments from the anonymous peer-reviewers. Chapter 2 is a revised version of a chapter originally published in the collective volume *Comic Art in Museums,* edited by Kim Munson (Jackson: University Press of Mississippi, 2020). A first, shorter version of Chapter 5 appeared as "Cut-Up and Redrawn: Reading Charles Burns's Swipe Files," *Inks: Journal of the Comics Studies Society* 1, no. 3 (2017): 309–33.

Introduction

The future of comics is in the past.

— Art Spiegelman

RT SPIEGELMAN'S APHORISM IS AN APT CATCH-ALL WHEN we talk about comics memory and the archival impulse in the contemporary North American graphic novel. With a playful adaptability typical of aphorisms, the sentence naturally lends itself to a wide variety of uses and contexts. If it makes for an opportune epigraph, there are more good reasons for using it as a starting point, especially if we resituate its invocation of a future within a particular present: at what point did it seem so urgent for comics to turn to their own past and why? Trying to locate one of the first occurrences of this aphorism leads us down a convoluted path to nearly apocryphal origins. Quoted again and again over the past two decades, Spiegelman's aphorism allegedly first appeared in print in Daniel Raeburn's short 2004 monograph on Chris Ware, where a footnote refers the reader to a telephone conversation between Ware and Spiegelman.[1] Besides its authoritative function, the phrase is used as a condensed description of the way innovation and tradition blend in Ware's graphic novels.

Dreaming up the future of comics requires a thorough understanding of their past, Raeburn argues, and if Chris Ware's experimentation with the form opens up new avenues, it is placed in a continuity with his intimate knowledge of the form's history. Accordingly, the monographic essay begins "in the 1820s," reaching back to Rodolphe Töpffer's *histoires en estampes* in order to draw a bridge with the graphic experiments of Chris Ware, whose *Jimmy Corrigan: The Smartest Kid on Earth* – a groundbreaking literary bestseller and prizewinner published in 2000 by Pantheon Books – ushered in a turning point for the graphic novel.[2] "Ware has escaped the comics ghetto," Raeburn quipped.[3]

By 2004, the graphic novel was indeed getting wider attention in the mainstream press, settling in bookstores, in classrooms and libraries, in galleries and museums. Graphic novels were being celebrated as the "next new thing, the new literary form," to quote from *New York Times* critic Charles McGrath's trendsetting article from that same year.[4] As much as they called for the new, the same graphic novelists were showing a joint fascination for older comics, making explicit their indebtedness to works, forms, styles, creators from the past, and hence nurturing a sense of tradition. For all their differences and idiosyncrasies, cartoonists such as Chris Ware and Art Spiegelman – but also Seth, Charles Burns, Daniel Clowes, and others – share a common visual heritage and an interest in passing it on to new readers and next generations. This interplay of new and old, innovation and tradition, rupture and continuity, is a puzzling phenomenon in the graphic novel, and yet one that has remained comparatively unaddressed.[5]

The generation of cartoonists who came into prominence at the turn of the millennium displays an intimate knowledge of comics history in their graphic novels. They have been actively engaged in producing, disseminating, and sharing this knowledge, assembling archives, and recirculating them in various contexts and settings, effectively acting as diplomats of comics memory for cultural and commercial institutions, for their peers, and for their readers. As Jan Baetens and Hugo Frey have observed, "the second career of major graphic novelists has been to act as historians of the field."[6] This book offers a full-length study of these contemporary cartoonists as comics historians. Graphic novelists are more often than not *auteurs* in the strong sense of the term: they usually strive to imprint their signature on all aspects of their work and operate as public figures.[7] Hence, there are plenty of situations, from interviews to museum exhibitions, in which they are licensed to display their appreciation of older comics and publicly assemble genealogies for their work – not to speak of the increasingly varied pedagogical settings, from art schools to university campuses, in which cartoonists are involved. In some cases, this might entail being drafted in by an institution to operate a selection from its archives, or by a publisher to repackage "classics" of comics history, or simply to contribute a preface to the reprinting of forgotten works.

Their canonical position in the field give their versions of comics history extra weight in the shaping of cultural memories of comics – and in their backward look, they inevitably leave out entire swathes of comics history[8] – and, given their public presence, make it tempting to follow the paths of declared influences. My main goal, however, is not to detail personal histories or individual artistic genealogies, or to produce lists of *who* or *what* makes up the personal pantheons of contemporary graphic novelists. Rather, I look into the variety of contexts and settings, practices and gestures through which contemporary cartoonists participate in the construction of historical knowledge about their own medium and in the transmission of this graphic heritage. This book thus offers a detailed description of *how* contemporary cartoonists draw from the archives of comics, examining the specific practices of collection, reproduction, exhibition, imitation, and appropriation that materialize and give shape to their engagement with the past. The diversity and intensity of this archival impulse demonstrate that older comics have continued to matter in the "new" graphic novels of the twenty-first century. This book goes after these acts of displacement and rediscovery, remembrance and monumentalization, with an eye for the variety of their objectives and material forms. This implies looking at settings in which traditional gatekeepers have a strong hold (the museum, the library, the book market) and where comics might willingly or not replicate the canonizing mechanisms of an official culture. But outspoken claims for legitimacy are not the only – or the most trustworthy – signs of a history in the making and this book pays particular attention to the smaller and little-noticed vernacular gestures that establish and sustain a relationship with the past in the margins of, or in collaboration with, more traditional mechanisms of preservation. These different contexts and settings impart different ways of mobilizing a comics history that needs to be understood as material visual culture. As cartoonists draw from existing archives, they rely on and enact different *gestures of transmission*: embodied acts that recirculate specific historical objects and, in the process, transform and adapt them to their new contexts.

COMICS MEMORY, C.2004

Before spelling out the theoretical and methodological premises of this inquiry, a cursory look at three examples – in line with Spiegelman's aphorism – will provide a first grasp on gestures of transmission in the post-2000 graphic novel. The same year that Raeburn's monograph came out, in 2004, Chris Ware edited an all-comics issue of the hip literary journal *McSweeney's Quarterly Concern*. The anthology was primarily a who's who of alternative comics artists and major graphic novelists, compiling sample contributions by leading figures such as Charles Burns, Daniel Clowes, Seth, Art Spiegelman, and many others. As much as it was building a sense of generational connectedness between contemporary authors, producing a community out of individual styles, the anthology was also tightening bonds with the past, tracing its own genealogy by integrating archival features on comics history, collecting drawn images, old newspaper articles, photographs, and short texts about departed cartoonists like George Herriman, Bud Fischer, Charles Schulz, and indeed the "inventor of the comic strip" Rodolphe Töpffer.[9] The self-definition of a generation is a matter of historical genealogies too.[10] The constant transformation of a medium and its changing social definitions necessarily reframe its history in retrospect. The institutionalization of the graphic novel has moved Töpffer's work – which was not completely unknown to North American fans but considered a kind of primitive antecedent to comics – to the center of its history. With its emphasis on authorial control over long-form narratives published in book form, the Genevan's "engraved stories" make for a more suitable starting point to the literary graphic novel than the traditional birth date of comics that fan-historians had situated in an 1895 *Yellow Kid* newspaper comic strip.[11]

While the *McSweeney's* anthology certainly participates in casting Töpffer as an inventor figure, the editorial choice to reproduce the first pages of *Mr. Obadiah Oldbuck* with its material idiosyncrasies (dog-eared, stained, colored in) somewhat muddles this linear narrative, highlights its contradictions, and undermines his status as the "benevolent father of the comic strip" (Figure 0.1).[12] Indeed, while Töpffer chose a printing technique that kept the spontaneity of his drawing (autolithography) and limited the circulation of his *romans en estampes* to a smaller group, his

Figure 0.1 *The Adventures of Obadiah Oldbuck* (New York: Wilson and Company, 1842), anonymously hand-colored.
Source: Collection of Robert L. Beerbohm. Digital scan of the facsimile reproduction published in *McSweeney's Quarterly Concern, Issue Number 13*, edited by Chris Ware (San Francisco, CA: McSweeney's, 2004), 24.

works were very quickly recirculated in unsolicited ways in more popular contexts, set to move beyond intellectual salons.[13] More than half a century later, the readers of the *McSweeney's* anthology find a facsimile reproduction of a pirated, translated, redrawn and engraved edition of Töpffer's 1827 *M. Vieux-Bois*, first published in the United States in 1842 using printing plates from an unauthorized British copy: "C'est lui et ce n'est pas lui."[14] The line from Töpffer to Ware appears to be a zigzagging one and, as Alexander Starre argues, the anthology schools its readers into a history of comics that is well aware of its material mediations, where the different reproductions, publishing formats, and unsolicited appropriations matter for the afterlives of such objects.[15]

Spring 2004 also saw the publication of the first volume of *The Complete Peanuts*, a comprehensive reprint of Charles Schulz's famous newspaper comic strip compiled by the alternative comics publisher Fantagraphics and designed by the Canadian graphic novelist Seth. By contrast, the point of the reprint was precisely to establish *Peanuts* as a complete oeuvre, spanning several decades, eulogizing the work of a cartoonist who had just passed away. The reprint was extremely popular and widely discussed, and met both significant praise and contesting voices, as Seth's graphic design reframed *Peanuts* in subdued colors, emphasizing its graphic poetry and its melancholy – a radically different choice from the popular gag-focused paperback collections of Schulz's comic strip. Not only did the commercial and critical success of the archival series reframe *Peanuts* for a new audience – compiling a daily comic strip as a classic to pass down for future generations – it also helped sustain its publisher in a new market, where the republishing of old material would find new steam as a commercial strategy within a burgeoning nostalgia industry.[16] Taken up in the literary publishing circuit – which graphic novels like *Jimmy Corrigan* helped substantiate – the mid-2000s would usher in a momentum of archival reprints, vintage editions, and other anthologies, many of them edited and designed by contemporary cartoonists.

Our last example returns us to where we started. Released in autumn 2004, Art Spiegelman's *In the Shadow of No Towers* set forth this archival impulse by juxtaposing a graphic memoir on post-9/11 New York and an anthology of Sunday newspaper comics from the early twentieth century within the same book. By reproducing, remixing, and redrawing century-old newspaper comics, *In the Shadow of No Towers* attempted to tap into these "vital, unpretentious ephemera" to try out different ways of making, adapted to an "end-of-the-world" moment.[17] The vulgarity and ephem-erality of old newspaper comics, alongside their responsiveness to polit-ical events of the day, embodied a liveliness and dynamism that cartoonists had come to long for in the era of the literary graphic novel. *In the Shadow of No Towers* indeed offered a radical departure from the main features associated with the graphic novel and that Spiegelman's 1986 *Maus* contributed to entrenching firmly. In terms of format, it was first serialized in newspapers and then collected as a large, bulky, cardboard book, closer to children's books than literary trade publications.[18] Instead of the long-length narrative that has been so important to the emergence of the graphic novel, we find a fragmented collection of single pages. Drawing-wise, while graphic novelists usually emphasize the handmade, personal quality of their drawn line, Spiegelman made a conspicuous use of computer graphics and image-editing software. The fountain pen and one-to-one ratio of *Maus* gave way to a combination of analog drawing and digital methods of copy and paste, duplication, rescaling, with these tools similarly applied to the reuse of comics fragments. Alongside this ragbag of hand-drawn panels and remixed comic strips, half the book further consists in a curated selection of full-color pages directly reproduced from Sunday newspaper comics supplements. The graphic novel's novelty lay as much in Spiegelman's graphic experiments as in the reproduction of these old newspaper comics at nearly full scale. Beyond the speculative dimension of Spiegelman's aphorism, *In the Shadow of No Towers* was very concretely set on allocating some kind of future to past comics by expanding the contact zone between archival practice and creative work in the comics world.[19]

At a turning point of its institutionalization and in a fast-changing media environment, the graphic novel thus prompted a fascination with the history of comics and a rediscovery of semi-forgotten works: by 2004, the graphic novel was a well-established phenomenon, and its stabilization opened up a moment when moving forward meant looking backward. This conjunction of forward move and backward look in the post-2000 graphic novel raises the larger questions that have guided this inquiry. How does the graphic novel retrospectively rework comics history? Why do contemporary graphic novelists turn to the past and what do they do with this heritage? How are cartooning traditions made and passed down? What means and techniques give shape to this transmission? What archives and materials do cartoonists handle in their creative and curatorial work? How do comics survive and circulate through time?

MEDIA CHANGE AND THE GRAPHIC NOVEL

The twenty-first-century North American graphic novel provides a compelling case through which to tackle these issues, precisely because the 2000s can be understood as a tangible moment of historical self-reflexivity. Placed against a more general background, there is a context of sweeping change and an accelerated pace for the lifecycles of cultural goods, where innovation has become a primer, if not an imperative, although this has simultaneously nurtured the fascination with memory and concomitant anxieties about loss.[20] This backward look further has to do with the wide-ranging transformations of the media landscape around the turn of the millennium and their more localized effects on the comics world. Comics have become increasingly brokered into larger cultural industries (Hollywood franchises in the case of comic book companies; the literary market and the general bookstore in the case of graphic novels and manga[21]) while timidly venturing onto new technological devices (digital reading platforms and viewing technologies, peer-to-peer networks, and the new genres of webcomics and digital-born graphic novels[22]). Every time comics are undergoing important changes, their history is opened up for revisions and reconsiderations.

Drawing on Thierry Smolderen's *Origins of Comics* for his history of French digital comics, Julien Baudry has pointed out the striking parallel developments of the twenty-first-century expansion of comics within a dense media ecology and the important historiographic debates of the last three decades: "our perception of what we can call 'comics' has considerably expanded in just a few decades, and the consequences of this expansion touch on its older history as much as its contemporary history."[23] These changes have put to test the narrow "sequential art" definition – one that remains implicitly widespread in Anglophone scholarship – in favor of more capacious and flexible models for envisioning the permutations of comics through time. The emergence and institutionalization of the graphic novel have had considerable effects in redistributing the boundaries that circumscribe our understanding of comics history. The space given to Töpffer in the *McSweeney's* anthology is a telling example of this feedback loop between the development of the graphic novel and historiographic debates in comics. Another striking example would be the history of the wordless novel, a form of visual narratives that had been nearly forgotten in the postwar era but that was vibrantly rediscovered with the graphic novel, providing new republishing opportunities and leading to all sorts of valorization of that global heritage by different stakeholders.[24] A good intermedial example of this process is Spiegelman's *Wordless!*, a musical slide-show lecture and "intellectual vaudeville show" on wordless comics by Wilhelm Busch, Frans Masereel, Lynd Ward, H. M. Bateman, and Milt Gross, all of which have gained a new relevance with the emergence of the graphic novel. The show worked simultaneously as public lecture and collective reading, as the image sequences were projected and accompanied by live music, providing for a different reading experience of these wordless comics – a hybrid scene that resonates with the messy mediascape of the early twentieth century, where film, animation, comics, and vaudeville acts dynamically feed into each other.[25]

By placing comics at the heart of complex intermedial entanglements, such media-genealogical approaches examine formal features as part of a complex and dynamic conjuncture of cultural practices, values and protocols, industrial and material constraints, technical and technological features, geographical topographies, and circulation infrastructures.[26] Definitions of comics are thus understood as functional and more or less tacit constructs that different groups, actors, and stakeholders develop "in a way that is directly related to the role they play in the form's existence."[27] Different definitions of comics suppose different histories: and these different tacit definitions, as they change over time, themselves are relevant traces for comics historiography.

Smolderen argues for the importance of a historical method to try to make these stakes legible, learning to recognize the "pieces and seams" that make up the "patchwork" of comics history, and which entails equal scrutiny for "sociological and technological bifurcations marked by the arrival of new commercial and institutional strategies" and for "the more constant 'traditions' that are transmitted from generation to generation of cartoonists, as well as the stylistic and thematic heritage – sometimes very old – from which they tap into for semiotic resources."[28] While histories of comics mark out sharp turns and focus on moments of rupture, they often struggle in accounting for the permanence of past works – or their neglect and erasure – beyond their moment of publication and for the processes of transmission that have allowed comics to sustain and adapt to change. To ask how cartoonists engage with the past, what they do with inherited works and traditions, is one way of considering the ceaseless interplay of mutability and stability, transformation and tradition that punctuates media history and its particular implications for the making of comics history.

The post-2000 graphic novel marks a moment of institutionalization of its "medium identity": it takes hold of a "radical change" while displaying a backward look to comics history as a means of palliating the potential violence of this distinction.[29] As Jan Baetens and Hugo Frey suggest, "comic books are far from dead, but the break that the graphic novel established (if even only symbolically achieved) has prompted much fascination with comic book history, literal and metaphorical."[30] In the United States, the graphic novel has been "indissolubly linked to a shift in status of comics from a low, minor cultural form to a very respectable one."[31] At its moment of coinage in the 1970s, the graphic novel was already a topic of debates in comics culture, spanning various uses and meanings and encompassing a much wider range of objects than the single example of Will Eisner's 1978 *A Contract with God,* as Paul Williams's detailed study of the period reveals.[32] Despite the variety of specific claims associated with the moniker since the 1970s, the graphic novel has been consistently associated with a distinctive logic and a strategic repositioning within cultural hierarchies, sometimes willingly embraced and reasserted, other times raising suspicion and caution among scholars, creators, and readers. In comics studies, the term has been and remains contested, as many see it as a problematic "narrowing of the field to a very small and unrepresentative canon."[33]

In *Arresting Development,* Christopher Pizzino critiques the narrative of "natural development from pulp infancy to literary adulthood" that has framed the understanding of the graphic novel. This dominant narrative brushes over a "history of conflict" marked by regulatory tendencies, heteronomous forces and cultural policing, illegitimacy and marginalization.[34] Pizzino's argument cautions us against the assumption that the cultural memories of comics manifest in today's graphic novels are a logical outcome of an organic development and a progressive legitimization, as if belatedly granting prestige to forgotten figures. Such development narratives tend to smooth out the complex and contradictory stakes of cultural memory. "Much is obscured when we look at the story of US comics as an organic process of growth towards adult artistic expression," as Pizzino writes, and contemporary cartoonists are often intimately aware of the pitfalls that come with legitimacy and respectability.[35]

Turning to the history of the form – one of "vital, unpretentious ephemera," to recall Spiegelman's words – can be a way of making visible these tensions.[36] In this regard, the fascination for the period building toward the 1954 Comics Code, when comic books were chastised as a bad influence on the youth, is telling for this memory of illegitimacy that has pervaded the graphic novel. Pizzino shows how contemporary cartoonists can efficiently bring up those painful memories by means of graphic citations: some panels reproduced in Fredric Wertham's *Seduction of the Innocent*, such as the "injury to the eye" motif, have for instance become iconic images that are regularly cited by contemporary creators.[37] Pizzino suggests throughout that contemporary graphic novels tend to foreground persisting discourses of illegitimacy on the page through a process he calls "autoclasm," a term he coins to describe "a commitment to working on the problem of illegitimacy in comics-specific terms and an expression of unwavering loyalty to the medium as such."[38]

While extending some of these claims by describing at length contemporary cartoonists' indebtedness to comics history, this book does not start from the same premises. If Pizzino's main interest is to highlight how the memory of illegitimacy works within the graphic novel to counter developmental discourses, the institutionalization of the graphic novel has gone alongside a wider range of engagements with the past and can be understood as a complex – if sometimes conflicted – negotiation between various stakeholders. In studying the specific gestures of transmission that express this commitment to the past, I argue that the variety of these situations cannot be completely subsumed under the expression of unwavering loyalty to the medium and a questioning of cultural authority. As cartoonists reframe, remake, or redraw past works in present times, such gestures can palliate the violence of cultural distinction in the context of the graphic novel, or perhaps enforce notions of cultural legitimacy, but also express interest, nostalgia, or attachment toward old comics for other reasons and purposes, and do so by particular means. Moreover, the backward look toward comics history in the graphic novel should not be taken as a straightforward indicator that the distinction between comics and graphic novels is a faulty one, superficially imposed from outside the comics world. That cartoonists acknowledge their indebtedness to comics history should not let us minimize the historical differences between various cultural objects and practices covered under the comics umbrella.

This is where the approach to the graphic novel advanced by Jan Baetens and Hugo Frey, who propose a non-essentialist and open definition, is useful because it helps "making room for differences" without endorsing an elitist stance and allows for a critical engagement with its various uses.[39] In this view, the graphic novel encompasses editorial and authorial attempts to explore different subjects, themes, and genres (memoir, autobiography, historical fiction, reflexive takes on popular genres), distinct ways of drawing (the choice and maintenance of a personal style) and telling stories (usually "uneventful" ones[40]). These features work distinctly only because of and in conjunction with particular techniques of production, distribution, and reception that have so far mainly embedded the graphic novel within literary circuits. For them, taking the graphic novel seriously has less to do with the disciplinary construction of graphic novels as new *texts* for literary approaches (sometimes blind to crucial elements of their working[41]) than with bringing a proper attention to the cultural and social *practices* that make a difference when it comes to understanding the graphic novel holistically. Hence, Baetens and Frey's suggestion that the graphic novel works as a distinct medium – recalling that a medium is understood as "something that changes all the time, although not always at the same rhythm, and that is characterized moreover by strong cultural variations."[42] Thinking of the graphic novel in this way allows us to bring out the stakes of drawing from the past: reframing old comics in the context of the graphic novel is a profoundly transformative operation because of the historical differences and material specificities that separate them. And, similarly, it invites us to complicate the terms of the dichotomy: this is less about marking a difference between graphic novels on the one hand and comics on the other than it is about acknowledging the multiplicity of historical objects and cultural practices that we regroup under the "comics" term.

This book casts new light on the contemporary graphic novel not by describing it in terms of innovations and transformations (whether in terms of content, style, narrative, format, editorial and cultural policies – by now a familiar story) but, rather, by placing at the heart of these transformations a reflexive relationship to its own historicity, concretized in the uses and appropriations of older comics that the graphic novel has lent to. When it comes to periodization, Paul Williams recalls in his account of the graphic novel in the long 1970s that "constructing comics history in terms of unified moments coming one after the other is otiose" as "historical periods are not homogeneous chunks of time that live for a season and are then replaced wholesale by a successor period."[43] He reminds us that the 1970s condenses a "wider network of backward glances and forward motions."[44] Looking at the post-2000 graphic novel, this book maps out such a network of backward glances and forward motions. It necessarily juggles two different temporal scales: a synchronic perspective, focused on the post-2000 graphic novel; and a diachronic one, necessary to account for the acts of transmission and the recirculation of cultural objects across time. The chronological boundaries of this research indeed encompass a recent temporal bracket, roughly set between 2000 and 2019, understood as a specific period in the longer history of the graphic novel. At the same time, by studying how the past is remembered and called upon at a particular moment, I look at how this contemporary moment is saturated with objects and images from a much larger chronology. This also requires understanding the longer histories of transmission that allow past works to survive in the present, and this book will frequently turn to older periods that have shaped today's cultural memory of the medium. Combining the synchronic and diachronic perspectives and maintaining these two scales in the analysis are fundamental methodological premises for understanding how transmission unfolds in time and mapping the changing conceptions of comics memory.

Attending to cultural memories of comics complicates histories of comics by thickening the issue of temporality, which can help us recognize different relationships to the past and to its density. As Will Straw argued in an article on popular music scenes: "Different cultural spaces are marked by the sorts of temporalities to be found within them – by the prominence of activities of canonization, or by the values accruing to novelty and currency, longevity and 'timelessness.'"[45] The cultural memory of comics – embodied in archives and material remainders, a reserve of graphic styles, genres, narratives, as well as techniques and social practices[46] – is a fundamental part of what has driven change and transformation in the North American graphic novel; if only already, as Charles Hatfield has shown, because fan nostalgia culture helped develop the very economic infrastructures that sustained and facilitated the emergence of the graphic novel.[47] But while the direct market was catering to a mostly male audience of comic book readers and collectors, alternative cartoonists turned away from the superhero comics that were dominating this market and reached out for other histories of comics, turning for instance to the newspaper supplements of the early twenty-first century. This choice of a different background is reflected in the preferred professional term that most authors of this generation go by, because of its connection with a particular tradition, as Seth declares:

> 'Cartoonist' I think . . . I always liked it because it had the right tradition behind it. Charles Schulz was a cartoonist and Frank King was a cartoonist. Harvey Kurtzman was a cartoonist. Doug Wright was a cartoonist. John Stanley was a cartoonist. Robert Crumb is a cartoonist. There's a long tradition to the term and I think it's an unpretentious term. Even 'comic book artist' has a bit of pretension to it because I think the seventies guys at Marvel and DC wanted to get away from the word 'cartoonist' since they thought it was a little bit derogatory. They saw the name 'cartoonist' as being connected to humor comics for kids or something like that.[48]

In describing his self-identification with the term cartoonist, Seth thus summons a list of "great authors" within his professional imaginary, echoing both fascinations shared with his peers (Schulz, King, Kurtzman, Crumb) but also more personal favorites whose work he has contributed to recovering and republishing (Wright, Stanley). Lists are common in comics culture, as Bart Beaty and Benjamin Woo have documented, and they indicate a particular way of distributing judgments of value.[49] Seth's list underlines an auteurist approach that is separated and distinguished from the authorizing strategies within superhero comics, but equally seeks to avoid adopting more pretentious self-definitions (rejecting the term "graphic novelist"). At the same time, this list should also call attention to some of its immediate blind spots: the profession that Seth adheres to appears as an all-male tradition.

"CANON" FODDER

If the post-2000 graphic novel has turned to the past with hopes to open up future directions, broadening the existing scope to accommodate new types of work, this retrospective gaze was also, unwillingly or not, founded on neglect and disregard, exclusions, and erasures. Today, the most striking blind spot in the historical interests of this generation of cartoonists is the absence of women. While female cartoonists have played a major and visible role in establishing the graphic novel and renovating its themes and forms in the twenty-first century, women's contributions to comics – in their occupations as cartoonists but also as publishers, editors, colorists, etc. – have largely been treated as expendable, sidelined and disregarded, when not actively erased from that history.[50] The generation of cartoonists examined in this book, all men who started producing work in the 1990s and gained wider recognition in the 2000s, has been largely oblivious to such omissions in comics history. Reading through the aforementioned *McSweeney's* comics anthology, Daniel Worden has described how it constructs a counterpublic of comics readers sharing in "intimacy, shame, and masculine melancholia."[51] While these cartoonists consciously turned away from superhero comics and the male-dominated fan subcultures, grasping for other models, they nevertheless ended up replicating some of those attributes in their own canons.

By then, the history of women cartoonists was not completely off the radar. Trina Robbins, who in the 1970s had been a major presence on the feminist underground comics scene articulated around *Wimmen's Comix*, had further started recovering the work of women cartoonists and of forgotten genres aimed at female readers: she coauthored a book on the topic with Catherine Yronwode in 1985, before following with her own *A Century of Women Cartoonists* in 1993 and *From Girls to Grrrlz: A History of Women's Comics from Teens to Zines* in 1999, bringing two landmark contributions that respectively charted a chronological overview of women cartoonists and the history of girls comics.[52] Robbins also devoted an entire monograph to the work of Nell Brinkley, a star illustrator and cartoonist of the interwar newspapers.[53] Aimed at a general audience, these books were repositioning women and girls within a comics culture from which they had seemingly been banned in the last three decades.

The difficulties in drawing from that heritage in the context of the graphic novel are telling when one considers *Neil the Horse*, a comic book series that, as Maaheen Ahmed argues, demonstrates the possibilities as well as the limitations of the 1980s direct market: written and drawn by Katherine Collins (then known as Arn Saba), the comic book series makes multiple references to comics for girls and for kids in its drawings styles and genre features, but engages with their paratexts, integrating paper dolls – drawn by Barbara Rausch and Trina Robbins – in order to introduce and present the "great women of the comics." In doing so, it tells a history of comics that "highlights the roles of feminine, girlish and childish elements, as well as the role of play and fan interaction to reconsider comics and comics memories."[54] Those elements were precisely losing currency in the "established order of what comics had become in the 1980s: serious, oriented towards the adult male, stamping out all the fun and games and variety."[55]

The overall omission of women in the canons, reworkings, and curations of the post-2000 graphic novel brings out a larger historiographic issue. If women's contributions to comics are sidelined and overlooked in histories of comics, this is because of the ways those histories have been written and conceptualized, biased by preferences for certain genres, formats, and models of authorship that have undermined the value of female roles and experiences.[56] The underground comics offer a case in point, precisely because they have provided "a foundation upon which both comics and comics studies have been built," replicating their exclusions.[57] Indeed, the generation of cartoonists studied in this book treads in the footsteps of figures like Robert Crumb and Art Spiegelman, as many of them contributed their first work in the magazines they coedited (respectively, *Weirdo* and *RAW*): they both manifested an interest in unabashed autobiography and in a tradition of cartooning that looked back to newspaper comics. Crumb has shaped the authorial model of the "modern art cartoonist" that lives on in the graphic novel today: "His use of traditional art materials, his affection for the history of cartooning and illustration, and his self-styled identity as a man out of time have informed the comics art and artistic personas of figures like Alison Bechdel, Ed Piskor, Seth, Noah Van Sciver, Carol Tyler, and Chris Ware."[58] By contrast, the heritage of *Wimmen's Comix* offers a very different reference point, founded on the collective and collaborative dynamic of an all-female periodical with rotating editorship rather than the promotion of a singular creative genius. As Margaret Galvan has argued, this collectivity is hard to account for in the archiving of these comics, as their archival record usually "falls short in usefully contextualising and representing the politics that structured the production of this series."[59] The grassroots networks of feminist and queer comics explore a different way of making comics at the margins of what has been remembered, and in so doing further call into question the formats, styles, narratives, and models of authorship that have been most valued in comics histories.[60] Writing a history of comics focused on women, but also on other marginalized identities and communities, sketches out a very different picture because it spotlights the importance of multiple workers (colorists and editors, for instance) and other publication venues (African-American newspapers), calling out the blind spots of the dominant narratives of comics history.[61]

It is important not only to acknowledge the gaps, exclusions, and erasures in the comics memory of the contemporary graphic novel but also to consider how this archival turn cannot be disentangled from the ethics and politics of troublesome pasts. Rebecca Wanzo's brilliant study of racist caricatures and citizenship in US comics threads the difficult legacy that comes with a medium that has relied so heavily on caricature for its graphic vocabulary and humor as a mode of visual imperialism. It makes for a problematic heritage to draw from, as "representations constructed in the past that haunt the present and still have the capacity to wound."[62] This capacity to wound remains vivid whenever contemporary cartoonists turn to a history of comics rife with racist and misogynist drawings. It is, after all, in the pages of the popular newspapers, which many contemporary graphic novelists are fascinated by, that such caricatures have thrived – and these are represented to modern readers whenever they are reprinted, reproduced, recirculated. Graphic novels like Chris Ware's *Jimmy Corrigan* and Art Spiegelman's *In the Shadow of No Towers* demonstrate that contemporary cartoonists are aware of the ethnic caricatures that come along with this American popular heritage and work through them to address the concerns of the political present and the legacy of state-based racism in the United States. Wanzo more specifically addresses these stakes for African-American cartoonists who, over the twentieth century and across various formats, have coped with this graphic vocabulary and the injury it has done and can still do: while it might sound counterintuitive, "many black artists and writers have responded to a popular resistance to the burdens of history by using stereotypical representations to explore the relationship between painful black pasts, presents, and precarious futures."[63]

The archival impulse in the graphic novel, in its most nostalgic undertones, thus raises a series of key problems and issues. As Baetens and Frey suggest in their analysis of nostalgia in the graphic novel, "the backward look to the past can seem limited and sometimes provoke more confusion than clarity," as "there is always a selection process around what is being recovered from the past and ... this is often about jostling for the future."[64] The retrospective gaze might flatten out comics history in a way that cartoonists themselves are sometimes aware of. Invited to contribute an afterword to an anthology of wordless novels, Seth confesses to the risk of anachronism and of an all too teleological understanding of the past: "Ultimately it's a mistake to see the sublimely crafted wordless novels as mere precursors to today's picture-novels. They stand on their own as fully realized artworks and don't need to be drafted into someone else's history."[65] This is a caution that we need to take heed of: the histories of comics that contemporary graphic novelists assemble in the present do not offer more truthful or accurate maps to the past (that is, after all, not their purpose). They always run the risk of reducing the complexity and historicity as well as the aesthetic value of such objects by recasting them as "mere" predecessors in a forward-moving history.

Jeet Heer has insightfully examined how Chris Ware, in designing and editing reprints of older comics such as *Gasoline Alley* and *Krazy Kat*, is "engaged in an act of ancestor creation, of giving a pedigree and lineage to his own work," through book designs that function "as a form of canon formation, a way of filling in the gap of missing archival and historical material and creating for comics a sense of continuous tradition and lineage."[66] The suggestion that Ware "invents" or "creates" ancestors follows Jorge Luis Borges's well-known essay on Kafka, which puts forward the idea that "each writer creates his precursors" in the sense that "his work modifies our conception of the past, as it will modify the future."[67] This combination of prospective and retrospective orientations underwrites a selective memory, to be sure: in the process of remembering, it voluntarily or unwittingly forgets many works and kinds of comics that do not easily fit within the contemporary context of the graphic novel, and recasts older comics in light of their current relevance. As Heer notes, "Ware offers an alternative canon that prizes cartoonists who practice either formal experimentation or focus on everyday life" and who, in this sense, "can all be understood as significant precursors to Ware's own artistic practice."[68]

It is here helpful to take the sociological hammer and strike while the iron is hot: those cartoonists best positioned in the field, those who have garnered most symbolic capital, will more or less implicitly contribute to setting the priorities and defining the canonizing policies of cultural gatekeepers. Different actors in the comics field will mobilize competing memories of comics depending on their position in this quadrature. The historical features of the *McSweeney's* anthology edited by Chris Ware or the reprint of Schulz's *Peanuts* by Fantagraphics dressed up by Seth hold stakes that are quite different from the management of "narrative memory" in the long serial catalogs of mainstream publishers such as Marvel and DC, for instance.[69] In this way, the past can sometimes be folded onto present concerns and the graphic novel can come to be seen as a reductive force, as when Beaty and Woo suggest that "recently reimagined as a kind of literature rather than a distinct medium or form, comics has borrowed so much from the literary field as to replicate it in miniature."[70] In the first decade of the twenty-first century, this literary upscaling of comics placed the graphic novel in a position of dominance, bearing on the weight given to comics history and the possibilities of its rediscovery: some past works appear more suitable than others as antecedents to the graphic novel, while others are not even envisioned as making part of that history.[71]

If the necessary critique of the contemporary comics canon has acted as a welcome and necessary invitation to expand attention to comics that have been overlooked and forgotten, such explorations of the archival past do not necessarily dispense with acts of selection and judgment values associated with canonization. As Beaty and Woo suggest, canonicity remains a relatively unstable notion in comics, as a field that is still moving fast and in the context of a digital "era of cultural plenitude," where the authority of traditional gatekeepers is in decline and which has seemingly facilitated widespread access (while raising new issues in terms of data monopolies and attention economy): but even then, "canons persist," if only as a "practical necessity."[72] Reminding us that "there are many ways to constitute a canon (whether personal or collective) in the margins of the traditional 'official' methods of literary historiography," Jan Baetens and Ben de Bruyn have underlined the importance of studying canonization as a heterogenous and contingent phenomenon that confronts us with the complex question of time in literature: cultural objects often belong to a multiplicity of temporal moments.[73] As John Guillory argues, in a comment on a classic essay by Erwin Panofsky, the dynamic interplay between "monumentality" and "documentality" – which we can rephrase here in terms of canon and archive – characterizes the object of study in the humanities as an object "given in time," marked by "its capacity to call to us over a gap in time": the object of the humanities, in this sense, "is always responsive to the present moment, to the ongoingness of historical time."[74]

COMICS AND THE ARCHIVAL TURN

While canonization has emerged as an important matter of concern in comics studies, comics in the twenty-first century also have to be considered through the corollary question of the archive. Comics archives take a new relevance around the 2000s. In his study of the nostalgic feelings of 1960s comics fanzine writers, Brian Cremins comes down to the following conclusion, in the face of the multiplication and institutionalization of comics archives in the twenty-first century: "The role of an archive is to make nostalgia obsolete."[75] The phrase itself has a nostalgic tinge to it: contemporary archives are making the stuff of the past accessible in ways that the same fanzine makers could only have dreamed of. Where fanzine makers of the 1960s were dedicated to recovering childhood readings that had often been lost, forgotten, or discarded, the twenty-first century opens up a time in US comics history when its archives are incomparably available: the institutional comics collections in the university libraries of Michigan State and Columbia; the Billy Ireland Cartoon Library and Museum at Ohio State; but also the many archival reprint collections from publishers; an extensive second-hand retail market; online public-domain repositories like the Digital Comics Museum as well as unauthorized networks of sharing and disseminating scanned comics. Since the 1960s, comics have indeed gradually assembled ways of sharing and accumulating their archives that have coalesced into established practices and sometimes moved into official institutions. Comics are in the midst of an "archival moment" that, as Stuart Hall reminds us, is a crucial one precisely because it defines the contours of its history: "The moment of the archive represents the end of a certain kind of creative innocence, and the beginning of a new stage of self-consciousness, of self-reflexivity in an artistic movement. Here the whole apparatus of 'a history' – periods, key figures and works, tendencies, shifts, breaks, ruptures – slips silently into place."[76] North American comics, which have been particularly tied to ephemeral formats of publication and rarely deemed worthy of preservation, make for an interesting case through which to grasp such a transition. Treading with caution, we should be careful not to fold this shift from "creative innocence" to "self-reflexivity" onto a story of progressive legitimization, as a normative course from a naively nostalgic engagement with the past to the development of a historical method or a self-conscious memory. Keeping in mind Pizzino's critique of development discourses, the historical self-reflexivity of the post-2000 graphic novel cannot simply be assumed as a logical consequence of a medium reaching maturity.[77] And, indeed, Stuart

Hall – writing about the archives of the black and Asian diasporas – is undoubtedly well aware of these concerns as he begins to pay tribute to those working "in very informal, personally taxing and under-funded ways."[78] Archiving and collecting, Hall further underlines, span a range of heterogeneous practices, "partly public, partly private," ranging from the "most buried, most inaccessible, most unrecoverable end of the archive" to the "conscious policies of collection and selection, of display and access" in public spaces.[79]

It is telling that the "moment of the archive" in comics overlaps with the broader "archival turn" that gained momentum in the late 1990s and that opened fresh avenues and perspectives both in archival practice and in conceptual reflections on the archive,[80] across a broad range of field and media from photography and film to contemporary art and the history of sciences.[81] By the turn of the millennium, traditional understandings of the archive as an institutional site of storage for historical records and documents were being unsettled, on the one hand by new critical voices that questioned their politics of memory, and on the other by the electronic and digital transformations pushing at the doors at the time. The cultural historian Ann Laura Stoler has described this turn as a "move from archive-as-source to archive-as-subject," a move dealt with differently on either edge of a disciplinary line between historians, for whom the archive is "a body of documents and the institutions that house them," and cultural theorists who have embraced the concept as "a metaphoric invocation for any corpus of selective collections and the longings that the acquisitive quests for the primary, originary, and untouched entail."[82] This "archival turn," as Kate Eichhorn suggested, was less the sudden change frequently ascribed to the idiom than it "has proven to be a much longer preoccupation than many other recent 'turns' in cultural theory."[83]

This division between two understandings of the archive – one practical and material, the other conceptual and theoretical – has similarly given ground to collaborations and convergences between both conceptions.[84] The necessary feedback loop between archival practice, conservation policies, and conceptual theorization has been accelerated by the spread of digitization and the impact of digital technologies of memory, intensifying the data glut while profoundly transforming the status of documents, their stability, and their uses.[85] The way digital archival practices have reshaped thinking about cultural memory is made clear in what Abigail De Kosnik, in a study of online fan fiction archives, has described as "rogue archives" in contrast with the main precepts we usually take for granted from institutional repositories or from enterprises of the heritage industry. Maintained by amateurs, fan-curated and bottom-up, rogue archives not only emerge to collect that which does not belong to official culture (they are anti-canonical by definition), they put more emphasis on circulation, proliferation, and reuse than on authenticity, longevity, and stability, they aim at strengthening communities and enhancing participation, and they uphold a loose or willfully disruptive relation to copyright law.[86] Rogue archives further unsettle the chronology of archives as records and sources: "Memory has gone rogue in the sense that it has come loose from its fixed place in the production cycle. It now may be found anywhere, or everywhere in the chain of making."[87] Athough De Kosnik's argument bears on digital cultural memory specifically, her description of "rogue archives" invites broader reconsiderations of the role played by amateurs and nonprofessional archivists in initiatives of cultural memory and transmission in the margins of official or institutional strategies of preservation.

Bearing in mind the heterogeneity of archival practices, between private and public, between institutional policies and grassroots initiatives, comics no longer appear as an "art without memory," as one of their most influential theorists once put it in an effort to pinpoint the difficulties in maintaining "classics" in print.[88] Thierry Groensteen had indeed identified a paradox of memory in comics: "if it artificially maintains alive some series whose popularity has been transmitted from one generation to the next, at the same time comics is an art that voluntarily cultivates amnesia and shows little concern for its heritage (*patrimoine*)."[89] The phrase hits a good point and reminds us of the disparities that necessarily organize and sort out what makes up the memory of the medium. Commercial imperatives, publishing practices, and material formats weigh in heavily on what is left forgotten and what gets remembered and how. While comics supposedly lack the modes of canonization and memorialization long available for higher arts, we cannot only retrace the history of their memory as the slow emergence of its cultural legitimacy, its dedicated libraries and museums, its recognition as a national heritage worthy of government policies, all of which have become new issues around the turn of the twenty-first century. This progressive legitimization builds on a longer history of preservation, transmission, and recirculation implicating a wide range of other actors – creators, publishers, fans, readers, editors, and book-sellers, among others.[90]

This "moment of the archive" for comics and graphic novels further needs to address the digital age, which has accelerated the twinned problems of accumulation and limited attention that have come with the modern mass-industrial production of cultural objects. According to Jared Gardner, who provides an extensive discussion of archives and collectors in graphic novels of the 1990s and 2000s, this new cultural paradigm requires "disciplines and skills" that "lie somewhere between 'data mining' and 'dumpster diving,' between analysis and scaven-ging," and that comics makers and readers have long been rehearsing.[91] For Gardner, comics creators and readers are indeed well equipped for this era of iconotextual overbundance because they have often had to engage with fragmented narratives and organ-ize their own archives through collecting. An important part of his argument indeed rests on the suggestion that comics share formal similarities with archives: as narratives made of fragments distributed in space (on the page, as well as across several pages and serial install-ments), they amount to "a visual archive for the reader's necessary work of rereading, resorting, and reframing."[92] The ubiquity of col-lectors and archivists in the pages of contemporary graphic novels indicates the relevance that these skills take in a digital media environment.[93] This archival impulse, I suggest, is not only at work in the graphic novel's thematic interest in collectors. If the formal kin-ship between comics and archives that Gardner describes indeed invites the work of "rereading, resorting, and reframing," contempor-ary cartoonists – as collectors and readers – have literally engaged in such material acts: comics not only hold a symbolic relationship to the archive as a "database form," they in fact substantiate archives to draw from in a myriad of ways.

GESTURES OF TRANSMISSION

By analyzing diverse material operations of sorting through the past, I draw attention to a wider scope of gestures that are brought on to recirculate materials from the archives (in the "loosest, messiest sense of the term" that such collections summon us to adopt) and to compose with comics as archives on their own terms.[94] The value that creators and readers find in past comics is inseparable from the gestures that compose their relationship to that past, the means and techniques used to recirculate, transform, reproduce, exchange, barter, preserve, or even destroy older comics.[95] Thinking about cultural memory and its transmission in terms of gestures emphasizes an anthropological approach attentive to the repeated actions, their materiality and situatedness, as well as their performativity in making what is being transmitted.[96] This places the very process of *drawing from the archives* at the heart of our inquiry: both as a process of selection out of whatever remains from the past and as a gesture that remakes its objects through distinct material acts of copying, reproducing, redrawing – a range of appropriations that entail a more or less significant kind of graphic intervention or manipulation.[97]

Comics gather a visual and a material culture, made of drawn lines and visible marks as well as techniques of inscription and reproduction.[98] Any engagement with their past necessarily involves an intervention into the visual and material properties of past works, and hence a more or less significant transformation of the ways of looking and reading that are brought onto them. The different gestures of transmission that displace earlier comics necessarily vary depending on the objects that are handled in the process, attending to their material properties and their particular contexts of inscription and preservation. Such gestures can engage various scales and breadth and different formats: from exhibiting original pages to reprinting entire series, from redrawing a single panel to sifting through large online corpora.

Seemingly small differences show the significant diversity and specificities that these gestures can take, depending on the particular histories of the works that are reproduced, copied, recirculated. Töpffer's nineteenth-century engraved stories and Schulz's *Peanuts* comic strip make for very different objects to grapple with: the first are in the public domain and were recently made available in digitized repositories; the second is an active brand with strong copyright and license policies and a global merchandising scheme. Past comics come with more or less accessible or usable archives, but also with their own formal and aesthetic questions, their histories of preservation and reproduction, various formats, readers' memories and expectations. When Chris Ware anthologizes a famed predecessor in the choice of a particular archival item reproduced in facsimile, when Seth manipulates image fragments sampled from Charles Schulz's fifty-year-long body of work, when Art Spiegelman revisits early-twentieth-century comic supplements, they not only distribute and construct canonical value but do so by selecting, handling, transforming, and actualizing a collective memory of comics embedded in graphic styles, narratives, publishing formats, and material objects. Such gestures of transmission, in the twenty-first century, take place on a large spectrum "between pen and pixel" – whether it is highly visible, as in Spiegelman's software design, or in less visible digital files, software, and reproduction technologies, as in the cases of *The Complete Peanuts* and the *McSweeney's* anthology.[99]

Without aiming for exhaustiveness and calling out to multiply the different gestures that give shape to comics cultures, this book proposes a taxonomy of gestures of transmission in the post-2000 North American graphic novel: collecting, curating, reprinting, forging, swiping, and undrawing as different possible ways of drawing from the archives of comics history. Through a series of case studies selected for their salient and heuristic value as examples illustrating specific practices, each chapter focuses on a gesture of transmission and the issues it raises for comics memory. Chapter 1 tackles collecting as a necessary premise for understanding the constitution and accumulation of materials to sustain further reuse. Chapter 2 explores the reframing of comics history in its most literal sense, by looking at the museum and the curated exhibition, institutional settings that have traditionally defined a curatorial engagement with past works as things to gather, collect, preserve, and display. While the reframing of older comics in the exhibition space raises issues of its own, the process of reprinting is a similarly delicate one as it displaces past comics from their ephemeral print context to the book – this shift is the core issue tackled in Chapter 3. Chapter 4 examines the forging of archives, looking at graphic novels that present their readers with a reflexive game of invented cartoonists and pseudo recoveries. Chapter 5 proposes aligning citational tactics in the graphic novel on the historical axis of swiping, which draws attention not only to the process of copying itself but also to that of collecting images and assembling reference files. Finally, Chapter 6 considers the increased interplay between archiving and making in the digital environment, as a productive space for the development of "uncreative" comics. The organization of the individual chapters follows a general move from the most institutionalized settings – the library and the museum, the editorial reprint market – to "rogue" practices of memory, less focused on long-term preservation and sometimes in the gray zones of extralegal activity – copying, appropriation, remix. It will quickly become clear that each of these practices in fact engages a variety of gestures and often implies various skills, techniques, and habits crisscrossing throughout.

The variety of these gestures illustrates what the French theorist and conceptual artist Franck Leibovici has called "*des opérations d'écritures qui ne disent pas leur nom*" ["writerly operations that do not tell their name"], highlighting a range of ordinary practices that engage with texts and documents in ways that have not been traditionally considered as writing because of the literary emphasis on stable and closed texts.[100] Thinking in terms of gestures similarly shifts the emphasis to actions and processes and calls for a mode of inquiry attentive to the local specificities and contexts for such practices. For comics, this calls for a reconsideration of drawing and the nexus of activities that accompanies it.

This book contributes to situating graphic style not so much as individual expression but as a highly socialized act, both in terms of synchronic collaboration and in the way that it participates in constructing historical communities of creators based on a visual heritage that is transmitted across generations. As recently highlighted in a collective volume on graphic style in comics, the notion of "heritage" in comics is essential because it "determines both the maintenance of practices, methods, artistic choices that condition the unity of a medium in time, and at the same time allows for its ceaseless evolution and hence actualization in the light of the readers' preferences, the evolution of techniques and other media."[101] The notion of "heritage" is central in producing a sense of the historicity of the medium, and understanding graphic style on a temporal and historical axis is crucial to grasping the complex dynamics of continuity and change. Central to their focus is the imitation and appropriation of individual styles that, in turn, become generic or collective: for all sorts of reasons, cartoonists often participate in the "fixation" of their own styles that makes them more easily adaptable and reproductible, defining particular filiations.[102]

To understand this interplay of individual and collective styles, and the changing rhythms that make up comics history, we have to push the study of such "stylistic circulations" beyond the examination of development of individual styles through the imitation of and emancipation from cartooning masters to broaden the scope of actors involved in the transmission and maintenance of graphic styles. We need to look at how past graphic styles as well as concrete comics images are passed down and recirculated through time, in sometimes little-noticed ways.[103] This requires us to consider second- or third-hand gestures of reproduction, circulation, appropriation, together with the redistribution of authorial and graphic identities they imply. To understand the inherited framework that sustains the work of many graphic novelists, we need to attend not only to the specific genealogies of their individual graphic styles (even if those do matter, of course) but also to the broader gestures of transmission that run alongside or within their cartooning practice, and that contribute to producing the very notion of a "heritage." In recognizing these different acts as specific gestures of transmission, this book argues for a material and vernacular history of how comics are remembered, shared, and recirculated over time.

CHAPTER 1

Collecting

I hate to argue for less cultural access but that was a time where the cartoonists of my generation were forced to find their own ancestors.[1]

Seth

C OLLECTING, AS SETH HAS SUGGESTED IN MULTIPLE INTER-views, was an important process for his generation, in pursuit of "a kind of artistic archeology that you were required to go through," because access to comics history was extremely patchy before the spread of personal computers, the Internet, and online retailing.[2] The import-ance of an individual process of collecting, of sifting through garage sales and second-hand bookstores to piece together a personal collection of ephemera as part of a "fundamentally autobiographic narrative," has been essential to this postwar generation of cartoonists.[3] Jared Gardner has underlined the ubiquity of such collectors and unofficial archivists in the contemporary graphic novel, taking as key examples the works of Ben Katchor, Kim Deitch, Seth, and Chris Ware, where "the adventures of superheroes and their villainous counterparts have been replaced with the seemingly more mundane tales of collectors, the compulsive combers of archives, warehouses, and dumpsters."[4] Extending Gardner's analysis, Henry Jenkins has analyzed in great detail the way Seth's graphic novels produce "stories constructed by and for collectors," normalizing certain practices that had been a common part of comics fan culture.[5] Both reveal the importance of collecting and collector culture within the contemporary graphic novel and sustain a relationship to the past that is tangible in material objects.

Those accounts, however, emphasize the private and personal dimension of collecting, as is told in the graphic novels of Seth, Ware, and other key figures of the contemporary graphic novel. This chapter charts a somewhat different aspect of collectors and the archives they assemble: I am less interested in the graphic novelist as a collector than in their indebtedness to previous collections and the new uses they invent for them. In order to understand the archival impulse in the contemporary graphic novel, I propose to attend to an earlier moment in the history of comics, one that precisely framed collecting as part of a media-historical conversation and in a context of changing ideas about cultural value, preservation, reproduction, and access.

COLLECTORS' ARCHIVAL WORK

For the largest part of their history, North American comics have been published on transient matter: the newsprint of comic strips and the low-end paper of comic books were not materials meant to last beyond the time it took to read them, making them more likely to be reused as wrapping paper or indoor insulation than preserved for posterity. "In the United States," as Alexander Starre notes, "the bond between comics and their storage and reproduction media has been precarious from the very start."[6] The importance given to serial logics and there being a ceaseless stream of new products within a recognizable framework have indeed been fundamental imperatives of both the comic strip and the comic book business (extending the same logics of modern cultural industries).[7] The serial logic of proliferation can be a powerful way of sustaining narratives and properties over long periods of time and across generations; it is also a mode of transmission that privileges circulation over continuity and preservation, making little case for archiving practices that have no justification in the economic rationale of publishing companies.[8]

In media-archeological fashion, Darren Wershler has unearthed a minute detail in the DVD archive for *Fantastic Four*, in which Marvel extended thanks to a collector who had provided the original issues for its digitization project (a mention that would disappear from later digital versions): "Certainly not having imagined a digital future in which an original copy of *Fantastic Four* would be needed again after its 1970 publication, Marvel was rather lucky that Eric Sluis was a better archivist than they were."[9] It might seem an anecdotal detail, but the case nevertheless speaks volumes about the extent to which tacit assumptions about the duration, obsolescence, and archival value of cultural objects will partly shape the possibilities of their future iterations. It indicates how archival practices might come from the ground up and highlights how the items in the "latent memory" of the archive hold the potential to be unexpectedly returned to light.[10]

The same serial logics that make yesterday's newspaper obsolete further habituate audiences and solicit dedicated consumers, producing affective attachment and fostering personal reading memories.[11] A landmark survey like Mel Gibson's "reader's history of comics," which analyzes readers' memories of girls' comics in the UK, demonstrates that the habits and ordinary practices of comics reading have a long impact on memories that are at once personal and collective.[12] The affinities of comics with serial culture have thus frequently elicited and supported ways of remembering works from the past, maintaining archives (even if precarious ones), copying, reproducing, and recirculating material – all activities that have embedded comics within a sense of historicity. Such acts of transfer, even if they have rarely been the work of professional historians and trained archivists, have nevertheless contributed to sustaining some form of transmission, passing down certain works, knowledge, and practices, transferring a particular know-how, or simply encouraging and inspiring others to take up these memory-making activities in turn.

The fan subcultures that emerged around comics in the United States in the late 1950s most visibly worked to embed the medium within a longer temporality, sometimes circumscribed by nostalgia for childhood reading. Such fan subcultures have produced particular forms of knowledge (such as identifying individual artists who worked anonymously, distinguishing periods that punctuate the history of comics and give structure to collecting practices) and facilitated the survival of selected works (by collecting, swapping, sharing, reselling, reprinting).[13] Comics archives have been mainly constituted by collectors, fans, and dedicated consumers assembling their own collections and records of their comics reading (often started in childhood). The constitution of organized fandom, with its fanzines, correspondence barter, second-hand retail, conventions, and price guides, has shaped postwar comic book culture. In this sense, "nostalgia ... has been structured into the trade in old comics."[14] Collecting is a well-known practice in North American comic book culture, described with great nuance in ethnographic and sociological accounts of comics fandom.[15]

It is also one that tends to segment its participants alongside gender lines. As Mel Gibson has demonstrated, comics fandom and its collecting culture have regularly sidelined girls' comics, which meant that they barely survived on the collectors' market and that anyone setting out to write their histories is necessarily confronted with the lack of archives.[16] As Galvan has further demonstrated in her compelling work on queer grassroots networks, comics historiography needs to look beyond the canon of "published and available texts," not only by digging into archives but also by searching elsewhere than in the archival comics collections, whose structure often replicates the gendering of comic book culture and the traditionally male-dominated spaces of its fandom.[17] Comics history is dependent on sites of memory that have cultivated a particularly gendered nostalgia, while actively forgetting many other works. The archives that the contemporary graphic novel often turns to are ones that, to a large extent, are sediments of these gendered collecting practices. And although graphic novelists have turned away from the direct market and the network of comic book shops as they were in the 1990s, their visions of comics histories are partly defined by fan practices in the 1960s and 1970s – as much so as they originate from the historical traditions that were renovated in the underground comix.

SAN FRANCISCO, 1968

In the United States, the underground comix movement is often understood as a turning point for the development of "adult comics," with the investment into alternative distribution models, the establishment of new values and ideas for emerging creators, and the cultivation of personal style and artistic expression against the comic book industry. As concisely summed up by Charles Hatfield: "The countercultural comix movement – scurrilous, wild and liberating, innovative, radical, and yet in some ways narrowly circumscribed – gave rise to the idea of comics as an acutely personal means of artistic exploration and self-expression."[18] It is a well-known story that underground comix have often tied their birthdate to a much-repeated anecdote: on February 25, 1968, Robert Crumb and his eight-months-pregnant wife Dana took to the streets of Haight-Ashbury in San Francisco to sell the first issues of *Zap* out of a baby stroller.[19] For all the legend tied to the artistic persona, Crumb is perhaps better understood in "his significant historical function" as an example of "a cartoonist who inherits, reworks, and maintains rather than invents certain American comic and visual traditions."[20] Indeed, Crumb's characteristic style was looking back to a range of newspaper-comic styles, from the approach to cross-hatching to the "rubber hose" style in comics and animation. As the underground cartoonist Sharry Flenniken, whose own drawing style was inspired by cartoonists like H. T. Webster or Clare Briggs, recalls in a 1991 interview: "Everyone was trying to develop their own original style, but, if you look, you can really see, like, Robert Crumb's influences in *Popeye* and all that stuff. Everybody had those things, but nobody was very blatant about it."[21]

While it makes for a duller anecdote, a few days after Crumb's distribution of *Zap* comics and several blocks away from Haight-Ashbury, newspaper-comics collector and historian Bill Blackbeard was assembling and signing the articles to officially set up the San Francisco Academy of Comic Art (SFACA) as a nonprofit association. The board for the association was composed of a sundry group of fans and collectors: friends from the science-fiction fandom in San Francisco; newspaper-comics aficionado Woody Gelman, also artistic director at the Topps company (where he put many cartoonists to work); comics fans Don and Maggie Thompson; West Coast jazz lover and French *bédéphile* Alain Tercinet, graphic designer for the comics fanzine *Giff-Wiff* launched in 1962. The list also included Crumb, although it is unsure whether he ever signed the articles.[22] The moment is nonetheless important: it marks the start of a significant shift in the archival status of newspaper comics. Creating a nonprofit allowed Blackbeard to become the legal benefactor of old newspapers that US public libraries were discarding in favor of their microfilmed versions.[23] Or, as Blackbeard later explained: "The library could not give any of its books or papers to any private citizen and they could not sell them, only transfer them to another institution or destroy them. So, I became another institution."[24] Over the next decades, he gathered a massive amount of newspapers from libraries all over the United States and assembled an archival collection dedicated to newspaper comics. In 1997, as Blackbeard was caught in a dispute with his landlord over leaky pipes, his six-semitrucks-load collection was moved to the Ohio State University Research Library (to become the Billy Ireland Cartoon Library & Museum).[25]

Blackbeard is somewhat heroically remembered today as "the man who saved the comics" against the threat of potential loss – whether by destructive disposal or simple disregard.[26] While we might retrospectively take for granted the value of the newspaper comics saved by Blackbeard, this is at least partly due to the sheer act of saving them. As some heritage scholars argue, it is not always clear whether an object is saved because it has intrinsic value or if it has value because it is being saved and taken care of.[27] Loss is continuous and persistent as much as it is necessary; it is more often the result of passive acts of forgetting, neglect, and indifference than conspicuous destruction. Hence, it takes a change in value and perception to actually see any loss as such. As Judith Schlanger writes: "[I]t is the judgement of loss that makes the loss, and this judgement is cultural – both local and historical, and very deep; both social and intimate."[28] Where some librarians saw in the microfilm an efficient progress, Blackbeard identified it as a major loss. For treasuring an archive assembled from disposed-of newspaper volumes, Blackbeard holds a particularly important place in the thickening of comics memory in the 1960s and 1970s, reframing ephemeral newspaper-comic strips as material cultural heritage and negotiating ongoing issues of preservation and reproduction, storage and materiality.

While Blackbeard was connected with a network of collectors with similar interest in old newspaper comics, he contributed to shifting this act of saving from private collecting to public archiving, assembling a collection of materials that was both a "one-man curatorship" and meant to be visited, studied, drawn from, used, and reused.[29] As Jenny

Robb remarks, Blackbeard flouted the lines between private collector and public curator: "[I]t seems the San Francisco Academy of Comic Art was something of a hybrid entity, not entirely private yet not wholly public either."[30] Cartoonists, collectors, and fans would have visited his treasure trove as Blackbeard had installed a reading room for the purpose, and the materials comprising his archive sustained the reprint enterprises of the late 1960s and 1970s, in most of which Blackbeard was closely involved.

The flurry of comic strip reprints in the 1970s often directly sourced their materials from the archive assembled by Blackbeard and the collection has continuously provided pages for many reprint projects up to now. Constituting an archive was not only a necessary step for renewing circulation of older comics, it fundamentally shaped how comics would be remembered and read for decades to come. It is in this context that reprinting and archiving became closely intertwined, yielding the very concepts of the "archival reprint," the "archive edition," and the "archival collection" that guide a significant wedge of today's editorial ideas about reprinting.[31] Beyond a question of cultural value, we would miss part of the picture by simply streamlining Blackbeard's role into the history of a progressive legitimization of comics. Rather, a genealogy of notions of historicity in comics culture demands that we situate Blackbeard's archive within a media-historical context in which the very meanings of archiving and reproducing were being opened up again, both within and outside the traditional institutions of memory. Without in any way diminishing his lasting contribution, it can be said that Blackbeard's role gains from being understood against a wider background that involves larger transformations in terms of preservation discourses.

COMICS FILES

For various media cultures in 1970s North America, as Lisa Gitelman argues in a media history of documents, "xerographic reproduction helped shift the meanings of reproduction from access to archive."[32] Photocopying was used not only as a technique of distribution but also, and most importantly, as a "technique of preservation, an embrace of plenitude and redundancy."[33] As such, the Xerox machines that came into widespread use in the 1970s bureaucratic environments put forward key questions of reproduction, preservation, openness, and self-possession in a way that also helps to explain the renewed role that microfilming would take in archival policies. A reproduction technique that libraries had been starting to use since the 1930s, microfilm started to become more widespread for archival use conjointly with the photocopier, which might explain how it came to be seen as a preservation technology in its own right in the 1960s. As much as the underground comix movement and the fanzine scenes were intimately related to cheaper offset printing and the new copy shops that settled around university campuses in the 1960s, the founding of Blackbeard's academy was at least partly a result of changes in reproduction protocols: his archive was indeed directly assembled as a response to changing preservation practices that organized the relationship between information, documents, and their media technologies in US libraries.

Confronted with an expanding proliferation of paper and in the context of an increasing "heritage overload," libraries understood microfilming as a cost-saving way of preserving documents by transferring them onto allegedly more permanent formats and, at bottom, as an efficient way of clearing up space.[34] This debate in information management has often unfolded around questions of storage durability and preservation. In the 1960s and 1970s came particular anxieties around the "slow fire" of acidic paper, the continuous deterioration of cheap newsprint from the early decades of the twentieth century, when sulfite pulp mills became the main paper providers for disposable print artifacts. Libraries and archives, after all, are "ecologies where the materials of remembrance are living, dying and being devoured" and where "fighting the decay and deterioration that time's chemistry brings" comes at great costs in terms of energy and storage space.[35] Preservation microfilming was in the end, perhaps, less a matter of fighting decay than a matter of space and scale. Blackbeard, in a biting comment on the management of public libraries, presented the microfilm transition as geared to the "benefit of library bureaucrats" and a means of getting "rid of the people they most disliked in libraries, which were the people that came in and sat in the newspaper room for hours and worked crossword puzzles in old newspapers and fell asleep on the volumes."[36]

Linked to the restructuring of library spaces, microfilm promised the miniaturization of large, heavy files into portable documents that could be stored in cabinet files.[37] In this, it essentially worked to ease transmission and make obsolete the kind of painstaking effort that Coulton Waugh otherwise describes with a pleasure evocative of Farge's "allure of the archives."[38] A cartoonist better remembered as an early historian of the form, Waugh urged his readers to go see the old comics for themselves, schooling them into the necessary steps to take, including how to navigate the public library from its administrative procedures to its archival catalog:

> The way to really understand the old comics is to lug out the musty newspaper volumes and have a look at them, even if you crack a few vertebrae doing it. ... In New York, go to the Newspaper Room of the New York Public Library, at 215 West Twenty-fifth Street, after having first secured a study card from the main office of the library, at Forty-second Street. The comic sections will be found bound together after the year 1924, before which it is necessary to get the full volumes. Many of them, owing to the inferior quality of the paper, are tattered and torn, and the researcher works in a dusty storm of yellowing fragments. But it is well worth while.[39]

Hefty, musty, and dusty – one might understand why libraries were keen to discard old bound newspaper volumes for the compressed portability of the microfilm. It also explains why the particular rituals that make up the "allure of the archives," for cartoonists, would have to shift from going to the newspaper rooms of public libraries to scouring used bookstores and garage sales – a process that is repeatedly depicted in the collecting narratives common in 1990s graphic novels (today this process of archival search is more likely to involve browsing online databases, microblogging platforms, and auction websites).[40]

The portability of transferring newsprint onto microfilm meant an intervention in scales: miniaturizing the newspaper onto film allowed for its magnification on screen, privileging scalability (the capacity to change scales smoothly) over local specificities of original size, proportions, and tactile texture. Also, colors were lost in the microfilming process, making it a particular challenge for newspaper comics whose history is bound up with color-printing techniques. Microfilm thus directly worked against these two aspects – scale and color – that are understood as key elements of newspaper comics, particularly when one thinks of the impressive broadsheet size and bright colors of Sunday comics sections. In postwar ideas about record management, "information had lost its body" – as Katherine Hayles puts it – and so the newspaper was primarily seen as a means of access to content or historical data, regardless of its material support, which was deemed to be of secondary interest.[41] Yet, as book historian Roger Chartier points out in relation to microfilming and digitization, "it is essential that the ability to consult texts in their successive forms be preserved"; otherwise, we are at risk of losing the capacity to apprehend the variability of texts and their social significance. Different forms of circulation and transmission "have their own dynamics that can, or may not, create a new audience ... and encourage a new appropriation of texts that previously circulated in other ways and among other readers."[42]

By salvaging the old newspapers from library dustbins, Blackbeard asserted the archival importance of their flimsy materiality and the "original" publication formats, partly stabilizing how fans have apprehended comic strips and producing new usages. Seizing the material that libraries discarded was also a way of remaking that material more or less publicly available, fostering different types of circulation and access than the ones allowed by microfilm preservation. Microfilming, as Auerbach and Gitelman suggest, was understood as a medium for preservation and transmission, but one in which transmission was relatively limited and secure because "cumbersome to retrieve" and necessitating particular reading devices. In this, micrographic reproduction was partly aligned on a strategy of containment and arguably contrasted with the relative openness of xerographic reproduction that enabled library users to keep books and documents for themselves (despite flouting copyright policies).[43] By recuperating discarded newspapers within a dedicated archive, Blackbeard was making old newspapers not only available in and for themselves but also available to other forms of reproduction: book reprints with various publishers and, in a more trivial but no less important way, "duplicate copies" that were made for fellow comics collectors and probably sold "at reasonable prices."[44] Blackbeard set out not only to sort out and store newspapers for the sheer sake of preservation, or in a struggle against time, decay, and loss, but also, and perhaps most importantly, to make possible their future uses.

Through his curatorial enterprise, Blackbeard contributed to reframing how we read, understand, preserve, and recirculate newspaper comics. Out of the vast amounts of newspapers that he was accumulating, he would trim his selection down to a specific (some would say narrow) focus on comics, privileging the comics sections (a separable section of the full newspaper). To do this, with the help of his wife and friends, he resorted to the well-learned tradition of clipping and scrapbooking that had been intertwined with the history of the newspaper since the mid-nineteenth century.[45] While keeping some fully bound volumes, Blackbeard clipped out daily comic strips and often separated comics sections from the rest of the newspaper, organizing the fragments into what he called "files" and trimming down their larger editorial and paratextual context, sometimes adding a quick note in the margin.[46] His aim was, by and large, to organize complete runs of particular comics titles and series, sometimes clipping them from various newspaper sources to complement his files, to find the best-printed versions or to replace decayed items with ones in a better state – all of this with notable exceptions based on his own preferences (there is no file for Bushmiller's *Nancy* in Blackbeard's collections, for instance).[47] These archival choices were largely sustained by the ambition to produce extensive "complete" archival reprints, despite the complexity and difficulty of stabilizing serial texts that, by definition, were open-ended, syndicated in various newspapers, and stretching across several decades. This very seriality was in itself the defining character for Blackbeard, who also collected dime novels and pulp fiction.[48] In the way Blackbeard curated his archive of newspaper comics, then, he contributed to defining how they would come to be further understood, read, and used.

The SFACA collections have been put to a wide range of uses. Blackbeard's initial motives were to assemble the necessary resources for his historiographic projects and thus to foster research, broadly defined, on newspaper comics. While Blackbeard wrote many essays and introductions, his book-long history of comics never came to fruition as it is quite likely that the labor involved in maintaining the archive took most of his time. The most visible use of the collections is found in the extensive archival reprints of newspaper comics that have come about since the 1970s and in which Blackbeard has been variously involved as editor and essayist, collaborating with a network of comics collectors and fans. Blackbeard indeed contributed to the successive waves of reprint series, from the early 1970s editions by Nostalgia Press and Hyperion, through the late 1980s and early 1990s volumes with Eclipse mostly circulated on the direct market, and picking it up with Fantagraphics Books at the turn of the century for reprints with a stronger hold in the general book trade. In the process, Blackbeard and other collectors have contributed to supporting the tacit understanding in comics culture that reprinting operates as an extension of archival work. Reprints, in this context, are situated at the twilight between private activities of collecting old papers and the public dimension of sharing and recirculating these privately treasured items. The same ethos largely guides contemporary archival reprints in which cartoonists are often actively involved in part on the basis of their own collecting endeavors. Taken up and recataloged as part of the special collections of the Billy Ireland Cartoon Library & Museum, Blackbeard's collection becomes part of an institution with clear public policies of availability, display, and access.[49] With the emergence of comics exhibitions in museums, the archival material also increasingly becomes a reserve for displaying newspaper comics on exhibition walls: and even then, the ethos of collecting as a liminal zone between the private and the public continues to inform the rhetoric of display. These two dynamics of curating and reprinting, as they draw from the archives assembled by Blackbeard and others, will come under closer scrutiny in the coming chapters.

"A USABLE PAST"

In a graphic eulogy of Bill Blackbeard, Spiegelman presents the collector dressed up as the Yellow Kid, with a scissor in one hand, his anthology *The Smithsonian Collection of Newspaper Comics* in the other, and newspaper tearsheets spread on the floor. The caption reads: "His vast archive of newspaper strips ... has given us a usable past – and since the future of comics is in the past – has provided the medium with a future."[50]

The image depicts the connected gestures of selection, preservation, and transmission that have organized Blackbeard's archival work. It also pictures Blackbeard with one of his most influential realizations, assembled from his collections: *The Smithsonian Collection of Newspaper Comics*, coedited with Martin Williams and published in 1977, a short ten years after the foundation of the San Francisco Academy of Comic Art.[51]

Under the caution of the prestigious Smithsonian Institution – the main governmental group of federal museums and collections in the United States – the anthology had a considerable impact on the construction and transmission of a cultural memory of newspaper strips. With its high print run, its advertisement in the *Smithsonian* magazine and availability through mail-order, its presence in general bookstores, it circulated widely and became a classic reference for many alternative cartoonists who grew up in the 1970s.[52] This decade of organized fandom is sometimes glossed over as predominantly organized around childhood nostalgia: comics readers growing up and longing to rediscover what they had known as kids. The younger comics readers and makers who were confronted with these anthologies, however, did not have a direct connection with newspaper comics from the first half of the twentieth century. By the late 1970s, the comics sections of newspapers, while animated by titles such as *Peanuts* and *Doonesbury*, had considerably shrunk in size and, by comparison, early newspaper Sunday pages would have come across as completely different objects. While not reproducing the old comics at their full scale, the *Smithsonian Collection of Newspaper Comics* contributed to monumentalizing both comic strips and Sunday comics, with lavish color reproductions and within an unusually large, hardcover book (35.8 cm × 26.4 cm and 4 cm thick) – a conspicuously sturdy format for comic strips otherwise preserved on yellowing newspaper (or indeed on black-and-white microfilm).

Its anthological composition differed from other reprint initiatives in that it precisely reprinted a wide array of various newspaper comic strips, rather than striving for completeness or substantial reprints of long-length serial comic strips. The only significantly longer episode to be included in the *Smithsonian Collection of Newspaper Comics* was a long segment of a hundred daily strips from Roy Crane's 1930s adventure strip *Wash Tubbs*. The rest has to do with a few contiguous strips, as the editors acknowledge: "By collecting and juxtaposing our strips as we have here, we do them some admitted injustice."[53] As a selection of a wide array of material, it made available glimpses of longer serial works that have since been the object of wider reprinting: the imbrication of anthology and archive not only spurred collecting interests but also reframed the work of poorly remembered comic strips and created a reference that later users would keep relying on. Many twenty-first-century reprints turn to semi-forgotten comic strips that were first excerpted in the *Smithsonian Collection of Newspaper Comics*; the most successful case of a modern rediscovery is undoubtedly Frank King's *Gasoline Alley*, but one could also quote a strip like Garrett Price's *White Boy*.[54] Their capsule reproduction spurred on new readers to take up the search for more.

The *Smithsonian Collection of Newspaper Comics* is indeed considered a landmark reference by those cartoonists who in the 1990s and 2000s were most closely involved in reframing and recirculating old comics, accounting in no small part for their particular interest in newspaper comics: Art Spiegelman, Chris Ware, Seth, Joe Matt, Trina Robbins, Mark Newgarden, Dylan Williams, and others have underlined their debt to Blackbeard's anthology.[55] As Jeet Heer observes, "this book would influence how a new generation of readers saw the history of comics."[56] It is telling, for instance, that one of Blackbeard's longest interviews was conducted in the 1990s by the alternative cartoonist and zine-maker Dylan Williams for *Destroy All Comics*, an alternative comics magazine published by Slave Labor Graphics and typically featuring long interviews with up-and-coming authors such as Ben Katchor, John Porcellino, Seth, and Chris Ware. Blackbeard and Williams's anthology is kept at hand and taken from the shelf for reference in an issue of Joe Matt's autobiographical comic book *Peepshow*, published in March 2000, as the cartoonist wants to browse its *Gasoline Alley* Sunday pages (Figure 1.1). Matt excerpts a few lines about Frank King's strip from the anthology, reading it aloud to his readers but leaving them to track down the visuals for themselves.[57] It shows how the anthology was used as a go-to reference book, and allowed the anthologized strips to become referenced in themselves.

It is in the *Smithsonian Collection of Newspaper Comics* pages that Ware first found out about the Sunday comics that he would engage with

Figure 1.1 Joe Matt, *Peepshow*, no. 12 (Montreal: Drawn & Quarterly, 2000), 8.
Source: Copyright © Matt. Courtesy of Drawn & Quarterly.

repeatedly in different ways. His main discovery in those pages was of course Frank King and *Gasoline Alley*, through a short selection of six Sunday pages that have since become iconic, and that would urge him to track down other tearsheets in various garage sales and nostalgia shops when he was studying at the University of Texas.[58] It is also in the pages of Blackbeard and Williams's collection that Ware found this single page from Charles Forbell's short-lived *Naughty Pete* series (Figure 1.2), which he later copied in a striking page from *Building Stories* that adopts the same layout ideas and evokes similar themes. Forbell's strip plays its running gag: the distracted Pete ignores his father's explicit warning and wreaks the expected havoc, a newspaper cartoon character smashing the sign of "imperishable culture" in a bourgeois home. The gag avails itself of the large space of the newspaper for a productive layout that aligns its gridded space on the architecture of a house – a visual trope that was very common in the early-twentieth-century comics sections and that Chris Ware has taken up and updated in the gentrifying Chicago of *Building Stories*. Ware's page uses the same organization of the page and aligns the character's movement through the house on the staircase, while also embedding the sequence within a long temporality and a narrative of aging, charting the entire lifetime of the landlady – from playing on the stairs as a child to scolding the African-American maid taking over the cleaning tasks she can no longer perform (Ware is quite aware that the heritage of newspaper comics he taps into was filled with racist caricatures and stereotypes). The allusion is both very subtle and

Figure 1.2 A Sunday page from Charles Forbell's "Naughty Pete" in *The New York Herald*, 1913.
Source: As reproduced in Blackbeard and Williams's *The Smithsonian Collection of Newspaper Comics*, 43.

elusive (knowledge of Forbell's page is not necessary for comprehending the page), as well as obvious and immediately recognizable for a generation whose eye for newspaper comics has been trained by the same anthology.

This allusion not only highlights the sense of a common heritage subtly expressed in the recognition of the allusion as such but also demonstrates the impact of the *Smithsonian Collection* in reframing newspaper comics as part of the visual languages that contemporary cartoonists could come to rely on. By reproducing selected pages in color and at a large enough scale, the anthological gesture presents many visually striking pages that can be read as individual fragments, separated from their serial history and from the day-to-day rhythm of the newspaper. Reframed as such, they lend themselves to new appropriations. This appears even clearer when we look at the handful of Sunday pages, six in total, reproduced from Frank King's decades-long *Gasoline Alley*, and which have greatly contributed to reintroducing the work of an otherwise forgotten cartoonist. From this small selection of Sunday pages, the strip would gather a small cult following among alternative cartoonists of the 1990s, for whom Frank King quickly became a "cartoonist's cartoonist" – a somewhat obscure reference enthusiastically circulated within a close-knit professional community. In the late 2000s, with the reprint series coedited by Chris Ware, Frank King would join in the canon of early newspaper comics, making the references more widely shared and available across the audience of graphic novel readers.

The pages reproduced in Blackbeard and Williams's anthology are now undoubtedly among the most famous pages in comics history, and key examples of the formal experimentation in King's work: on the one hand, for his gentle parodies of modernist art; on the other, for his "polyptych" pages where the grid is used to represent a single panoramic image from a bird's-eye view fragmented into small sequences that can be followed in various directions and reading orders (Figure 1.3). Seth and Chris Ware have directly adopted this model in some of their pages, citing some of King's most iconic Sunday pages in a way that would have been unspoken and yet evident for readers sharing a similar interest in the history of newspaper comics. The formal principle is used on several occasions by Chris Ware, perhaps most famously in one of his "Big Tex" pages, which elongates the temporal distances between the various fragments, dispatches the various panels to wildly different moments of the story time, as indicated by seasonal changes, dead characters, a ruined roof, a tree that has just been planted, a missing

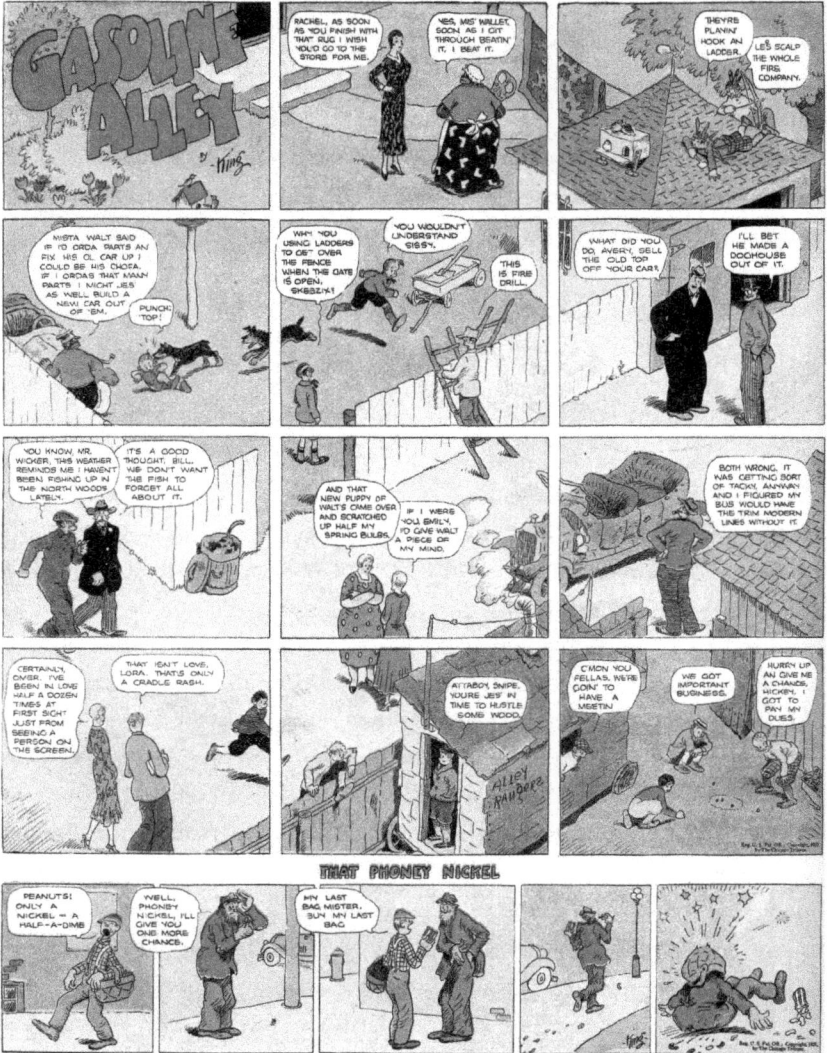

Figure 1.3 Frank King, "Gasoline Alley," *The Chicago Tribune*, May 24, 1931.
Source: As reproduced in Blackbeard and Williams's *The Smithsonian Collection of Newspaper Comics*, 110. 1931 Gasoline Alley © Tribune Content Agency All rights reserved.

fence. The depictions of trees, shadows, and attention to seasonality are themselves recurring tropes in the *Gasoline Alley* Sunday pages, but here King's comforting, idealistic view of small-town rural America gives way to a much more dismal view of countryside life (it seems telling that where

King was drawing the middle class for middle-class readers, Ware shifts attention to a different social class, in a demeaning stereotype of the hillbilly). The formal dialogue of these pages has already been commented on many times, in analyses that nearly systematically read King's pages alongside Chris Ware's.[59] By citing and revisiting King's Sunday pages, perhaps more influentially than through his editorial and design work on the reprints of the daily black-and-white comic strips, Chris Ware has inevitably constructed an image of King's work that centers on its formal experimentation. The Sunday pages of *Gasoline Alley*, moreover, lend themselves more easily to reproduction in the present because they are self-contained objects, relatively autonomous from an ongoing storyline and from the synchronous rhythm of the newspaper (and often dissociated from the bottom gag at their margins). This makes them easier to display in exhibitions, as well as to reuse and cite them, or to reproduce them in anthologies and essays – all of which adds value to what could be thought of as intericonic capital.

It is useful to turn to a more obvious and direct allusion by Seth in a 2008 issue of *Palookaville*, coming when King's work was being reprinted, and which discretely references its own allusive process. The main character Simon Matchcard – who, here, closely resembles Seth's author persona – revisits a yard that has been abandoned. The combination of fence and backyard, if a common picture of rural North America, is a direct echo of King's page from 1931, including in its last panel as the character crouches to the ground in the same way that the kids in King's page play marbles on the floor (Figure 1.4). The crowded scene of *Gasoline Alley* and the desolate yard in *Clyde Fans* offer a strong contrast in terms of tone, imbuing the page with a nostalgia typical of Seth's work.[60] Seth tips off the reference on the preceding page by including a "King" real estate board at the entrance of this abandoned lot, which is a subtle way of crediting the source image. It is also and perhaps more importantly a way of suggesting that the visual reference works as a way of using and inhabiting a space that is not one's own but that is open for nostalgic remembering as well as new creative uses. The character's vague familiarity with the surrounding further resonates with the ambivalences of an allusion that might also "elude rather than allude," and thus effectively depends on an expectation of shared knowledge.[61] Both the

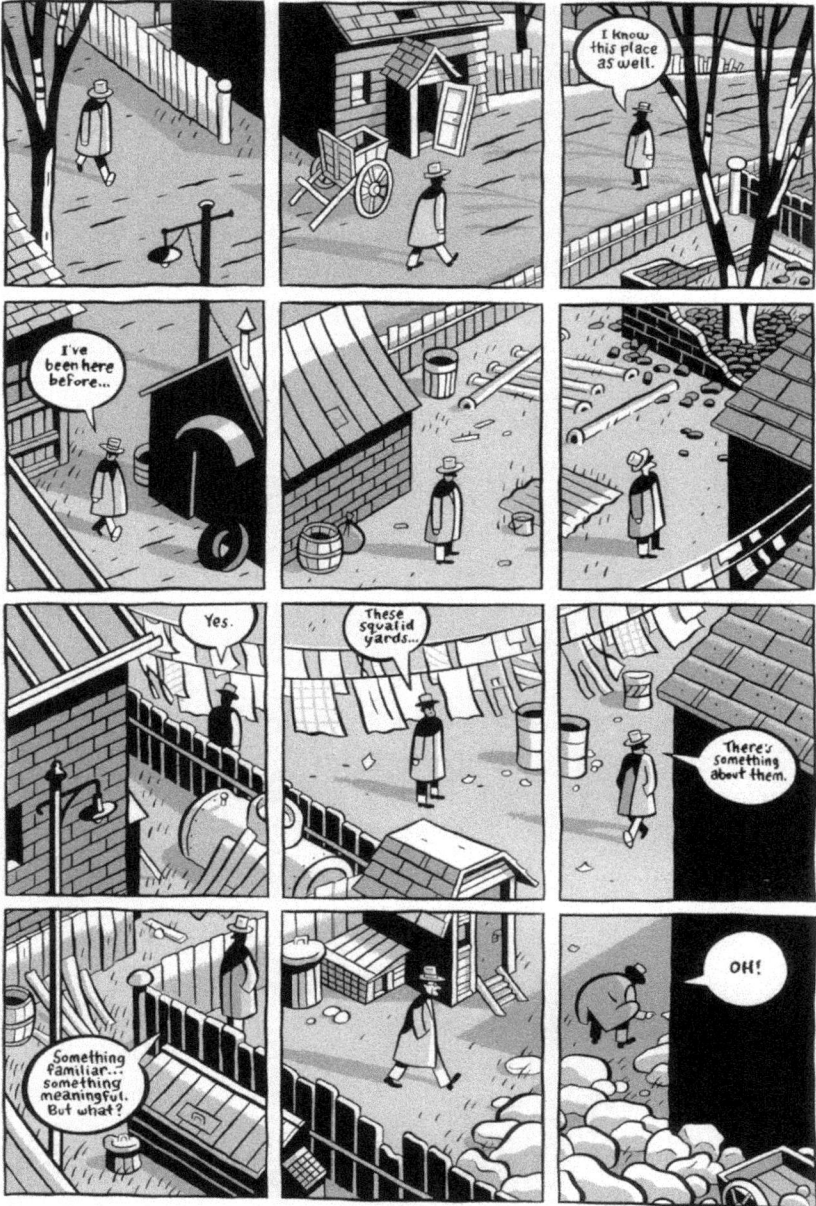

Figure 1.4 Seth, "Clyde Fans," *Palookaville*, no. 19 (Montreal: Drawn & Quarterly, 2008), 74. Source: Copyright © Seth. Courtesy of Drawn & Quarterly.

examples of Chris Ware and Seth foreground the transitive effects that such an allusive reutilization of a formal principle can hold: the allusion to King's Sunday pages here works as a gesture of transmission that embeds their work in a genealogy of images, pointing to a common visual culture.

While this kind of comparison traces lines of influence between Frank King and contemporary graphic novelists (ones that are necessarily elected in retrospect), it is important not to forget the mediation of *The Smithsonian Collection of Newspaper Comics*, which indeed in its very makeup emphasized what Blackbeard called its "gallery" dimension, drawing attention to the graphic experimentation of early newspaper cartoonists – even when Blackbeard, in his role as archivist, was primarily striving to reconstitute reference files for popular cartoon characters with long serial lives, stretched across newspapers and over decades. Blackbeard was well aware of this dimension, of course, as the introduction makes its own editorial choices clear, highlighting how preservation and collection choices also entailed particular ideas of what comics were and how best to commemorate them:

> The dual purpose of this collection reflects the remarkable dichotomy of the strip medium itself, shared only with cinema, in that its best works can be enjoyed both as 'gallery' art and in continuity as fiction or drama. Indeed, this division of esthetic possibility in the divergent emphases on the only two national institutions at present devoted in full or great part to comic-strip art: the Museum of Cartoon Art in Greenwich, Connecticut, which is largely concerned with rotating displays of original strip drawings; and the San Francisco Academy of Comic Art, which files all of the printed strips, so they can be studied in relation to other printed narrative arts, as story-carrying material.[62]

Blackbeard's definitions and ideas, which prioritized the idea of American comics as a vernacular idiom born with the *Yellow Kid* as a narrative art of iterative characters, might now seem somewhat outdated. His preference for character-based serial storytelling that situates comics as part of a large culture of serial narratives, connected to pulp and adventure novels (which Blackbeard also collected), was more typical of his generation.[63] Yet, it also appears clear that, as much as this social definition of comics was translated to his archival strategies, the recirculation of its pieces he had collected and the "gallery" assemblage of the *Smithsonian Collection of Newspaper Comics* played an essential role in establishing other understanding of comics and producing new usages.

BROADSHEET SCALES

Three decades after Blackbeard set up his semi-private, semi-public institution in 1968, the process of microfilming in libraries had continued its course (indeed Blackbeard also facilitated the process by helping with the salvaging of the hefty volumes). It found a renewed relevance with the emergence of digitization projects at the turn of the millennium. In 2001, novelist Nicholson Baker published *Double Fold*, a critical and controversial essay about microfilm, inquiring into "the assault on paper" in libraries; it stirred up the debate to a critical point, attracting reviews (and support) from such distinguished pens as the book historian Robert Darnton.[64] The preface of Baker's essay recounts his encounters with Bill Blackbeard, whose archival enterprise is credited as giving the original impulse for his inquiry. Following suit, Baker had in 1999 founded his own nonprofit archive, the American Newspaper Repository, which integrated the special collections of the Duke University Libraries in 2004. By then, Blackbeard's collection was being processed in the special collections of the Ohio State University libraries. Incidentally, those amateur and professional archivists are all profusely thanked, with "broadsheet-scale gratitude," in the acknowledgments of Art Spiegelman *In the Shadow of No Towers*, published in alternative newspapers on both sides of the Atlantic and collected as a large book in 2004.

In the Shadow of No Towers is a vibrant homage to the newspaper comics of the early twentieth century that have been preserved by Blackbeard and his collaborators. A large and thick, hardcover, cardboard book, *In the Shadow of No Towers* collects and brings into dialogue two serial objects: Spiegelman's own autobiographical pages about 9/11 and its aftermath, originally published in the German broadsheet *Die Zeit* and other newspapers, and a "comics supplement" typical of early-twentieth-century newspapers, featuring color pages from well- and less well-remembered cartoonists, all working for William Randolph Hearst's *The New York American*: Winsor McCay, Lyonel Feininger, Richard F. Outcault, Carl E. Schutze, Gustave Verbeek, George McManus, and Frederick Burr Opper. The graphic novel reads as a vibrant homage to early newspaper comics and their resonance in a post-9/11 North America. As Spiegelman writes in a famous segment of his preface to the "comics supplement" of *No Towers*:

> The only cultural artifacts that could get past my defenses to flood my eyes and brain with something other than images of burning towers were old comic strips; vital, unpretentious ephemera from the optimistic dawn of the 20th century. That they were made with so much skill and verve but never intended to last past the day they appeared in the newspaper gave them poignancy; they were just right for the end of the world moment.[65]

What made newspaper comics such appropriate reading in what felt like the end times was precisely their ephemerality and surprising persistence. While it certainly strikes nostalgic overtones, the relief found in the old comic strips is not an escapist refuge into the past and the items selected for *No Towers* directly echo the political concerns expressed in Spiegelman's own pages.[66] Old comics produced at the heart of New York's newspaper empire come to haunt a landscape of collapsed towers. The early-twentieth-century contexts of urbanization and immigration, with the brutal gags that cartoonists spanned around vertical architecture, tumbling-down towers, dynamite explosions, and ethnic stereotyping, suddenly take on new meanings as they are reread under the light of 9/11 and the ensuing war on terror. A Sunday page from George McManus's *Bringing Up Father*, featuring a dream sequence in which Jiggs is crushed by the leaning tower of Pisa, is paralleled by Spiegelman's account, drawn in McManus's style, of his paranoia-induced sleep disorder.

Further on, the conspicuous use of digital image editing software (Quark) contributes to producing the "collagelike nature of a newspaper page" that *In the Shadow of No Towers* is imitating.[67] This collage aesthetic in *No Towers* precisely helps Spiegelman to draw parallels between a layout typical of the early-twentieth-century print culture and the contemporary new media ecology. *No Towers* relies heavily on a copy-paste process, with multiple repetitions, scale transformations, and distorted images that make its computerization plainly visible, "guarantee[ing] the readability of the image's technological origin."[68] This emphatic use of digital editing, however, is also geared to reproduce on glossy paper the effect of newsprint. In order to mark out his borrowing of serial comics characters, Spiegelman colors them with digital half-toning, which exaggeratedly mimics the analog Ben Day dots used for the color supplement of early-twentieth-century newspapers.[69] The size of the digital dots is much larger and hence they appear as more conspicuous than their analog counterparts in the newspaper section reproduced in *No Towers*, effectively drawing attention to a material aspect of newsprint that has become so strongly associated with old comics. Similarly, while Spiegelman's pages are printed on a clear white background, the comics supplement is underlain by a generic newsprint background layer that emulates the look of yellowed papers. These might seem like technical details, but if "past and present jostle and layer each other, 'smashing' into each other to make graphically legible their coexistence," this smashing is organized by digital means of production, post-production, and reproduction.[70] Printed on the thick glossy pages of a monumental cardboard book, *In the Shadow of No Towers* contrasts with the ephemerality of newspaper-comic strips; it produces their pastness while simultaneously constructing an argument for the need to remember them. The "graphic legibility" of what is experienced as past and present is based on complex material acts of redrawing and reproducing that frame our understanding of and relation to the past of comics.

While Spiegelman's own pages are saturated with visual effects, in a way that was very uncommon for graphic novelists who often privilege a hand-drawn effect (even when using a graphics tablet), the graphic reproduction of the newspaper pages follows a facsimile approach and quite importantly aims at reproducing them as close as possible to their original size and dimensions. The book indeed folds out in double-page spreads so as to maximize the available space, requesting the creativity of designers, production assistants, and printers in finding a "workable format," credited accordingly in the colophon. A year after the publication of *In the Shadow of No Towers*, comics collector and self-professed "accidental publisher" Peter Maresca (thanked alongside Bill Blackbeard) ventured into assembling anthologies of digitally restored early-twentieth-century Sunday newspaper comics reprinted at their original broadsheet scale.[71] The hyperbolically large and sturdy books, printed and the binding hand-sewn overseas in Asia, illustrate how much the digital age has contributed to refocusing attention on particular aspects of the original materiality of newspaper comics that microfilming had cast as irrelevant: color, reproduction and printing techniques, yellowing paper, size.

This situation highlights the complex relationship to digitization in the graphic novel and in its engagement with archives of comics history: contemporary producers are painfully aware of the loss that might come with technological transmutations such as microfilming or digitization of existing archives, especially of their implications when thought of as storage operations. At the same time, the graphic novel fully avails itself of the new possibilities and opportunities – in terms of design, composition, and production – that the digital affords to print publications.[72] Books like *In the Shadow of No Towers*, but also Peter Maresca's large-size Sunday Press Books, owe their makeup to digital software, printing technologies, and globalized economies of production. In this context, digital technologies of reproduction and graphic design software make it easier to reproduce drawn images in higher quality and in a way that makes seemingly evident the materiality of their native publishing format – provided one has access to usable archives, of course.

RAUCOUS ARCHIVES

We can conclude this chapter by turning to a last debt owed to Bill Blackbeard, which also confronts the limitations of his archival endeavors. In his 2018 *The Goat Getters*, cartoonist Eddie Campbell (best known for his collaborations with Alan Moore on *From Hell* as well as his autobiographical series *Alec*) proposes a history of the sports cartoon in San Francisco newspapers around the turn of the nineteenth century – a messy period in comics history and one that pushes against the limits of

Blackbeard's definition.[73] As Campbell notes, Blackbeard and other collectors "tend to be focused single-mindedly on the comic sections."[74] As a result, the historiography of "the comics" has largely focused on the comics section as a separate unit of the newspaper, one that can be removed from the other parts, putting at a distance the messier appearances of cartoons and graphic works elsewhere in the newspaper.[75] Core to Campbell's argument is that the sports page requires the contemporary comics historian to put between brackets features that have been essential to its popular and scholarly definitions, such as sequentiality and narrative, in favor of a more holistic understanding of picture making in the newspaper.[76] The sports pages might have bred many of the cartoonists who later became famous in the full-color Sunday pages (such as George Herriman and Jimmy Swinnerton), but this should not make us forget that, between 1890 and 1920, cartoonists primarily worked at first as "all-round newspapermen."[77] The institutionalization of the comics sections and the syndication of content in newspaper across the country produced some of the most impressive Sunday pages (the ones that contemporary graphic novelists have been most keen to collect and copy). This development was concomitant to a process of format standardization that had an important impact on the connection of newspapers to their local anchorage and to the labor opportunities for cartoonists outside New York.[78]

Because Campbell was interested in the 1890s and 1900s cartoons in the sports pages – which appear in a cluttered variety of forms (from single-panel caricatures to narrative sequences) – rather than in the institutionalized comics section, he had to complement his archival research in the Billy Ireland Cartoon Library with the newspaper microfilms that are being digitized and made available online through library programs, and that offer more holistic archives of the newspaper publications, hence a larger access to the paratextual contexts for these comics (but also lacking, as Campbell puts it, a "jungle guide" to help in navigating this "great big wodge of microfilm").[79] As a result, Campbell had to patiently restore and redesign the poor-quality images of the microfilm in order to reproduce the various cartoons and comics in *The Goat Getters*, which occasionally preserve scratches and smudge traces from their microfilm sources.

The process yields a book that is as inventive in its design as in its argumentative propositions; the title page moreover states "written and designed by Eddie Campbell," placing both activities on the same level and in a mutual relationship. The material design of the book is indeed essentially related to the ideas that are formulated in it. Rather than presenting individual newspaper comics and cartoons (clipped out and reframed), *The Goat Getters* unsettles both the traditional anthological presentation and the history book, with its strong divided line between text and image, between the reconstructed historical narrative and the reproduced documents or illustrations.

Campbell's design and image reproduction choices communicate a sense of the iconotextual and intermedial density of the old newspapers, stressing the local specificities of drawing for the newspaper between 1890 and 1920. The black-and-white images are nearly always represented in their paratextual and visual context, always giving a hint of their size, where and how they would fit in relationship to the columns of text and to the typographical choices of the typesetters and printers. Just as often, though, Campbell also singles out smaller cartoons and fills the margins with doodles, close-ups of panels, (typo)graphic details, and so on, which populate all parts of the book and mimic something of the "raucous" energy of the 1890s newspapers. Images frequently bleed out of the page and across double-page spreads, acknowledging the size differences between the book and the broadsheet material it reproduces.

Campbell makes use of all the elements of book design, in a playful dialogue with the many images that he reproduces, both in the many direct references between the text and the drawings and in the typographical imitation of their newspaper layouts. Campbell organizes this dialogue between word and image by a strong cohesion between the text and the surrounding images within double-page spreads, but also across the entire volume, which is clearly meant to be read in nonlinear ways, as evidenced by the index organized by page and image numbers. The design of the pages confronts the reader with a rowdy reading experience that effectively contributes to conveying the historicity of the cultural objects it reproduces.

Eddie Campbell's *The Goat Getters* is both a logical outcome of the previous ways of engaging with archives and a critical reconsideration thereof as it opens beyond the full-color Sunday pages that still form our ideas of the golden age of comics. In the process, he comes to highlight the social definitions of comics that undergird gestures of archiving. Alongside paying attention to the site-specificity of the page, to the local anchorage of smaller newspapers and the pull toward standardization through increased circulation, Campbell also touches on a key tension in comics that the digital age is bringing to the front again. As Aaron Kashtan suggests, the "tension between 'fixity' and 'flexibility'" is also a "characteristic formal property of comics": just as "comics are irreducibly tied to the material form in which they are embodied," this does not prevent them from moving from one format to another.[80] This is something that comics readers are particularly aware of but that also has stakes for how we remember comics: as Sylvain Lesage and Bounthavy Suvilay have recently noted, "the question of the heritage preservation of comics is tightly intertwined with the stakes of materiality in comics studies."[81] But while preservation microfilming has made us aware of the material importance of preserving successive versions, it should also turn our attention to the uses that are made of the archive. As François Brunet, a historian of photography and an expert on North American visual culture, suggested in a perceptive inquiry into the "post-2000 archive fever" around photographs, "archives in general are less about the goals and the mechanisms of their production and preservation . . . than the economy of their future usages and the readerly operations that will bring meaning and value onto them."[82] In this chapter, I examined both the constitution of comics archives and their usages, an interplay that was in itself already key to Blackbeard's approach, which archiving was directly linked to other practices of reproduction and dissemination. The following chapter extends this thread, looking more deeply at particular practices that engage with those archives in different contexts.

CHAPTER 2

Curating

I didn't want to be a curator per se, to decide who should live and who should die in that context.[1]

– Art Spiegelman

BECOMING A CURATOR IS NOT A POSITION THAT MANY CARtoonists intuitively adopt. Yet, *Le Musée privé d'Art Spiegelman* ("Art Spiegelman's Private Museum"), organized in 2012 at the Musée de la bande dessinée in Angoulême, and *Eye of the Cartoonist: Daniel Clowes's Selections from Comics History*, which took place in Columbus, Ohio in 2014 at the Wexner Center for the Arts in collaboration with the Billy Ireland Cartoon Library & Museum, offer two clear examples of a specific kind of comics exhibition where cartoonists are precisely invited to act as curators and provide "their" own vision of comics history. This curatorial framework moreover functions as a valorization of the comics archives that are treasured within the institutions involved with both exhibitions: the cartoonist-as-curator makes selections from the archives, repurposing their materials for display in the space of the museum. This chapter looks at these cartoonists-curated exhibitions of comics history through the lens of the relationship between canon and archive, arguing that these exhibitions move away from an overt attempt to establish a canon but ground this act of canonization within cartoonists' own idiosyncratic look at comics history, emphasizing the individuality of these authorial canons. Based on interviews and archival research, this chapter offers an in-depth analysis of the layout strategies and museological discourses around the two exhibitions, describing how curating shapes a particular visual transmission of comics history.

MUSEIFYING COMICS

Curating has today become part of the "practice of everyday (media) life" expanding beyond the confined art world institutions and permeating all areas of consumer culture, as users are increasingly invited to select, share, and reframe cultural items and build their own lists and archives.[2] As David Balzer argues, "if curators began to dominate the art world in the 1990s, they began to dominate everything else in the 2000s."[3] This expansion of the curatorial to everyday life in the twenty-first century has given rise to a widespread "curatorial culture" transforming various media and cultural industries, from music to television, questioning the authority of cultural mediators and redefining traditional forms of connoisseurship.[4] Comics have often relied largely on their readers and fans to act as "curators" of their history, collecting fragments in scrapbooks, folders, and long boxes. In a complex correlation with the deinstitutionalization of high culture, the place of curation in the context of comics has perhaps been most profoundly changed by its recent institutionalization and the growing role played by "high" cultural mediators shaping the "newfound sociability" of comics, to borrow an expression from Erin La Cour and Rik Spanjers's issue on the relocation of comics in the social worlds of art and literature.[5]

This "newfound sociability" has found a keener ally in the literary circuits of production, distribution, and canonization than in those of the art world – as Beaty and Woo's inquiry has further made clear.[6] The claims to literary value built into the definition of the graphic novel since its very first uses have effectively helped situate comics within literary institutions like the book market, the public library, and the university in ways that US comics have not exactly done in the art world, despite various blockbuster exhibitions in major museums. The fact that the graphic novel has been more readily embraced in North America as a form of literature than as visual art remains a puzzling historical phenomenon, one that has to do with the intermedialization of literary culture on the one hand and with the antagonism between comics and art as separate social worlds on the other.[7]

There is one area related to the art world and its practices where comics have been investing with more success, however, and that is the auction house, the collector's market, and the galleries. Until the 1970s, original art pages were not thought of as art in themselves but were primarily understood as templates for subsequent reproduction; indeed, original art was produced with its print outcome in mind. Over the past decades, original art has become a much more integral part of the practices in the comics world, for creators as well as publishers, agents, curators, and readers. For creators, original art can be a valuable source of additional income in difficult market conditions, and this alone might impact the very way one draws and produces the art (depending on the revenue that it might generate), not to speak of the entire market that supports it, implicating a longer chain of stakeholders. Original art has become so widespread that it has spawned a surprising trend in comics publishing: the issuing of facsimile reproductions of original artwork, often termed the "artist's edition" or the "studio edition" of a particular graphic novel.[8] And, most importantly, as Beaty and Woo note, "the market for original art is also a major point of contact between the comics world and art-world institutions"; it contributes to generating cultural value. The artists whose works top the sales of auction houses, however, are not necessarily the same whose pages will be put up on museum walls. In the end, "while auctions hold a high degree of consecratory power, they pale in comparison to museums, which generate prestige by acquiring works for their permanent collections and by dedicating shows to artists."[9] And, on that front, the exhibitions dedicated to comics in major museums have remained part of an ambiguous process, with the outspoken consecratory power of museums often received with resentment or skepticism in the comics world.

As Beaty indeed concludes in *Comics versus Art*, in the twenty-first century "the most powerful legitimizing institutions in the traditional art world have been able to incorporate comics, albeit in frequently vexed and vexatious fashions, into their work."[10] This would primarily involve a curatorial process of selecting "masters" of the form, in an act of canon-formation that has been a capital bone of contention between comics and museums, as Baetens and

Frey suggest: "[t]he question of what, who, and how of commemoration processes has loomed large when major art galleries have mounted shows featuring comics and their history."[11] The *Masters of American Comics* show, held in 2005 at the Hammer Museum and the Museum of Contemporary Art in Los Angeles, coalesced the tensions and debates surrounding the appropriation of comics by art-world institutions.

The show was an explicit attempt to "define a canon of comic artists in the traditional art historical manner," as documented by Kim Munson.[12] The show thus reflected a growing trend in art historical and museo-logical discourse, which has tended to specialize its canons according to specific subfields, "requir[ing] its own organization and hierarchy in order to convert information into usable knowledge and create a historic understanding of a particular tradition."[13] Integrating comics into art history and establishing its canon thus appeared as a necessary preliminary step. Accompanied by a lavishly illustrated catalog, the *Masters of American Comics* exhibition relied on a narrow selection of fifteen cartoonists elevated to the status of creative geniuses in a clear act of canon formation that also attracted criticism.[14] Bart Beaty has underlined the ambivalences and tensions in the curatorial choices for *Masters of Americans Comics*, questioning not only the decision to establish a canon of individual artists but also the exhibition layout, which "assents to the formal biases of its museum setting, displaying frustratingly partial stories in the midst of the white cube museum space as if they were paintings."[15] The *Masters of American Comics* show and its explicit dis-course of canon formation, if momentous, has had few follow-ups, but remains a reference that museum curators will measure against or imitate.[16] As Jeet Heer has suggested, "[p]ost-*Masters* there is much more interest in looking at individual cartoonists as their own thing or part of a scene – the grand narrative of comics history seems too large. As artists like Ware, Spiegelman, and Crumb get canonized, they are seen as their own thing and divorced from their comics contexts."[17] Cartoonists are themselves often aware of these tensions. Art Spiegelman acted as a consultant for the *Masters of American Comics* show but precisely refused to be further involved and credited as curator so as not to take on the explicit role of canon-maker: "I didn't want to be a curator per se, to decide who should live and who should die in that context."[18]

CARTOONISTS AS CURATORS

What, then, would bring exhibitions that situate cartoonists precisely in that uncomfortable position? It is important to pay attention to the larger framework of the two exhibitions, which is connected to the positions of Clowes and Spiegelman as canonical figures in the contemporary graphic novel but also to the specificities of the museum that commissioned the exhibits. In both cases, their comics history exhibits were connected to larger retrospective shows devoted to Clowes's and Spiegelman's own work. *Modern Cartoonist: The Art of Daniel Clowes*, originally curated by Susan Miller and René de Guzman for the Oakland Museum of California, was hosted in Columbus in 2014 at the Wexner Center for the Arts, providing the opportunity for a collaboration with its neighboring institution the Billy Ireland Cartoon Library & Museum to set up *Eye of the Cartoonist.* Similarly, *Le Musée privé d'Art Spiegelman* was organized for the 2012 International Comics Festival in Angoulême alongside the *Co-Mix* retrospective, following the graphic novelist's Grand Prix award. While *Le Musée privé d'Art Spiegelman* was a one-shot tied to the specific context of the Musée de la bande dessinée in Angoulême, the *Co-Mix* retrospective subsequently toured at several prestigious institutions like the Pompidou Centre in Paris or the Jewish Museum in New York City. In both cases, there is a manifest status discrepancy between the retrospectives and the comics history exhibitions, as the former clearly occupy the dominant position in terms of circulation and visibility.

While the retrospectives are ambitious shows touring at various fine arts centers and art-world museums, accompanied by lavish art books, the comics history exhibitions are more modest one-shots that are more closely associated with specific institutions of comics memory.[19] This distinction approximately runs along the dividing lines of the "comics world" and the "art world," showing the different visibility pull that each type of exhibition is akin to setting forth, as the comics history exhibitions function, to some extent, as peripheral sections complementing the "main" retrospective exhibits by showcasing the authors' influences.[20]

It is undoubtedly the canonical position of Clowes and Spiegelman that gives "their" histories a particular weight. In framing their own perspectives on the memory of comics, comics and art museums back up their role as historians and mediators of their chosen medium. As Henry Jenkins reminds us, "within the realm of comics, few exercise the amount of cultural capital Spiegelman commands, and thus, few have his capacity to transform yesterday's 'trash' into the contents of a 'treasury,' archive or canon."[21] In other words, some cartoonists' histories of comics will fare better than others depending on the cultural capital of the individual as well as on the larger standards of greatness and criteria of value that are active in the field at a certain time.[22] And so, in a sort of feedback loop, the museum both benefits from and relays the comics artists' canonical status, while simultaneously putting the mechanism of canonization into the authors' hands by inviting them to act as curators.

Le Musée privé d'Art Spiegelman and *Eye of the Cartoonist* thus hold a particular relationship to canonicity, based on its traditional principles of "selection, curation, and distinction," while affirming its subjectivity and contingency.[23] Without catalogs, and thus relatively few public traces documenting them, the comics history exhibitions offer a "personal canon" of comics that is all the more contingent given the ephemerality of its exhibition, contrasting with the canonizing effect and higher cultural impact of the retrospective shows. In this way, they contrast with the kind of top-down act of canon formation reflected in the curatorial decisions of *Masters of American Comics*. Rather than attempting to build "the" canon, such exhibitions conspicuously emphasize the plurality and subjectivity of canons while backing up the institutions' own memory-making role. Indeed, this specific curatorial approach is not a radical rejection of canonization as it also serves to valorize the heritage work performed by the Musée de la bande dessinée and the Billy Ireland Cartoon Library & Museum. Rooted in the comics world, both institutions have developed what Jean-Matthieu Méon has called a "comics-specific museum approach," privileging "exhibitions that are not meant to be substitutive but complementary and explanatory of the comic works."[24] This discursive dimension reinforces the scientific and patrimonial function of these museums, which are specifically dedicated to the preservation of comics as cultural heritage and have grown to be among the largest archives of comics. Clowes's and Spiegelman's selections from these archives acknowledge this memory work, while proposing to activate its materials through the lenses of their own pantheons.

Both exhibitions thus negotiate the relationship between canon and archive that, according to Aleida Assmann, embodies two modalities for the presence, function, and usage of cultural memory: the canon, as the "actively circulated memory that keeps the past present," and the archive, as "the passively stored memory that preserves the past past."[25] This distinction is not a rigid one and what matters most is the dynamics it sets in motion: "the active and the passive realms of cultural memory are anchored in institutions that are not closed against each other but allow for mutual influx and reshuffling."[26] Such reorganization of the comics canon is precisely what animates the two exhibitions under scrutiny, which, by showcasing comics creators' perspectives on the history of comics, explicitly highlight how the past of comics functions as a "cultural working memory" for contemporary graphic novelists.[27]

In the case of the two exhibitions under scrutiny, this reshuffling of the "storage memory" of comics happens in the space of the museum, activating it in a particular way. As the title of Spiegelman's comics exhibit makes clear, these exhibitions suggest to turn the museum into a "private museum," emphasizing the double nature of their engagement with comics history – at once subjective and collective, personal and collaborative. Furthermore, the phrase coalesces the curatorial logics at work in the exhibitions, pointing to two different "ways of curating": it positions the cartoonist in between the traditional museum curator, as a caretaker of the heritage preserved in the institution, and the curator as exhibition-maker, following the redefinition, in the 1980s and 1990s, of curating around the individualized "curatorial gesture" as creative work.[28] These two curatorial logics emphasize the growing contrast between the museum as a somewhat rigid institutional space, strongly regulated by traditional art history, and the temporary exhibition as a potentially freer play with those art-historical conventions.[29] In the same way, while Clowes's and Spiegelman's "private museums" evoke the authoritative framework of the museum as a guardian of memory, their "privateness" cues an idiosyncratic and thus contingent perspective on comics history. While helped by the institutions' own professional curators for the material and practical organization as well as the designs, Clowes and Spiegelman are invited to act as curators in order to frame what is conspicuously presented as their own versions of comics history.

By enrolling artists as curators and inviting them to operate a selection from their archives, the institutions thus demonstrate their own role as sites of the cultural memory of comics while simultaneously encouraging an active engagement with this memory through creative practice. The curatorial strategy of the "artist-curator" is one that has become wide-spread in the art world and that comics museums adopt and adapt for their own purposes.[30] In doing so, they shed light on the role that cartoonists themselves play in the transmission of comics heritage. Reclaiming these cartoonists' perspectives to motivate a dynamic appropriation of comics heritage, the exhibitions themselves frame those histories in quite specific ways, relative to their material and institutional contexts. In what follows, I examine more closely how institutional contexts, design strategies, and (para)texts participate in shaping the mutual relationships between canon and archive in both exhibitions, as these elements give different inflections to the cartoonist's personal histories of comics.

SPIEGELMAN'S PRIVATE MUSEUM

Le Musée privé d'Art Spiegelman is based on a very specific appropriation of the museum space that is aptly described by the author in the introductory video screened at the very entrance of the exhibition: "it seems that I have been allowed to highjack the Centre of Bande dessinée Museum [*sic*] to replace what is primarily the Francophone patrimony of comics with my own perverse and private map of what comics are. . . . So this is the alternate universe, Bizarro version of a patrimony."[31] This statement directly emphasizes Spiegelman's idiosyncratic take on the history of comics and presents how the author was invited to take over the curatorial organization of the museum and "replace" its contents with his own selections.

While his own oeuvre was meant to become the object of a major retrospective during the International Comics Festival of Angoulême in 2012, after having received the Grand Prix the year before, Spiegelman early on manifested his interest in showcasing more than just his own work and being able to collaborate with the Musée de la bande dessinée.[32] Constrained by the available space, the proposition of its curators was to offer Spiegelman a carte blanche to refashion the permanent exhibit of the museum.[33] Hence, *Le Musée privé d'Art Spiegelman* invested the space that is otherwise used for its permanent exhibition into the history of comics: Spiegelman's "perverse and private map" proposes to question and redistribute the otherwise "official" version of comics history presented in the vitrines of the museum, which had taken its contemporary format only since its reopening in 2009.

While the origins of the Musée de la bande dessinée can be traced back to 1983 and subsequently to its first inauguration in 1990, it went through a major transformation and was reopened in 2009 in buildings renovated for that purpose. This transformation accompanied a profound museographical reflection and a redefined patrimonial project, fine-tuning its comics-specific museum approach and strengthening its historiographic discourse.[34] The main part of the museum accommodates the "Musée d'histoire de la bande dessinée" (the comics history museum) in one large room divided into four chronological sequences, featuring European, American, and, to a lesser extent, Japanese comics, organized according to periodizing criteria: the origins of comics from 1833 to 1920, the "golden age" from 1920 to 1955, the emergence of "adult comics" from 1955 to 1980, and contemporary "alternative" comics and manga since 1980.[35] In the exhibition space, this history of comics not only is made visible through a selection of original art but systematically combines original pages with the related books, albums, periodicals, and other print artifacts, as well as derived products and other transmedial exploitations of comics, hence drawing attention to the variety of comics formats. This narrative of comics history is further echoed and documented by the companion volume *La Bande dessinée: son histoire et ses maîtres* written by Thierry Groensteen and richly illustrated with original art from the museum's archive.[36] Driven by a state-funded patrimonial mission and backed up by authoritative comics historians such as Groensteen and Jean-Pierre Mercier, the Musée de la bande dessinée in Angoulême presents in many ways the official history of comics – and so the background against which Spiegelman's appropriation of the space becomes alternative and subjective.

The architecture of the Musée de la bande dessinée indeed orients and constrains the exhibition design of *Le Musée privé d'Art Spiegelman*, which, to a large extent, adopts and replicates its material presentation. Following the spatial organization of the museum, the exhibition is divided into six segments that, similarly to the permanent exhibit, lead the visitor chronologically through a history of comics divided into periods. Co-curated by Thierry Groensteen, who organized the spatial disposition of Spiegelman's selections,[37] the exhibition follows a periodization that runs relatively parallel to that of the permanent exhibit, but that is more closely aligned with the history of American comics. The four sequences that segment the central room (Figure 2.1) are split into four periods corresponding with pregnant moments for different formats:

- "Comics and caricature, from 1830 to 1914" goes back to the origins of comics from Rodolphe Töpffer to the *Yellow Kid*, with a particular emphasis on European caricature periodicals such as *L'Assiette au Beurre* or *Simplicissimus*.
- "The Golden Age of American Comic Strips" mostly covers the first half of the twentieth century with canonical figures such as Winsor

Figure 2.1 Exhibition shot of *Le Musée privé d'Art Spiegelman*, Musée de la bande dessinée, Angoulême, 2012.
The photograph depicts the display furniture and vitrines, here filled with various examples of Jack Cole's *Plastic Man* publications, from cheap comic books to archival reprints. The video monitor features a commentary on Jack Cole's work by Spiegelman.
Source: Photograph by Caroline Janvier, Cité international de la Bande Dessinée et de l'Image (CIBDI). Courtesy of the CIBDI.

McCay, George Herriman, Chester Gould, or Harold Gray, as well as lesser-known cartoonists such as Charles Forbell and Harry J. Tuthill. It also includes postwar newspaper strips as Schulz's *Peanuts*, Watterson's *Calvin and Hobbes*, and Bill Griffith's *Zippy the Pinhead*.

- "The Origins of Comic Books and E.C. Comics" focuses on a variety of comic books, from funny animals to horror comics with only a few references to the superhero genre. It gives a distinct place to Harvey Kurtzman's *MAD* and its collaborators, stressing its oft-cited influence on Spiegelman.

- "Underground and Post-Underground" catches up with Spiegelman's own beginnings on the underground scene in the 1970s but foregrounds its transnational circulation by including many European underground comics magazines, such as the Dutch *Tante Leny presenteert* or the Spanish *El Víbora*.

- These four segments build up toward more recent developments that have shaped the emergence of the graphic novel with which Spiegelman's work is narrowly intertwined. The two additional rooms that make up the permanent collection of the museum are less used to present periods in comics history than objects with a particular place in Spiegelman's career.

- "*RAW*, or the Assertion of an International Avant-Garde" displays the cartoonists that Françoise Mouly and Spiegelman published in their groundbreaking magazine and features a video interview of Mouly to cast light on its editorial history. The selection not only represents a variety of now-canonical figures such as Chris Ware or Charles Burns but also emphasizes *RAW*'s role in translating European comics for US readers.

- "The *Binky Brown* Revelation" displays the forty original pages that made up Justin Green's 1972 autobiographical comic book *Binky Brown Meets the Holy Virgin Mary*. It stresses the eye-opening influence that the book had on Spiegelman as an unprecedented exploration of the potential for life-writing in comics. The press release of the exhibition presents *Binky Brown* as a necessary step for Spiegelman's *Maus* in a section tellingly entitled "The Justin Green Revolution: From *Binky Brown* to *Maus*." Moreover, the fact that all original pages are exhibited indirectly echoes Spiegelman's

Co-Mix retrospective, simultaneously on show during the Angoulême comics festival, where the complete set of original pages for *Maus* were being shown.

Le Musée privé d'Art Spiegelman, then, follows a relatively linear progression organized along periods and material criteria, where the presentation of Spiegelman's selections adopts the usual display used for the permanent collection of the Musée de la bande dessinée. The alternative cartography of comics history that Spiegelman presents is not exactly a kind of "Bizarro" historiography in the sense of an alternative history-writing: the museum design shapes his selections into a historical pattern that aligns with its usual layout, following the "official" historiographic model developed by the institution and as mirrored in Groensteen's *La Bande dessinée: son histoire et ses maîtres.*[38] Rather, Spiegelman is given a carte blanche to replace the contents of the permanent exhibition so that it reflects his own perception of the past of comics, giving it an American yet transnational twist and spotlighting his personal canon of great comics artists.

Spiegelman's "highjacking" of the museum, however, not only goes through the imposition of his own pantheon of "greats" but also requires the importing of comic art otherwise unavailable in the holdings of the CIBDI. While the local archive furnished a significant part of the displayed material, the author's primary affinities with North American comics required him to gather and bring over many items from other collections, from the Billy Ireland Cartoon Library & Museum (for newspaper comics) as well as from a handful of collectors, such as Glenn Bray (for underground comix), Thierry Smolderen (for nineteenth-century cartoonists), and the Spiegelmans themselves.[39] In this way, by bringing new material into the space of the Musée de la bande dessinée, the exhibition spotlighted some of its inevitable blind spots and showcased comics otherwise absent from the museum. By extensively relying on the collections of Bill Blackbeard and Glenn Bray, *Le Musée privé d'Art Spiegelman* furthermore paid homage to the crucial role played by fans and collectors in preserving the memory of a medium that did not use to have an institution like the Musée de la bande dessinée. The exhibition features a display case specifically dedicated to the archival work performed by "obsessive collectors," containing Spiegelman's short essay on collecting, "In Praise of Pathology," as well as his obituary comics page in homage of Bill Blackbeard, "the collector who rescued the comics" by salvaging newspapers that libraries were throwing away in favor of micro-film and whose vast collection is now hosted at the Billy Ireland Cartoon Library & Museum.[40] In his introductory video, Spiegelman further declares his admiration for Blackbeard, presenting his "private museum" as a homage not only to the history of comics but also to the passionate collectors who made that very historiographic discourse possible.

While the exhibition celebrates the memory work of these collect-ors, Spiegelman simultaneously moves away from the perspective on comics history fronted by the first generations of organized comics fandom. In the same introductory video, he states that his own canon is neither the one dominant in the United States nor that of the French *bédéphiles* of the 1960s and 1970s, who held a particular fascination for 1930s adventure comics artists like Burne Hogarth, Alex Raymond, Milton Caniff, Lee Falk, or Hal Foster – names that represented a "golden age" of comics for both European and American fans.[41] While they are well represented in the archive holdings of the Musée de la bande dessinée, they are strikingly absent from *Le Musée privé d'Art Spiegelman*, except for a single Caniff original. Similarly, the superhero genre is explicitly and deliberately kept at bay, safe for a few represen-tative examples and the exceptional place given to Jack Cole – for whom Spiegelman's fascination was already made clear in his long essay on the creator of *Plastic Man*.[42]

Featuring more than a hundred cartoonists, the exhibition reconfig-ures the museum following Spiegelman's personal canon, giving particu-lar weight to certain "masters" of the form. The selection directly followed from Spiegelman's version of comics history as he has been refining it since the very beginning of his career. The cartoonist has indeed contributed significant essays on comics history, notably his appraisal of Bernard Krigstein's "Master Race," and has reprinted "old" comics from Winsor McCay to Basil Wolverton in the post-underground comics magazines he coedited (*Arcade* and *RAW*).[43] From 1979 to 1987, Spiegelman lectured a class on the history of comics at the School of Visual Arts in New York and recapped that material into a key article published in *Print* tellingly titled "Commix: An Idiosyncratic Historical and Aesthetic Overview."[44] Condensing Spiegelman's interest for the past of comics in a few pages, this panoramic essay retraces a chronological but fragmentary history of the medium, as shaped by a pantheon of great cartoonists caught "in the crossfire" between the "demands of Profit" and the "demands of Art."[45] Alongside this overview piece, Spiegelman would further pen down numerous prefatory essays on individual cartoonists, often for reprint volumes: these essays have been collected in *Comix, Essays, Graphics and Scraps* and, taken together, offer a kaleidoscopic history of comics.[46] Focusing on individual cartoonists with highly personalized styles, Spiegelman's comics history privileges, as Beaty and Woo would put it, the "exceptional" over the "typical."[47] As Spiegelman said about his lectures, "in teaching this thing I'm teaching supposedly the history of comics, but I'm primarily dealing with the aberrations in the history of comics."[48] What emerges from this engagement with the past of comics is thus a personal canon that is aligned on Spiegelman's aesthetic interests and understanding of what comics are.

Le Musée privé d'Art Spiegelman directly draws on the artist's essays by making them available in French through an e-book version released as an exhibition catalog. In turn, Spiegelman gives the works that he spotlights in these essays a privileged place within the exhibition by singling them out in specific vitrines, reproducing complete short stories, and adding detailed video commentaries. Shot in the author's studio in New York, the videos portray him in his usual posture – black vest and shirt, cigarette at hand – surrounded by his collection of framed original art, displayed objects, and overloaded bookshelves, alternating with pans of the comics he comments upon and décor shots of New York City.[49] Guiding the visitors throughout the exhibition, these videos intertwine this historiographic discourse with a process of self-exposure through which Spiegelman discloses his curatorial choices and explicates the role that certain comics have played in his own life and work, thus giving a certain relief to his version of comics history. While the entire exhibition features an impressive breadth of cartoonists from various traditions, a handful of cartoonists are also given particular attention, thus reflecting Spiegelman's personal pantheon. Lyonel Feininger's *The Kin-der-Kids* and George

Herriman's *Krazy Kat*, for instance, not only get a dedicated spot but their individual positions and their place in Spiegelman's canon are further made clear in short videos screened next to the vitrines, in which the graphic novelist uses their works to illustrate the tug-of-war between commerce and art that, to him, has been essential to comics.

The display of complete (short) stories, such as Harvey Kurtzman's 1952 war story "Corpse on the Imjin" and Justin Green's early autobiographical comic *Binky Brown*, has a different canonizing effect in that it pinpoints individual comics as masterpieces that can be read by the visitor in the exhibition context: this follows from one of the main concerns of the Musée de la bande dessinée, which has always tried to respond to the narrative challenges of exhibiting comics. The screened videos further guide the visitors in their reading of the material: Spiegelman not only gives contextual information on the production of these works but also performs short close-readings. In one instance, he details the intersection of content, affect, and form in Kurtzman's "Corpse on the Imjin" by describing how its vertical and horizontal lines give it a distinct rhythm and visual power: the video shows Spiegelman's hand retracing the direction of the different lines on a facsimile of Kurtzman's original art. Adapting comics to the museum context, the exhibition simultaneously underlines their visual, literary, and narrative dimensions, which allows Spiegelman not only to place an individual short story like Kurtzman's within its historical context but also to demonstrate and signal its continued relevance for today.

Le Musée privé d'Art Spiegelman demonstrates its author's second career as a comics historian and consistently couples this historiography with Spiegelman's own authorial image and posture. Following on *In the Shadow of No Towers*, which enmeshes Spiegelman's double career as graphic novelist and comics historian by offering a "comic supplement" of early-twentieth-century Sunday pages alongside Spiegelman's own pages, *Le Musée privé d'Art Spiegelman* further highlights the breadth of Spiegelman's "canons": if it remains idiosyncratic and personal, the framework of the Musée de la bande dessinée doubles it as a patrimonial gesture. More than a strictly "private" history of comics, the canonical position of Spiegelman himself has given "his" history a particular resonance, given his "capacity to influence" beyond the comics world.[50] Considering

Spiegelman's engagement with the archive of comics, Henry Jenkins has shown how the author's own understanding of comics history has helped stabilize a certain narrative articulated around a few great cartoonists: "[a]s a critic, editor, and curator, he has been instrumental in shaping the emerging canon of his medium."[51] A very clear example of this dynamic, and the way Spiegelman's take on comics history also shapes art-world commerce, is the record auction selling of the full original art for "Master Race" to a private Belgian foundation (supposedly aiming to open up a museum of graphic arts) for $600,000.[52] The comprehensiveness of the short story, which can be displayed as a complete item, and Spiegelman's endorsement of its historical importance have made of "Master Race" a desired museum exhibit with a hefty price tag in the art market. Just as *Le Musée d'Art Spiegelman* bears the marks of a complex entanglement of individual collectors and heritage institutions, this case also reminds us of the financial stakes that seam through the relationships between private collectors and public state-funded initiatives.

THROUGH DANIEL CLOWES'S EYE

While sharing the same basic idea of inviting a cartoonist to act as curator to showcase his "own" history of comics, *Eye of the Cartoonist: Daniel Clowes's Selections from Comics History* took place in a very different institutional context, that of a fine arts center collaborating with a comics museum and library, which made for a contrasting appropriation not only of the museum space but also of the archive. While Spiegelman transformed the Musée de la bande dessinée by bringing in material from outside of its collections, Clowes selects material from a single archive, the Billy Ireland Cartoon Library & Museum, in order to curate an exhibition at the Wexner Center for the Arts in parallel with the *Modern Cartoonist* retrospective on Clowes's own artwork. The setup for the exhibition is made explicit at the very entrance to the exhibition room, which welcomes the visitors with the following text:

> The Wexner Center's proximity to the Billy Ireland Cartoon Library & Museum – the world's largest repository of original cartoon art – presented us with a wonderful opportunity. We invited American

cartoonist Daniel Clowes (b. 1961) to curate a personal reflection on the history of the art form with examples culled from the library's one-of-a-kind collection, giving visitors an even deeper appreciation of his work. ... The exhibition is not an exhaustive overview of comics history by any means, but it is a quite personal curatorial gesture that reflects both Clowes's tastes and his refined eye as a cartoon artist.

These lines delineate the specific institutional context that frames Clowes's perspective on the history of comics, situating his "personal curatorial gesture" in the cartoonist's experience, his taste, skill, and vision. Disavowing any pretense to an "exhaustive overview of comics history," the *Eye of the Cartoonist* exhibition presents Clowes not primarily as a historian but rather as a cartoonist with a distinct eye for the history of comics as visual culture.

The exhibition leaflet similarly emphasizes the visual process of choosing and selecting the pages from the archive by including a large-size "behind the scenes" picture featuring Daniel Clowes sifting through original pages in the stacks of the Billy Ireland Cartoon Library, assisted by exhibition organizers David Filipi and Caitlin McGurk. The photograph and description text give insight into the Billy Ireland as a key institution for the patrimony of comics and frame the exhibition as a way to valorize the archive. Recalling Assmann's description of the dynamic relationship between storage memory and active, living memory, Clowes's selections from the stacks of the Billy Ireland draw out a kind of personal canon and thus animate the archive in a particular way. As Filipi and Jenny Robb remark in the leaflet, "enlisting an artist, one with a cartoonist's expert eye and appreciation for the medium's history is an illustrative and enriching way of activating a selection of the archive's holdings. This is one artist's quite personal take on comics history."[53] The archive necessarily shapes and frames this activation, as does the exhibition context: the specific focus of the Billy Ireland on cartoons and newspaper comic strips is reflected in the selection of original art, which emphasizes short comics forms that rely on narrative compression and brevity that thus adapt well to the "white cube" of the Wexner Center for the Arts (Figure 2.2).

Figure 2.2 View from the entrance to the gallery, Exhibition shot of *Eye of the Cartoonist: Daniel Clowes's Selections from Comics History* (Columbus, OH: Wexner Center for the Arts, 2014). Source: Photograph by Mark Steele. Courtesy of the Wexner Center for the Arts.

As the exhibition title already suggests, Clowes's curatorial gesture lies not simply in the act of selection but in a selection primarily oriented by the skilled eye of the cartoonist. It emphasizes *looking* at comics, immediately underlining an understanding of comics as visual objects. From the start, then, the exhibition subscribes to the idea, aptly worded by Svetlana Alpers, that the "museum effect . . . is a way of seeing."[54] The space of the museum repurposes its objects for an aesthetic of the visual and Clowes's choices follow this logic by foregrounding the visual and design elements of the comics he selects. The items are indeed chosen according to their capacity to "hold the wall," following an expression of the French comics critic Christian Rosset when talking about the potential of comics to work visually when hanging on the walls instead of being held at arm's length.[55] Along similar lines, Clowes follows Spiegelman's suggestion that "art museums won't necessarily want to hang the same works that might be studied in lit departments. It is not the same work that will live happily on a wall and in a book."[56] Adapting to the space of the white cube, the cartoonist's two-day process of sifting through a large quantity of original art and comics tearsheets pulled out from the archives was oriented toward "what strikes the eye," as Clowes described it: "looking for pages that had either an X-factor quality – something that would point out an odd specificity in the artist's work in an immediate, eye-catching way – or those that were perfectly emblematic of their best (or most visually interesting) work."[57]

Prioritizing its visual dimension, the exhibition does not display the same kind of historiographic ambition as *Le Musée privé d'Art Spiegelman*, which was aligned with the tenets of comics historiography upheld by the Musée de la bande dessinée. By contrast with Spiegelman, who often acts as "the face of comics to the cultural establishment," Daniel Clowes comes across as a different type of comics historian, whose mediation of the past appears less cohesive and more ambiguous.[58] Although his work displays a keen understanding and obsessive fascination for the past of comics, he has often voiced his relationship to that heritage in ironical terms, harboring a cynical relationship toward comics criticism. In his preface to a reprint collection of Bushmiller's *Nancy* strips, Clowes marks his distant approach toward both academic and fan discourse when he writes: "while I fully support even the most thorny-headed discourse on Sluggo and the Male Gaze, I have no such offerings to that vigorous body of thought, nor do I possess any 'interesting information' or 'useful knowledge' about The Great Man."[59] The preface demonstrates a lack of interest in the academic (post-structuralist) and fan-historiographic discourse and instead focuses on Clowes's personal history with the strip, its minimalist drawing style and continued relevance for contemporary readers. We could also think of the comic book critic Harry Naybors appearing in Clowes's *Ice Haven*, whose pompous discourse is half-serious, half-nonsense, and further ridiculed by his graphic representation.[60] Clowes's own text on comics history in the pamphlet-like *Modern Cartoonist* (1997) adopts a similar discursive style, putting forward bold claims about comics history as driven by recursive fifteen-year cycles of innovation while stressing the ambiguities of the cultural recognition of comics.[61] His ironical position appears as an example of what Christopher Pizzino has termed "autoclasm," designating "the illegitimacy of comics not as a theme that can be safely contained but as a reality inside which the comics creator must struggle."[62]This autoclastic tendency in Clowes's discourse on the history of comics transpires through the systematic "self-breaking" of his own legitimacy.

Accordingly, *Eye of the Cartoonist* gives less room to extended commentaries on the history of comics than *Le Musée privé d'Art Spiegelman* and does not mobilize an overt critical apparatus. The exhibition design leaves out a direct juxtaposition of the author's comments and the exhibited artworks: instead, Clowes's reflections are neatly laid out as a fold-out of the gallery guide (Figure 2.3), which includes short comments on each artist alongside a fragment of the exhibited item. The snippets reflect the curatorial focus on visually striking images, often praising the drawing, the line, or the design elements of the page. Quite tellingly, even when including pages from the suspenseful adventure strip *Terry and the Pirates*, Clowes insists on Milton Caniff's chiaroscuro mastery: "I'm not so interested in these stories I must confess, but no one ever made more thrilling use of black ink on white paper." Furthermore, he frequently refers to the very process of selecting the pages, as when he writes: "The *Little Nemo* original in this show is one of those holy grail pages of comic art that you can't forget once you've seen it. I almost passed out when I opened the drawer and found it sitting there."

Just as the fold-out spreads the featured artists regardless of schools or periods, the exhibition setting similarly eschews organizing its elements into a chronological sequence. Rather, it clusters the work of each artist and juxtaposes these clusters next to each other, unrelated by period or artistic affinities: the early-twentieth-century cartoonist T. S. Sullivant, for instance, stands alongside a *Buck Rogers* Sunday page from 1937 and original art from the 1960s by Henning Mikkelsen (*Ferd'nand*) and Gus Arriola (*Gordo*). Each frame is placed at a relative distance from the others, but the exhibition nonetheless favors a comparative experience of Clowes's "selections from comics history" offering a kaleidoscopic view that does not add up into a narrative development. Neither the exhibition layout nor Clowes's comments emphasize the position of these cartoonists within a linear narrative of comics history; rather, they repeatedly appeal to their transtemporal value. Clowes indeed calls Otto Soglow's strips "timeless, eternally truthful, and just as funny today as

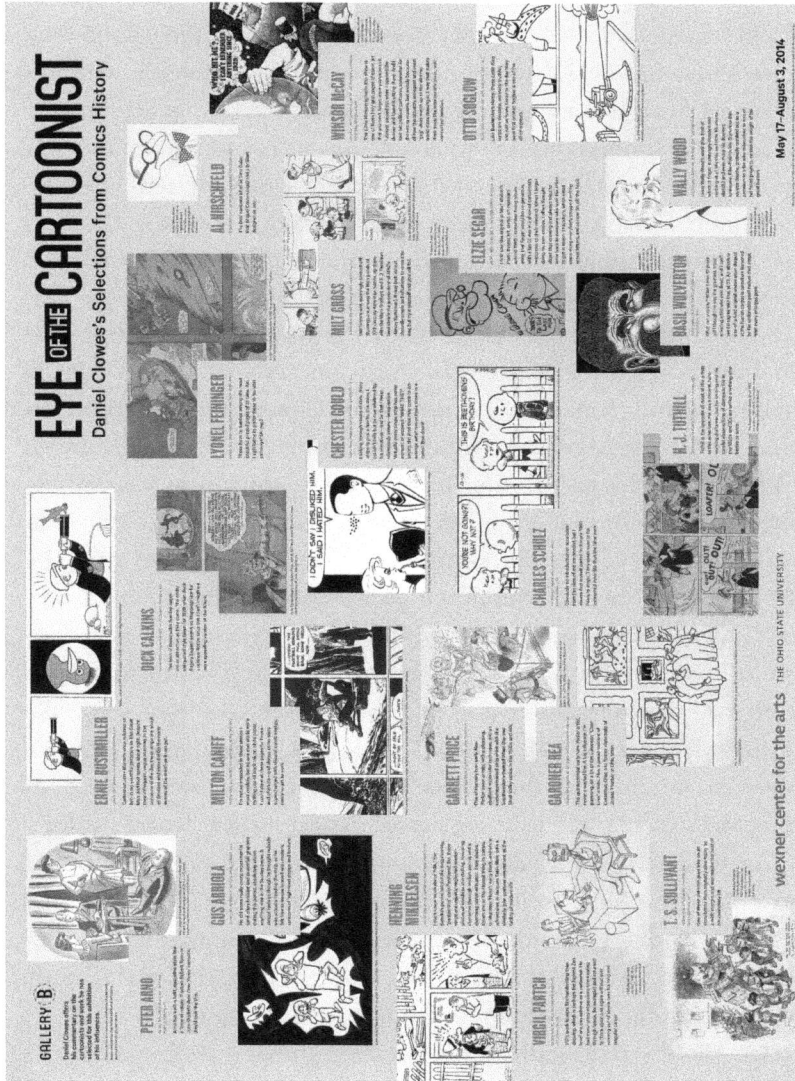

Figure 2.3 Inside fold-out part of the gallery guide for *Eye of the Cartoonist* (Columbus, OH: Wexner Center for the Arts, 2014), designed by Mike Greenler for the Wexner Center.

Source: Courtesy of the Wexner Center for the Arts.

the day they were first printed," presents Al Hirschfeld as "the best caricaturist of all time," and states about Lyonel Feininger's *Kin-Der-Kids* that "these have to number among the most beautiful printed pages of all time." These shorthand notices speak out Clowes's fascination for and attachment to these "old" comic strips while simultaneously affirming their continued relevance today. Invoking the canon logic of curation, selection, and duration, Daniel Clowes draws attention to what speaks to his own practice in the past of comics in order to present what amounts to a personal canon.

Despite this canonizing logic and the highly legitimate setting of the museum, there is also an "autoclastic" tendency subtly at work in Clowes's curatorial choices: albeit never short of praising and celebrating the artists, the exhibition never monumentalizes their works and the curator's comments consistently suggest what is worth remembering and why in only a few lines. Among the vast amounts of Winsor McCay originals in the Billy Ireland Cartoon Library, Clowes surprisingly selects only one *Little Nemo* page and includes five of his later cartoons, drawn toward the end of his career after his venture in animation was flailing. Although it is an unusual curatorial choice, Clowes explains that what interests him is precisely the contrast between McCay's art and the specific situations they are supposed to humorously illustrate: "I love his political cartoons, somewhat for the wrong reasons, but mostly because of how the absurdly inelegant and overt 'gag' ideas match up to the all-time world-class drawing in a way that makes them seem like intentionally ironic, well-concocted parodies." Similarly, Clowes's choices also foreground the works of lesser-known artists, such as Henning Mikkelsen's "unjustly neglected masterpieces of wordless storytelling" or Gus Arriola's "really crazy, experimental (and often brilliant and beautiful) graphics," in that they demonstrate the mastery of formal elements within the constrained context of the newspaper. As Clowes further writes of Arriola: "It almost feels as though he thought nobody was actually reading the strip, so he felt free to amuse himself."

In fact, Clowes repeatedly connects the exhibited images with the craft, work, and skill of their cartoonists, sometimes further connecting them to his own practice of cartooning: in this way, *Eye of the Cartoonist* not only showcases his interests and tastes for comics history but demonstrates how Clowes is profoundly embedded in a tradition of drawing comics that is also a history of its *métier*, of its production and reception. Quite telling in this regard are the two drawings he includes by Elzie Segar and Wally Wood, which are not "proper" works, comics, or cartoons, but doodles quickly brushed for fan readers: in his comments, Clowes thus emphasizes the act of drawing as something that extends to a specific relationship to the readers. These references to the culture of comics work and the constraints of commercial art counteract the problematic importation of "old" comics, as visual culture, within the white cube of the contemporary arts exhibition. A vitrine of comic books – from Virgil Partch and R. O. Blechman's cartoon books to DC *Jimmy Olsen* and *Lois Lane* comic books as well as the underground comix of Jay Lynch and Robert Crumb – recalls to mind for visitors that comics are readable objects, even compulsively read as their deteriorated covers suggest.

Ultimately, the exhibition also leads visitors back to Clowes's own works, which, just as the museum room allows for transtemporal juxtapositions, often mix dissonant styles drawn from the history of comics: *Ice Haven* and *Wilson*, in particular, offer a compilation of various graphic styles that are more or less explicit references to certain cartoonists.[63] Yet, the exhibition also refrains from making those juxtapositions too evident for the visitor, allowing Clowes's personal selections from the history of comics to work beyond their simple function as influences. Quite on the contrary, *Eye of the Cartoonist* invites visitors to look at the history of comics with a fresh eye, uncovering new ways of looking at and reading those familiar and less familiar works.

WAYS OF LOOKING

Both exhibitions thus manifest different ways of enacting a complex dynamic between canon and archive, showing the importance of both the institutional context and the "curatorial gesture" of the cartoonist. Enrolling cartoonists as curators, these institutions avoid the pitfalls of a top-down canon formation, as heavily debated for the *Masters of American Comics* show, and in the process propose a more flexible, relative act of selection linked to the practice of individual graphic novelists. The case of cartoonists-curated exhibitions proves particularly useful for understanding such mechanisms of canonization as they negotiate the relationship between the contingent, personal canon of the individual cartoonist as a subjective take on the comics history and the institutional framework of museums as guardians of memory. Both exhibitions deliberately seek to present "personal" canons. Distinguishing between "memory as background" and "memory as force," Judith Schlanger puts forward the notion of a "personal canon" that crystallizes a subjective "living memory" by contrast with official historiographies: "Personal affinities subvert the didactic canon, which would be the representative list of great books to teach and transmit, in favor of a personal canon polarized by admiration, a canon that is above all inspirational."[64]

Instead of a didactic canon, the museums present "personal canons" that tap into a living memory of the medium and help to draw connections between the past of comics and their present. Asking cartoonists to act as curators is not only a way of situating the act of selection; it is also a particular way of *looking* at comics history in the context of exhibition display. Most importantly, what these exhibitions offer to their audiences is another way of looking at older comics when they are torn from their original contexts and hung on the wall: if the comics are radically decontextualized, they also promise new ways of looking at them, drawing attention to other aspects of their history while also bringing into the art world other types of image that were never meant to be presented in such a context. It is also an invitation to look at comics pages through the "cartoonist's eye," framing the expertise of the professional cartoonist as a particular skill in assessing and evaluating comics as visual objects.

CHAPTER 3

Reprinting

It's all part of the economics of it; why books have to be made of things that appeared already in magazines or in newspapers, besides just making an archive of the work or some kind of collection of the work. It's a good question.[1]

– Ben Katchor

ANTHOLOGIZING THE WORK OF A QUASI-FORGOTTEN CAN-adian cartoonist popular in the postwar decades, *The Collected Doug Wright* is a book that is conspicuously made to endure: it is unusually big, towering at 38 cm × 29 cm, its thick cardboard covers are plastered with a brilliant red foil, it features a cut-out medallion with an embossed drawing of Wright's comic strip character Nipper, and the title is hand-lettered on a paper ribbon delicately wrapped around the edges (Figure 3.1). By bibliophilic standards, "Canada's Master Cartoonist" is given an impressive paper monument by his younger counterpart Seth, who edits and designs this lavish "collected works" edition. The enormous book is a telling example of the monumental quality of contemporary comics reprints. If literary classics and their many pocket editions can be conveniently described as "portable monuments," this would be a heavy one to carry around.[2] It is even more telling when you learn that the design of the book was in fact based on an actual stone-and-marble monument.

In an essay on his general approach to book design, Seth disclosed how he chose to structure the composition of the book after an imaginary visit to the Vimy Memorial Ridge in France. The logic

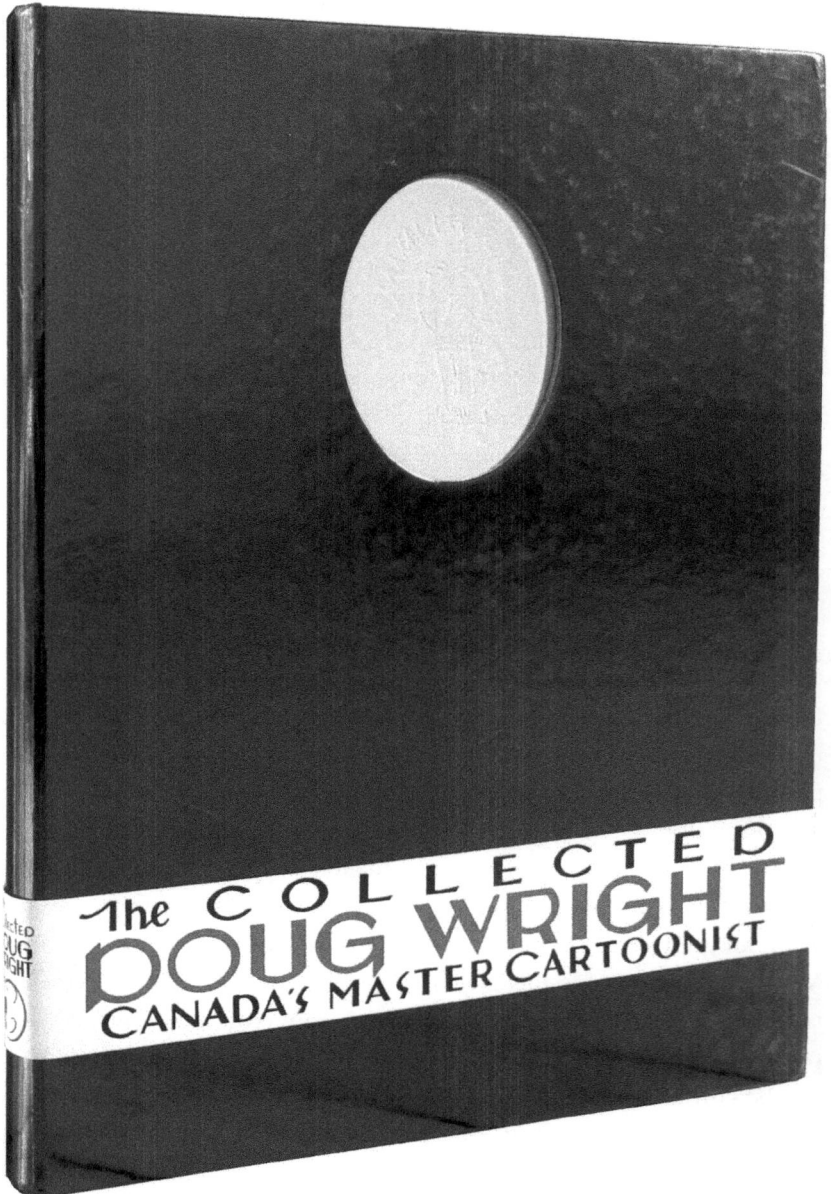

Figure 3.1 *The Collected Doug Wright,* edited and designed by Seth (Montreal: Drawn & Quarterly, 2009).

behind it is slightly anecdotal, but is nevertheless worth mentioning briefly: it implies a connection between Seth's reading of a newspaper article on the memorial and the biography of Doug Wright, whose father was killed in the First World War (although in different circumstances than the ones commemorated in Vimy). As Seth concludes, it really is an underlying logic that is more useful to him in his creative process than it is to the readers:

> Smart or a stretch – the decision was made. The book would be built around the appearance of the Vimy Memorial. It wouldn't be overt. No one would ever guess it to look at the finished book but it *would* give a deeper underlying meaning and a clear visual plan that would allow me to structure the concrete design of the book itself.[3]

The details of the underlying biographical story are not what primarily matters, they are supposed to remain covert. And yet, the choice to use a monumental memorial – one commemorating the deaths of 11,169 soldiers and a foundational "site of memory" for the Canadian nation – is anything but a superficial one and it certainly undergirds a patriotic desire to establish Doug Wright as a distinctly Canadian cartoonist.[4] The biographical specificities are less interesting than what the working model tells us about the final product itself.

The sheer fact that a monumental memorial has served as the basis for crafting a reprint precisely calls attention to the architectural quality of the book, which can be read as an attempt to offer a more durable resting place to what was once an ephemeral comic strip. It highlights the commemorative dimension of this gesture of transmission, which can also be seen as a form of mourning, reclaiming a place for a somewhat forgotten comic strip, while being fully aware that this kind of recovery relocates a comic strip into a very different context. In the preparation sketches that Seth shares in his *Devil's Artisan* article, he shows how much book designing is about guiding the readers' attention, leading them through a material space, imbuing a certain sense of rhythm and movement in the framing of the material. Reorganizing a comic strip previously published on flimsy newspaper into a hardbound monument also means defining how contemporary readers will remember or discover this archival material.

For the way it draws links between book design and memorial architecture, this example offers an interesting foray into the complex, interlinked, but conflicting dynamic between document and monument that Erwin Panofsky charted in the mid-1950s and that still effectively captures something of the tensions at the core of contemporary comics reprinting.[5] As John Guillory suggests in his comment on Panofsky's document/monument distinction: "The relation between monumentality and documentality is always dynamic, which is to say, unstable; documents change our understanding of monuments and sometimes even destroy them or, better, demote them to documental status."[6] This tensive dynamic between monumentality and documentality brings an additional layer of meanings that is useful to consider when addressing reprints. Guillory notes how Panofsky's text is underwritten with material metaphors: metal or stone for the monument, paper for the document. Contrasted with the ephemerality of their original publication formats, contemporary archival reprints of old comics are more often than not high-production-value books, more or less large and expensive, heavy to handle. They are books conspicuously made to withstand the wear of time. For all their monumental stature, they nevertheless also risk either a form of "calcified monumentality" or appearing as documents of a comics history that is dead and gone.[7]

The current wave of comics reprints reflects these tensions. It monumentalizes a few works from the history of comics and consecrates them in lavish editions, and in doing so often necessarily caters to what is more urgent or obvious in present needs and interests. Reprinting is certainly a crucial mechanism of canon formation. As Bart Beaty and Benjamin Woo argue, "reprints frame what works are important within the field of comics and why."[8] But the attempt to "monumentalize" comic strips from the past – which can sometimes lead to a kind of "mummification"[9] – just as frequently signals the pastness of these objects, relocating them in the latent memory of the archive. It is in this sense that "archival reprint" or "archival anthology" appears as the preferred vernacular term in the comics world to refer to such books. "Archival collection" is indeed the term used for a steadily evolving section of the Eisner Awards since 1993 that has greatly contributed to instituting the very concept as a generic category in comics publishing. While terms like "classics" have also been part of the editorial branding strategies of comics publishers, it is striking that the term "archives" seems more frequently used as an editorial category in its own right, similar to volumes of "complete" works, which in both cases stress the idea of recovering extensive works rather than selecting and handpicking "canonical" stories. Before taking their legitimizing discourse at face value, we have to recognize how reprints, in that way, are always on an edge between monumentality and documentality, canon and archive.

By looking at publishing practices and graphic design, this chapter works toward a "historical poetics of media" and leans on book-historical approaches attentive to the social, material, and commercial practices that organize the circulation of texts.[10] Emphasizing the "poetics" dimension, it more specifically studies how these reprints present ways of reading, with questions of graphic style and narrative that are just as crucial as questions of economy and cultural status.[11] In this, it follows Emmanuël Souchier's notion of "editorial enunciation," which underlines the material, visual, and social dimensions of texts, their circulation, and successive editions, urging scholars to examine their "enunciative plurality."[12] Where Souchier, writing in a context dominated by text, has to assert and remind us of the "visual dimension" that necessarily organizes any form of writing, this is blatant if not banal information for comics readers. This evidence of a visual materiality in comics publishing raises interesting issues when it comes to reprints: when cartoonists take over book designing they necessarily engage with a plurality of other graphic marks, including their own. Reprints rub graphic styles against each other, contributing to produce renewed understanding of old comics as well as tracing lineages and collaborations between past and present.

To understand this enunciative plurality means to take a holistic approach to reprints, paying attention to both their economic and their commercial circuits, to their book design, to the archives into which they tap. In this view, it also becomes important to embed the contemporary archival reprints within a longer history of reissuing, precisely because every new phase in comics reprinting is described as a new "golden age" of reprints, which tends to undermine the historical continuity between the various reprint initiatives.[13] The reprint works by Seth, Chris Ware, and others are inseparable from a longer construction of the "archival reprint" itself as an editorial concept in comics, emerging from the fan subcultures of the 1970s. Works that have already been reprinted are always more likely to get reprinted, and the way they have been reprinted might provide guidelines on how they are going to be reprinted again.[14] Across these successive reprint initiatives, it thus becomes essential to analyze the works and their surrounds, grasping the key role that the paratexts serve in reframing the history of comics and the archival work that reprints perform for contemporary readers.

NOSTALGIA CORNERS

Before tackling the specific situation of the early 2000s, which saw the distribution of new cards for reprinting older works, it is crucial to return to a previous time in the history of reprints linked to the organization of fandom and the first republishing initiatives of then already decades-old material. The 1960s indeed witnessed the structuration of fan scenes, the strengthening of the second-hand retail market and its practices of correspondence, exchange, and barter – all of which would gradually build into a series of nostalgia books devoted to comics. In 1965, *New Yorker* cartoonist Jules Feiffer's *The Great Comic Book Heroes* reprinted for the first time some of the earlier stories from the dawn of the comic book in the 1930s.[15] Published by the Dial Press with E. L. Doctorow as editor-in-chief, and with Feiffer as a successful staff artist of *The Village Voice* with several book collections of his cartoons and comic strips, the anthology marked a momentum. As Hugo Frey and Jan Baetens have demonstrated in an article that rehabilitates the impact of Roy Lichtenstein as part of a more productive "feedback loop" between pop art and comics, the widespread success of pop phenomena in the late 1960s (they single out the 1965–1968 bracket) had contributed to opening up new commercial opportunities for repackaging old comics under different formats, from cheap paperbacks to bulky hardcovers, with cover designs and page layouts that often mimicked a pop aesthetic. In the process, these reprint initiatives contributed to creating a market for reprints of historical material by helping to "establish older, more historically aware and reflexive readerships."[16]

On that front, Woody Gelman provided a seminal contribution in 1967, founding Nostalgia Press, one of the first comics publishing houses dedicated to reprinting old comics. Frey and Baetens mention a variety of editorial initiatives, including various paperback publications, but underline the groundbreaking role of Nostalgia Press for its book-length reprinting of prewar comic strips, beginning with *Flash Gordon* (arguably the most obvious predecessor to the modern comic books that were at the center of pop aesthetics). The bulk of Nostalgia Press's reprints would follow up in the 1970s, with the "pop design aesthetic" of its early years slowly fading away.[17] Woody Gelman navigated several roles as collector, publisher, creative director, and entrepreneur. As a collector, his collection of tearsheets from Winsor McCay's *Little Nemo* had sustained an early and ambitious reprint of the classic newspaper comic, coordinated across an international network of *bédéphiles*, groups and clubs of amateurs whose primary function rapidly evolved from exchanging and swapping older comics to finding ways of preserving, reproducing, and reprinting them. The first anthological collection of McCay's *Little Nemo*, based on Gelman's collection of tearsheets, was thus initially published in Italy by Garzanti in 1969 then taken up in French by Pierre Horay before it finally found its way to the United States, when printed by Gelman's company Nostalgia Press in 1972.[18]

As a creative director of the product development department at Topps, a Brooklyn-based bubble-gum producer that developed original packaging and collectibles, Gelman hired several cartoonists from the early underground scene, providing them with work, sometimes spotting them out through their high-school fanzines – as was the case for Jay Lynch and Art Spiegelman, for instance.[19] Gelman was thus closely connected to the pre-underground scene that had emerged in the bosom of Harvey Kurtzman's *MAD* (1952–1956) and his subsequent magazines *Trump*, *Humbug*, and *Help!* – all published between 1957 and 1965, extremely short-lived but laying the groundwork for underground comix. It is in the crucible of these magazines, moreover, that a culture of reprinting old comics was kindled: *MAD* featured a "Rare Old Cartoons" column with works from late-nineteenth-century and early-twentieth-century cartoonists such as Wilhelm Busch, Caran d'Ache, and H. M. Bateman; and *Help!* was even more prolific in its reprints of older comics, featuring cartoonists such as Milt Gross and T. S. Sullivant, cartoons from *La Vie Parisienne*, and giving prominent spots to Winsor McCay's *Little Nemo* and George

Herriman's *Krazy Kat* a few years before Nostalgia Press would take to reprinting their work in book format. Following the logic of Kurtzman's magazine, with whom he had worked on one or two "nostalgic vignettes," Gelman reached out to underground cartoonists for help in his own archival enterprise.[20] While Robert Crumb contributed the logo and letterhead, while Art Spiegelman was involved in the design of and curated a column in Gelman's magazine-format title *Nostalgia Comics*: "Noble Efforts" was presented as a "a miscellaneous selection of comic strips by artists better known for other works."[21]

In their collecting endeavors, collectors like Bill Blackbeard and Woody Gelman helped sustain historically aware readerships and, in turn, new creative work began flowing from this historical reflexivity as underground cartoonists started to dig into the piles of "musty, old comic strips" – as pictured for instance in Spiegelman's 1973 short comic "Skeeter Grant," in which the cartoonist depicts himself drowsing off on *Happy Hooligan*. Following the models provided by Kurtzman and Gelman, later "post-underground" magazines such as *Arcade*, *RAW*, and *Weirdo* (and their twenty-first-century counterparts *Drawn and Quarterly* and *Kramers Ergot*) all feature an "archive" section reprinting old comics alongside their contemporary experimentations. When Spiegelman and Bill Griffith set out to publish *Arcade*, they included an "Arcade Archives" column, curated in the same vein as Spiegelman's contribution to Gelman's anthologies and casting light on forgotten comic strips (such as *Nibsy the Newsboy*, George McManus's pastiche of *Little Nemo*).[22] The feature would be taken up again in *RAW*, expanding to a larger conception of comics by including works that had traditionally been thought of as on the margins of comics history (outsider artists such as Henry Darger; painted narrative works by Jerry Moriarty and Chéri Samba). The historical genealogy that *RAW* assembles is nevertheless clearly grafted onto the heritage of Kurtzman's magazines: Caran d'Ache and Bateman were favorites, and *RAW* issues also included pages from Winsor McCay's *Dream of the Rarebit Fiend* and, later on, a longer episode from George Herriman's *Krazy Kat* ("Tiger Tea," famous in underground circles for its possible analogies with hallucinatory drugs).

The magazine has always been an important cutting-edge for exploring and experimenting with new forms (including, in the

context of postwar American comics, as a practical way of circumvent-
ing the comics code), and this also goes for reprinting where magazine
publication often worked as a laboratory of sorts.[23] The important
impact of Nostalgia Press undoubtedly lay in its envisioning this archival material not as a side section of magazines but as long-length
reprinted books, laying a foundation for the various reprint publishing
initiatives that would follow up in the decades to come, somewhat
facilitated by the installation of the direct market in the 1980s.
Gelman's connections with countercultural networks of underground
creators and fans did give Nostalgia Press a wide resonance, including
across the Atlantic, as his reprint editions were frequently taken over in
Europe.[24]

Another key venture in this context, in which Gelman and
Blackbeard were both involved, was the "Hyperion Library of Classic
American Comic Strip Reprints" put out by science-fiction publisher
Hyperion Press. In 1977 Hyperion released no fewer than eighteen
titles with reprinted selections of long-running comic strips such as
from E. C. Segar's *Thimble Theatre* and Harold Gray's *Little Orphan
Annie* as well as shorter experiments and lesser remembered titles
such as Ed Wheelan's *Minute Movies* or Percy Crosby's *Skippy*. It provided a reprinting model that today's "Library of American Comics"
(IDW) has approximately taken over by following similar guidelines
(reprinting, for instance, a single year's worth of a particular comic
strip title). The project is telling for the ambiguities and tensions that
shaped this early reprint market: a quick burst of books making old
comics available but within editorial strategies that are often quite
short-lived. As Jean-Paul Gabilliet observes about the comics histories
written around the same time, "the multiplication of works on comics
during the 1970s testified less to the emergence of a durable interest
on the part of the public and the academy than to a fad effect in the
wake of the counterculture."[25] If many of these books had gone out of
print by the 1980s, these early books on comics history and the
reprinting efforts had planted seeds that would take a few decades to
burgeon.

In a decade where the "graphic novel" label was being used by
a variety of comics publishers and creators to push for new experiments

that were difficult to market and distribute in the editorial context of the time, the monumental dimension of many reprint books emphasized different readerships and played a distinctive logic in a way similar to the peritextual use of the graphic novel label.[26] As much as reprints were turned to the past and catering to widespread nostalgic feelings, they nevertheless reframed comics in important new ways, playing a relatively unacknowledged part in the history of the graphic novel. According to Paul Williams, the 1970s reprint collections were largely understood separately from the graphic novels of the time and their explicitly literary aspirations. When it comes to reprints, "the overwhelming leitmotifs were that these books are repositories of American cultural heritage and/or a time capsule whisking the reader back to childhood."[27] Even when they did not explicitly reframe long-length serial comic strips as novel-like products, these reprints did contribute to cultivating historically minded readers and ultimately led to uses that framed these comics in different terms from those of nostalgia or American cultural heritage. This shift is envisioned by Eddie Campbell in his autobiographical *Alec* series, published in the 2000s, which explicitly mentions the comics history books and reprint collections available in the bookstores of the 1970s (gathered on "that particular shelf in *Bookends* of Camden") as invitations to create "a monumental kind of comic strip" and "add his own chapter to the story in these days when you will still have believed art to be a continuous narrative."[28] Questioning the necessity of a sense of historical progress, Campbell xeroxes, cuts up, and clips out comic-strip panels in his pages, reproducing black-and-white citations from the older comic strips that these reprints made available, literally as material for new uses (Figure 3.2). The loose formatting, with juxtaposed panels reproduced from a variety of comic strips, is evocative of a scrapbook of clippings: in the same work Campbell depicts himself giving this scissor-and-glue treatment to comics history books and collections, crafting his own files out of the unbound, cut-out fragments. With annotated date, copyright mention, and artist, each panel is linked to a cartoonist and acts as a kind of metonymic citation for their work: it both echoes the anthological variety of some 1970s nostalgia books and seems to counter the very idea of a comprehensive reprint.

Figure 3.2 Double page from Eddie Campbell's *Alec: The Years Have Pants* (Marietta, GA: Top Shelf, 2009), 244–45.

RESELLING AND REPACKAGING

The foregoing pages have shown how the archival endeavors of collectors and fans in the 1970s contributed to opening up a space for reprinting that ran parallel to the early inklings of the graphic novel, supporting a sense of historical reflexivity and introducing new audiences to older comics. The development of the graphic novel as we know it today, though, would need the support of a market to further take hold: for comics to exist viably as books, as Charles Hatfield has argued, it would require the development of the direct market and the reorganization of comics culture around stores, and finally the sustained attention of the literary distribution circuit. The changing market conditions for the graphic novel from the 1980s into the 2000s would deal a new set of cards, strengthening the links between reprint collections and graphic novels.

Taking a firm hold on the comic book market in the 1980s, this distribution circuit for specialized comics stores had grown out of "a hobbyists' network concerned with bartering *old* comic books and the underground distribution methods established by comics" in head shops and similar countercultural stores.[29] By contrast with the short life that comics were afforded in newsstands, soda shops, and pharmacies, the comic book shop put a brake on their ephemeral circulation by providing access to back issues and lengthening their shelf life. The role of the comic book shop can be fruitfully compared to the "inertial force" of the video stores that emerged around the same time and that, as Will Straw argues, "ha[ve] acted as a drag of sorts on the forward movement of cinematic culture, slowing the disappearance and commercial obsolescence of films as they pass out of their theatrical runs."[30] While comic book shops were undoubtedly paced at the serial rhythm of weekly releases, they were also "dedicated to the nostalgic preservation of the old and outworn" and, in contrast with the video rental store, emphasized "getting and keeping" and instituted practices of collecting, structured around price guides, back issues, long boxes, mylar bags – rehearsing a set of archival gestures particular to comic book culture.[31] By slowing down the obsolescence of comics, stores participated in the transformation of comic book culture, the consolidation of dedicated fan communities, the production of historically reflexive narratives for know-ing audiences.[32] The direct market also allowed for new independent publishers to emerge and structurally nurtured archival reprint initia-tives such as those of Kitchen Sink Press, Fantagraphics Books, Russ Cochran, Eclipse Comics, or Flying Buttress/NBM. Coming from the underground scene, Denis Kitchen's comic book reprints of Will Eisner's *The Spirit* – who was then nearly completely forgotten – brought the cartoonist back on the scene and encouraged him along to produce the graphic novel work that he is now most remembered for.[33] Favorable to such interactions between old and new, the comic book store, as Hatfield argues, effectively contributed to bringing along new experi-ments in comics publishing in the 1980s and triggered the development of long-length narratives by sustaining their serialization.[34]

The installation of the direct market in the 1980s, however, would also calcify into a reductive focus on a particular understanding of comics history – dominated by the comic book and by publishers prioritizing the superhero genre, leaving large swaths untouched – and a specific audi-ence defined by highly "gendered collecting patterns," narrowly target-ing male readers and by and large keeping female readership away.[35] By the early 1990s, this "narrowing in" would usher the industry into a recession that would lead to the economic integration of comics culture into larger cultural industries (the book trade, for graphic novels).[36] The "inertial force" of the comic book store is also one that has borne on comics historiography, defining boundaries to its archivable past and to understandings of what and who makes history in the form.[37] Even as it partly takes roots in the head shop distribution of underground comics, the US "store memory" tends to forget the publishing experiments of the 1960s and 1970s that happened outside of the mainstream comic book industry.[38] Collections of newspaper comics, for instance, were rarely found in comics stores and were more likely to stand in the humor section of general bookstores. While the circuit of the direct market provided a space where "old" and "new" would conflate and converge, sustaining the publication of objects like reprint editions and graphic novels, it would take the turn toward the book trade in the early 2000s to open up a new moment in the short history of archival reprints of comics. Partly as a result of the recession of the direct market in the 1990s, after which mainstream comics publishers merged into bigger media industries, alternative comics publishers strongly shifted to integrate a literary market that was increasingly welcoming to the graphic novel.[39] The sea change came when North American alternative comics publishers such as Fantagraphics and Drawn & Quarterly rewired their production and distribution methods for the book trade, shifting from periodical to book publication in the early 2000s.[40] The literary institutionalization of the graphic novel, in other words, not only contributed to shaping the publication of new works but also fostered the repackaging of old comics as graphic novels.

At bottom, the graphic novel has been intimately related to reprinting strategies if only for the sheer practical constraints of serialization that have organized its production and distribution. In his 2005 *Alternative Comics*, Charles Hatfield was telling a cautionary tale of the graphic novel, warning of the dangers of overlooking its economic constraints: "importing comics into prevailing canons of literary value, without regard to their special formal characteristics and the specialized circumstances of their making, may mystify their origins and impoverish our appreciation of the medium."[41] This issue remains a red flag for the current field, which tends to work by close readings that uproot graphic novels from their production contexts. It is, moreover, a revealing document for the tensions that were pervading the graphic novel as it was assimilating into literary culture.[42]

If we take reprinting to be a basic mechanism of graphic novel publishing across the board, the interactions between original one-shot graphic novels, collections of serialized stories, and archival reprints become much more evident and tightly connected. Archival reprints here fit within larger commercial strategies of reprinting, drawing on their constituted stock of periodical publication. Fantagraphics Books, for instance, is well known for constantly repackaging the work of its bestselling authors: any firstcomer to the work of the Hernandez brothers or Daniel Clowes will have to navigate their way through a long and sometimes confusing list of multiple reprints, between the original comic book series, "complete" collected editions, anthologies of selected short stories, and multiple editions of their flagship graphic novels.[43] As Fantagraphics shifted from periodical to book publisher, with an extra boost given by integrating the W.W. Norton distribution, it has learned to repackage its back catalog for that market, with long serial comic books such as *Love and Rockets* and *Eightball* providing fragmentary material that can be repeatedly collected in different ways. The same strategy is at work in Fantagraphics' extensive "classics" catalog, which moreover includes important licensing contracts with media franchises such as Disney and Peanuts.[44] The bestselling success of *The Complete Peanuts* – or *Moomin* in the case of Drawn & Quarterly – also helped these publishers to overcome some financial and economic difficulties as they ushered into a new market: in 2004, Fantagraphics sold at least 25,224 copies of the first volume of *The Complete Peanuts*, and the series would remain a steady source of sales revenue.[45] It also shows how alternative publishers have been able to secure rights for producing reprints that the companies or rights holders have otherwise no interest, expertise, or priority in doing by themselves – which does not let us forget that reprinting always involves a complex set of negotiations between publishers, literary agents, copyright holders, and collectors who all have a stake and a say in who or what gets reprinted and how, and who can possibly stall the process.[46]

Where the success of *The Complete Peanuts* demonstrates the commercial interest that alternative comics publishers can find in contracting rights for popular comics, the majority of archival reprints rely on smaller, dedicated audiences in a business model that has become known as the "long tail": it aims to offer a greater diversity of products to niche audiences on a longer basis, which makes reprinting obscure works from the past commercially viable (if not profitable).[47] The development of a relatively healthy market for archival reprints should not hide the "precariousness of comics publishing" that continues to shape their practical reality.[48] Given the massive amount of material that "complete" reprint editions aspire to republish and the difficulty of maintaining such series in the book trade, reprinting comics that were often not intended for book publications raises a number of commercial and formal issues. The *Walt & Skeezix* reprints, for instance, have settled, after the success of their first volumes, around a smaller dedicated audience, leading the publisher to gradually increase retail prices in order to break even.[49] Similarly, some complete reprint series either are abandoned or have their publication schedule lapsed over time because it is too hard to sustain.[50]

For publishing houses like Fantagraphics and Drawn & Quarterly, reprints are also a way of constructing a heritage and enhancing their position as quality publishers with a high reputation and an agenda in positioning comics as an art form on the literary market.[51] In this context, the history of these two publishing houses can be compared to the shift identified in the catalog of their partner French publication house L'Association, which moved from a "logics of war" to a "logics of patrimonialization," as Björn-Olav Dozo has insightfully suggested, by reprinting older comics from the 1970s (but also in editorial endeavors to document its own history as in its "Archives" series, compiling the early works of its foundational members).[52] By contrast with the new French and Belgian comics publishers that have often understood design choices as a principal way of constructing an editorial image and building a catalog, publishers like Fantagraphics and Drawn & Quarterly do not uphold a strong visual identity for their internal catalogs and tend to change design choices depending on the works they publish; they are also prone to let cartoonists take in hand the design and production choices for their works.

For all these reasons, the importance of heteronomous and commercial imperatives in particular market conditions can hardly be overstated in the context of archival reprints. And as Bart Beaty has suggested, part of the stakes in these reprinting strategies also holds to the necessity of reframing past works as graphic novels – hence the choice to have contemporary graphic novelists design and repackage works from the past, acting as "symbolic bankers."[53] As Seth suggested in an interview a few years ago, however, the symbolic caution offered by contemporary cartoonists seems to have somewhat lost its necessity or its appeal: publishers are now more likely to rely on in-house designers to repackage the old comics for which they have obtained reproduction rights. Yet in the mid-2000s, as Seth continues, "it was somewhat standard to draft a modern cartoonist in as the designer to give some special 'flavor' to the books."[54] Within the "economy of prestige" that has come to shape literary production, the graphic novel has been pushed by a small subset of celebrity award-winning cartoonists whom it becomes useful to enlist to repackage old comics and to draw in new audiences by sponsoring a more contemporary look on the covers and by reaching out to the designing authors' own readership.[55]

This seems particularly true for Drawn & Quarterly, which has by and large constructed its editorial identity around autobiographical cartoonists, perhaps by contrast with Fantagraphics, which – with its roots in North American fandom – already had a longer tradition of engaging with comics history (both with *Nemo*, a magazine stunt that republished "classic comics" between 1983 and 1990, and with various book reprints in the early 1990s). Hence, in the Drawn & Quarterly catalog, each reprint is tightly connected to one of "their" cartoonists: Chris Ware has coedited and designed the *Walt & Skeezix* volumes; Seth has repackaged *The John Stanley Library* and Doug Wright's works; Adrian Tomine does the book designs for the translations of Yoshihiro Tatsumi's *gekiga*. Even if its expansive reprint catalog displays more diverse approaches to design, Fantagraphics too has regularly relied on the same contemporary cartoonists to design some of its archival collections: Seth has devised a bold visual identity for *The Complete Peanuts*; Daniel Clowes dressed up Crockett Johnson's *Barnaby*; while Chris Ware has designed a handful of reprints from the *Krazy & Ignatz* series as well as little-known works such as Gajo Sakamoto's prewar action manga *Tank Tankuro* and A. B. Frost's *Stuff and Nonsense* (the last was a bit of a flop on the US market, which reminds us that it takes more than a famous cartoonist to successfully resell past works).

In some cases (and particularly with the Drawn & Quarterly reprints), the association established between a contemporary cartoonist and the reprinted comics is so strong that Ware, Seth, and Tomine have further acted as full-blown cultural mediators, promoting these works and telling their readers why it matters to read these works in a contemporary context. As Jeet Heer has argued, what such reprints instantiate is a kind of "linkage between past and present," whereby a particular version of comics history, with its various key ancestor figures, becomes tightly connected with a distinct group of alternative cartoonists.[56] Cartoonists do more than provide the dressing; they contribute to defining the reprinting priorities of their publishers by promoting certain works from the past. All have recognizable individual graphic styles that are more or less strongly present in their design work, effectively shaping contemporary readers' first encounters with these reprints.

PERIGRAPHIC NOVELS

The way contemporary graphic novelists have repackaged past works appears as a key trend of the early twenty-first century, raising a more complex and diverse set of questions. The economic logic behind these choices is clear: it signals an obvious and clear-headed strategy to capitalize on the success of celebrity cartoonists and their recognizable individual graphic styles to rebrand works that might otherwise be difficult to sell to alternative comics readers. In turn, design and illustration work has become an important part of graphic novelists' professional activities in the twenty-first century as it helps them sustain their practice in a context of dwindling serialization.[57] Yet, it can be somewhat limited to view these mid-2000s reprints only through the lens of their cultural economy. The design work of contemporary cartoonists clearly goes beyond a surface effect and cannot be understood without accounting for a larger redefinition of the relationships between format, form, and content that the graphic novel helped establish. The fact that cartoonists are drafted in as designers derives from their greater involvement in the design of their own works, whereby Seth's, Ware's, or Tomine's books, for instance, have come to have their own visual signature.

In the context of the graphic novel, cartoonists are likely to get involved in the design and production process of their books as physical objects, precisely because format and materiality are more likely to bend themselves to the needs of their narrative and aesthetic project, in contrast with the tighter format constraints of comic strips and comic books (where the cartoonist's aim is to skillfully fill in a well-defined and measured space, usually against tight deadlines). Combined with the emphasis put on personal graphic style in the graphic novel, this means that the relationship between text and paratext becomes particularly strong, as Baetens and Frey suggest: "The most striking difference between an average novel and a graphic novel is the (visual) continuity between paratext and text."[58] The perfect example is of course Chris Ware, who not only adopts different formats for every issue of his periodical *ACME Novelty Library* but also consistently undermines the distinction between text and paratext by approaching perigraphic elements as an integral part of the narrative and the overall aesthetic project.[59] In most of Ware's graphic novels, it is often hard to tell where text and paratext start as the cartoonist blurs the boundaries between the two by making key paratextual components (the title, to start with) less immediately legible than most book design imperatives usually command and, in the process, by strongly folding text and image onto each other, strengthening the iconotextual dimension of the paratext in a way that is consistent with his holistic approach to comics making as writing, drawing, and designing.[60]

While Ware does push things an extra length and weaves text and paratext together in an extremely consistent way, many cartoonists of his generation have developed a strong do-it-yourself ethos from the small-press and zine scenes that remain important sources for the contemporary graphic novel.[61] It also speaks volumes about how much the graphic novel entails an *auteur* or what is usually referred to as a "complete author," responsible for all aspects of production, writing, and drawing as well as putting together the entire book design.[62] An attention to design elements and material components, the narrative use of the perigraphy, and the combination of text and image are all common features of the contemporary graphic novel. This graphic continuity between text and paratext has also undoubtedly contributed to the convergence between graphic novels and literary culture in the 2000s, which was strongly permeating visual culture but had also rekindled an interest in "bookishness" amidst debates around dematerialization (even when all this materiality is sustained by digital printing technologies and their globalized economies).[63]

Jan Baetens and Hugo Frey have already underlined the important role played by the New York book designer Chip Kidd, but it is useful to briefly come back to this example and stress again his lasting contribution at the intersection between graphic novels as well-designed objects and the production of archival reprints. Working as a designer for Random House's various imprints, Kidd further got involved with the editorial direction of Pantheon Books when it turned to comics again in the late 1990s (a decade after having published *Maus*), bringing many of the names from *RAW* (Burns, Katchor, McGuire, Ware, ...). As a designer, Kidd not only facilitated the integration of comics into literary publishing and its market but also defined the perigraphic approach to the graphic novel by helping cartoonists craft the designs of their own books, and hence influencing cartoonists in affirming their own design choices. Moreover, Kidd was also involved in launching the twenty-first-century reprint wave in 2001 with two noted collections. Prior to these, he had installed a benchmark with his collaborating photographer Geoff Spear with *Batman Collected*, a coffee-table book devoted to the collector culture, merchandising, and collectables around DC's superhero icon – largely based on Kidd's own extensive collection of *Batman* items.

A small book in plastic covers, *Jack Cole: Forms Stretched to Their Limits* featured at its center a long essay written by Art Spiegelman.[64] First published in *The New Yorker*, the biographical *text* was important in redirecting attention to a somewhat forgotten figure within comic book history and to its author's complicated life story: the comic book artist Jack Cole shot himself in his car in 1958 for reasons that have remained unclear and that Spiegelman partly tries to untangle. But the book itself is a particularly fascinating hybrid: Spiegelman's essay is typeset in an aptly disorderly fashion, mixed with a large number of Jack Cole's drawings (of all types) and with an anthological selection of *Plastic Man* stories printed on a different paper stock, mimicking the effect of newsprint (of which the degraded quality has been kept if not deliberately reinforced). On top of it, Kidd constantly juxtaposes and intersperses the various types of material in a playfully confusing way that culminates with a number of cut-ups and collages that function as a tribute to the zaniness of Jack Cole's comics. Here, too, the lines that traditionally separate text and peritext are not so clearly defined and the designer takes advantage of this perigraphic space to set out his own contribution: it underlines the vital contribution of graphic design to the construction and interpretation of the work it packages.

Following a similar design, if only toning down its zaniness, Kidd's second 2001 book commemorated the death of Charles Schulz, drawing on a collaboration with the photographer Geoff Spear, who visited the archives of the Schulz estate in Santa Rosa (CA) and, in addition, tapped into Chris Ware's large *Peanuts* merchandising collection to assemble a homage book celebrating the "art of Charles M. Schulz."[65] In fact, in all of his design work, Kidd emphasizes the materiality of the ephemeral objects he takes to monumentalize in coffee-table books, as Spear's photographs strategically play up the different types of paper, the four-color printing technique, the yellowed tapes holding *Peanuts* in place on the pages of a scrapbook, the ink-stained brushes, the dull glow of plastic dolls. By photographing these archives in their actual state, playing up the way they are preserved and kept, Kidd and Spear eulogize and commemorate the deceased creator of *Peanuts.*

Kidd's books in many ways magnify the archives from which they are assembled, drawing attention to the activity of collecting and to comics less as narrative works than as material culture. The same emphasis is not as strong in the complete reprints that followed up only a few years later, but these do display some of the same concerns, especially in their perigraphic strategies, by providing full-fledged autobiographical essays and by showcasing the material diversity that makes up a popular comic strip (where original art and toys are set on the same graphic foot). While Kidd's books are certainly different from the "complete" chronological reprints, they undoubtedly helped establish the genre of the archival collection as we know it today: it is in this sense, as Baetens and Frey put it, that Kidd is "one of the preeminent inventors of the form, certainly as a saleable book commodity that looks good on a bookstore shelf or an adult's desk or side table."[66]

Cartoonist-designed reprints are situated at the crossroads of these two field-defining trends in the twenty-first-century graphic novel, which has turned some graphic novelists – such as Chris Ware, Seth, and Adrian Tomine – into sought-after illustrators and designers. Signature style matters in the realm of graphic novels and this also shows how drawing style, as much as it is connected to a storytelling voice, not only is constructed as part of a comics production but always evolves in dialogue with other graphic work, from illustration to graphic design – always participating in a specific situation of editorial enunciation. In the case of cartoonists who systematically design their own books, and whose work has come to be partly defined by this attention to materiality, their "author function" comes to encompass a visual identity that stretches to the perigraphy. In the case of Chris Ware, Seth, and their peers, part of their authorial identity also lies in the way their books are designed. This is a matter not only of graphiation and drawing style but also of a certain

approach to layout, the recurrence of discrete motifs, geometric compositions, typographic styles and lettering, the expression of particular
material preferences (a specific paper stock, a certain printing technique) – all of which are often shaped by references to past print cultures:
Ware is very often alluding to 1920s modernism; Seth conspicuously
references cartoon books and a larger segment of paper ephemera
from the first half of the twentieth century; and Clowes collects 1960s
paperbacks that shine through in his typographical experiments and
color choices. The perigraphic style of their own books hints at old
designs, and further strengthens how that signature style can be used to
repackage old comics that they admire.

"TOO MUCH SETH – NOT ENOUGH SCHULZ"

Given the continuity between text and peritext in contemporary graphic
novels, it might seem slightly counterintuitive to commission cartoonists
with a strong graphic style in order to repackage older works, precisely
because it tends to disrupt the graphic continuity between the work and
its surrounds, the wrap-up and the contents between the covers. The
exercise can be seen as walking a tightrope, trying to keep a difficult
balance between appropriation and fidelity. When working as designers,
cartoonists necessarily have to handle the existing visual material and
a different graphic style, whether it is one strongly identified with a single
individual author or one that has given way to multiple appropriations to
which the design adds another layer. Book design, here, fits within the
larger media dynamics of continuation, expansion, and adaptation that
necessarily transforms and modifies the life of an oeuvre and subsequently renegotiates a relationship to its graphic rendering.[67] When
partly put in charge of repackaging an old comic, cartoonists become
important actors in the editorial enunciation of the reprinted comics and
thus contribute to distributing its "author function," both by asserting
their own selective affinities with a particular work and by contributing to
(re)defining that same work and its authorship.[68] The linkage rarely goes
unnoticed, even if the cartoonist's intervention can be minimal and
discreet, and tightens the act of reprinting with a work's contemporary
relevance, its value as a monument of comics history.

Seth's work as a designer precisely foregrounds these questions because his designs have become such a strong part of his own authorial identity that they are instantly recognizable as "Seth books" whether it is his work that one finds inside or not. The Canadian cartoonist has described his personal approach to design in an article for the typesetting journal *Devil's Artisan*. His thinking about design is shaped by his collections of mostly "commonplace sources," regional paper ephemera from the 1920s to the 1960s that he "steals" as direct source materials for his design motifs and patterns: "I don't want to downplay the stealing aspect. I collect for inspiration, and inspiration in design is often a synonym for 'thievery'."[69] The "recognizably Seth" aesthetic directly derives from a process of collecting print ephemera from a particular period, just as his graphic style is interlinked with his sense of comics history – all of which does not make them less personal. There is a recognizable set of material and compositional preferences that make Seth's books easily stand out: a systematic use of sans serif, hand-drawn fonts; a limited palette of flat, subdued colors; thick, grained hardback covers; a particular flavor for uncoated and matte paper stocks and for rarefied (but increasingly affordable) printing techniques as metallic foil stamping and embossing or debossing; a particular use of the inside covers and the peritextual spaces, privileged for their horizontal flatness and often used to integrate landscapes.

Seth's readers quickly learn how to immediately spot a work of his on a bookstore table, and it is perhaps partly for this reason that Seth has been regularly commissioned to design many other publications and graphic matter beyond archival reprints of old comics: he has, among others, provided cover designs and illustrations for new editions of short story collections by Dorothy Parker (as part of a collection of Penguin classics illustrated by contemporary graphic novelists) and Stephen Leacock.[70] Although Seth asserts a neat difference between his personal work and the commissions he does for various clients, his reprints are often situated somewhere in between the two.[71] More often than not, he has done more than "simply" repackaging; he has helped to revive interest in old comics by writing essays that preceded the reprints. In various cases Seth not only has designed the reprints but has actively contributed as a coeditor, directly participating in the recovery of forgotten segments of comics history. It is common to find, among the paratextual essays that often go along with such volumes, a "designer's note" or an "introduction by the designer" in which Seth elaborates on his relationship to the reprinted comic and the design approach adopted to reframe it. This level of engagement is perhaps most evident for Doug Wright, whose work he had collected for years before the reprinting project actually came together. *The Collected Doug Wright*, in turn, is designed with an amount of care and with a personalized approach that are telling of his investment in the project and that give the book a particular place in Seth's own trajectory.

When it comes to *The John Stanley Library* project at Drawn & Quarterly, which collects a selection of comic books written by John Stanley for Dell Comics, Seth had already devoted a long essay in a 2001 issue of *The Comics Journal* to one of Stanley's forgotten series, *Thirteen Going on Eighteen*.[72] The essay analyzes his teen comics, eulogizes the humor, composition, and storytelling craft of Stanley. Following up on Carl Barks, the cartoonist was similarly reconstructed and celebrated as an *auteur* as part of fannish epistemologies. Seth further contributes to this historiography, identifying Stanley as an individual cartoonist within the Dell comics production, underlying his idiosyncratic writing.[73] In this work as a comics historian – "exposing forgotten comics history" is the subtitle of his essay – Seth further contributes to defining and organizing the archive of comics history: reprinting shifts here from a focus on a popular series (as collected in the late 1980s by Another Rainbow publishing in their *Little Lulu Library*) to a focus on a particular cartoonist whose contribution to comics history is primarily understood as that of a writer (with stories drawn by a variety of cartoonists, including a few by Stanley himself). Out of the graphic heterogeneity of the Dell catalog, the *John Stanley Library* creates a unified collection dedicated to a single author. This reframing is effectively taken out by Seth's designs, which develop a consistent material look for the series; Seth takes a particular license by contributing his own mark to the paratext of *The John Stanley Library*, drawing his versions of the characters on the covers and title pages of the different volumes as a way of uniformizing the look of Stanley's various collected series (Figure 3.3).

Figure 3.3 Double page from the frontmatter of Seth's book for John Stanley's *Thirteen "Going on Eighteen,"* edited by Rebecca Rosen (Montreal: Drawn & Quarterly, 2010), n.p. Source: Copyright © Seth. Courtesy of Drawn & Quarterly.

By upholding a strongly personal style in his graphic design, Seth firmly asserts his own intervention in the reprinting process. Hence, also, the criticism that readers have sometimes voiced toward his design for *The Complete Peanuts*, founded on the idea that his take on Schulz's work was "too dour" and unduly marked by his own aesthetic: "Too much Seth – not enough Schulz."[74] This visual presence is counterintuitive to the traditional role of book designers, who usually have to remain "invisible."[75] But this admonition also shows how these reprints evidently work as adaptations: as such, they are prone to spark judgments of value depending on the readers' implications about what constitutes a good or a bad adaptation. In reaction, Seth has commented on this affirmation of a personal approach to design in his reprints, describing it as an expression of love and homage:

> The truth is, when I design something it really is too much about me. I'm responding to Stanley with the love of another artist. I'm trying to create

a package for him that is a tribute to him. It's not really how designers classically work. I think the best graphic designers try to remove themselves from the picture and create a package that is suited to the work being packaged. I don't really think that way – I can't keep myself out of the process. My designs end up having a bit too much of me still in the picture. It's that way with Schulz, it's that way with Stanley, and it is certainly that way with Wright. I'm probably not a very good graphic designer for that reason.[76]

Although it might seem counterintuitive to standard practice in book design, this is of course also precisely what makes Seth a sought-after designer. Moreover, if the publisher's aim is to revive interest in old comics and reframe them for contemporary comics readers, the blending of old and new that defines Seth's aesthetics proposes a useful solution to the problems of repackaging works from the past; it can help publishers not only find the balance between material that looks authentic without seeming completely old-fashioned but also reframe kid comic strips for an adult audience.[77]

This process of reframing brings out different stakes and is thus at the heart of the debates around *The Complete Peanuts*. Schulz's comic strip was so popular that it had already expanded into a considerable number of paperback collections, screen adaptations (fondly remembered television specials), and, as widely displayed in Kidd's book, a large merchandising empire.[78] The long serial life of the comic strip meant that it would be able to integrate this merchandising development into a profitable feedback loop with the comic strip itself (the popularity of Snoopy would gain the dog character an increasingly prominent place in the newspaper strip in the 1960s). Schulz actively collaborated with United Media to bring about "the expansion of consumer products related to his characters" and set up a studio of creative associates to help him produce the graphic work that such an expansion required.[79] At the same time, Schulz kept on drawing the newspaper comic strip himself, refusing to have it taken over by another artist. The graphic afterlife of the strip continues to be managed by the Peanuts Studio (headed by Paige Braddock), which today hires a handful of graduates from the Center of Cartoon Studies.[80] Schulz's heritage and legacy, about which the author was well aware and which he did contribute to organizing, is managed on a daily basis not only by business associates and heirs withholding or distributing copyright but also by creative teams liable for the graphic afterlives of the author. Schulz's graphic style, in other words, is reaffirmed and reinvented whenever there is need for a Linus coffee mug or a Snoopy book collection. In doing this, the Peanuts Studio team constantly manages, organizes, and revisits the reproduction of *Peanuts* images. Where the importance of studios in producing and distributing "individual" styles collaboratively is well known, however, there has been less interest in the continued work done by these studios in maintaining the legacy and heritage of cartoonists after their death, updating and refitting images for licensed uses and in a way being endowed with the role of visual caretaker for their cultural memory.

The Complete Peanuts consists in an extraneous contribution to that memory work, but one that is fully entrusted with permission from the Schulz estate and creative associates – by contrast with the vibrant realm of extralegal recirculations and appropriations of his work, such as the *Peanuts* parody anonymously done in the early 1990s by Seth, Joe Matt, and Chester Brown. As already indicated in that parody, *Peanuts* is not a light, happy, and funny comic strip in the eyes of many alternative cartoonists who have rather turned to the melancholic and depressive quality of the strip that echoes their own concerns. As Charles Hatfield notes, "*Peanuts* has been reclaimed with a vengeance, inspiring homages and parodies from a great many alternative comics artists ostensibly working for adults."[81] Before doing the designs for *The Complete Peanuts*, Seth had already paid multiple homages to Schulz in his comics, citing his work on various occasions. The graphic design for *The Complete Peanuts* was thus positioned in the continuity of a particular understanding of Schulz's comic strip that has further guided the creation of the packaging. The project was also an explicit way of commemorating Charles Schulz's death in 2000; the fact that the heirs and creative associates granted Gary Groth permission to edit and publish a complete chronological reprint fits within the mourning work that Schulz's copyright holders have embarked on (and which found its expression not only in a variety of projects, notably the Schulz Museum and many others dedicated to the cultural memory of the creator, but also in financial support provided to institutions of comics history in general, such as the Billy Ireland Cartoon Library & Museum).[82] The sober aesthetics of *The Complete Peanuts* certainly partakes in this commemoration; it also opens a dialogue with other readers' remembrance of the comic strip by inviting celebrities to write prefaces, and by involving Seth in the design.

The covers of the series reflect Seth's personal approach to design, marking particular preferences in terms of color, composition, and lettering. By featuring blown-up drawings of Charles M. Schulz against single-flat-color backgrounds, Seth also follows in the long tradition of paperback collections and other reproductions of *Peanuts* images (one can think of the Fawcett paperbacks or the famous covers of the Italian magazine *Linus*). The paperback collections, however, regularly hinted at a well-known gag or recurring situations in the *Peanuts* comic strip: the Fawcett paperback covers are a gag in themselves, in their combination of an excerpted drawing and a well-known catchphrase from the comic strip. By contrast, the covers of *The Complete Peanuts* only feature close-ups of the characters' cartoon faces, putting on expressions familiar to the readers. The subdued colors, even if relatively varied, also give a different tone that contrasts with the colorful images of many paper-backs. The covers, then, instill a melancholic mood into the reprint of *The Complete Peanuts*, which to many readers would have seemed odd. As Bart Beaty observes: "To many, the *Complete Peanuts* books seem like an incongruous way to celebrate the work of a man who sold more than a million copies of a book titled *Happiness Is a Warm Puppy*."[83] Yet, *The Complete Peanuts* also shifts the reading from a focus on Schulz's comic as a gag strip to reading it as a long-length oeuvre, emphasizing the series as a personal and unified work – thus reframing the comic strip in the context of the graphic novel.

This is not just an effect of the cover design, of course, and Seth's perigraphic contribution goes beyond the hardback covers. In fact, as in most of his book design work, Seth follows advice from Chip Kidd who apparently suggested to him that "the space between the half-title page and the title page is the book designer's chance to make poetry."[84] These couple of pages are always used by Seth – as already seen in the case of *The Collected Doug Wright*, he uses them to produce a particular sequence and rhythm, leading the reader in and out of the book. In this case, the compositional and horizontal flatness of the title pages and inside covers is used to depict landscapes and background from the comic strip, describing the "neighborhood" that makes up the consistent "microcosmic world" of Schulz's kid characters.[85] Over the entire series, these double pages consistently use the horizontal quality of the oblong books to emphasize the landscapes of the *Peanuts* strip, contrasting with other reprints that tend to primarily focus on the cartoon characters. As such, they not only lead the readers into the paper world of the comic strip but also emphasize how much the strip was dedicated to creating a suburban background, how much small but recurring details (grass, falling leaves, snowmen) were also fundamental parts of the graphic world of *Peanuts*. The stillness of these pages further sustains a poetic reading of *Peanuts* as a comic strip essentially about everyday life, aligned with the concerns of alternative cartoonists about "what happens when nothing happens," to borrow Greice Schneider's apt phrasing.[86] By creating a perigraphic sequence that underlines the visual poetry of *Peanuts*, Seth relies on "visual, verbal, and design strategies that slow down the time of reading and call attention to the materiality of the book as object," inviting the reader to a "quiet contemplation."[87] In the process, then, Seth attempts to school the reader into reading *Peanuts* differently.

Seth's approach can be usefully contrasted with other reprints by contemporary cartoonists, whose design work is often less strongly connected to their own graphic style. By contrast with Seth's designs, Daniel Clowes's design work for Fantagraphics' reprint volumes of Crockett Johnson's kid comic strip *Barnaby* appears as relatively unobtrusive.[88] The design work speaks out Clowes's collaboration in recovering a newspaper strip for which he has regularly declared his passion. Fragments of his extended collection of *Barnaby* clippings were further exhibited in one of Ivan Brunetti's anthologies.[89] And yet, Clowes has less assuredly taken on the role of comics historian than Spiegelman, Seth, or Ware have done, keeping some distance in a way that already appeared clear in his ambivalent positions toward exhibiting (see Chapter 2). Accordingly, his design on the *Barnaby* volumes is not marked by his own graphic style but proposes in fact a clever adaptation of the popular *Barnaby* book reprints of the 1940s, published by Henry Holt & Co., into a larger graphic novel format. *Barnaby* started running as a comic strip in April 1942 in the left-wing newspaper *PM*: its everyday circulation was quite limited, but it gathered a dedicated audience of public figures – none other than Duke Ellington and Dorothy Parker – but some of the key episodes were very quickly remade into a first book by Holt in 1943 that would become a real bestseller.[90] The two volumes published by Holt anthologized a selection of episodes, sometimes redrawn, from the daily comic strip. These reprints would be reissued and extended by other publishers in the 1960s (Dover) and 1980s (Ballantine), until the Fantagraphics project – sustained by Eric Reynolds and Crocket Johnson's biographer Philip Nel – started to reprint the entire newspaper strip in chronological order.

While the volumes are very different objects from the 1940s books, Daniel Clowes nevertheless revisits their covers, relying on the same background color choices (yellow, red, black) against which the cast of characters is set off and on the same combination of condensed and medium versions of the Futura typeface. Clowes's back cover does rely on a familiar trick in his book design toolbox (as used, among others, for the back cover of *Ice Haven*) by displaying a grid of square panels (quite close to the layout of most *Barnaby* comic strips), hued in primary colors and including cartoon heads and speech balloons that seamlessly integrate the necessary paratextual information (blurbs and endorsements, credits, price and barcode). The governing principle, however, is to strengthen the graphic continuity between text and paratext. In so doing, Clowes's designs reinforce the main aspects associated with Johnson's "graphic cool."[91] Crockett Johnson indeed shares with Ernie Bushmiller (*Nancy*) and Otto Soglow (*The Little King*) – all exhibited as part of Clowes's selections of comics history – a minimalist approach to cartooning that strips graphic style down to its bare communicative efficiency, purging from their drawings any distracting details. Clowes's designs are extremely perceptive in understanding the strength of this graphic style and adapting it to the paratext.

The cover is in keeping with this clear minimalist style: regular and uniform lines, a geometric composition, and single-value colors. It understands that this approach is also reflected in the choice of the geometric sans-serif Futura typeface, designed for the Bauer Type Fondry and released in 1927 by the German Paul Renner.[92] The use of the typeface is a distinguishing feature of *Barnaby*: at a time when cartoonists mostly relied on lettering by hand, Johnson worked with the *PM* type shop to set his dialogues in italicized Futura medium. By placing "Volume One" within a speech bubble on the cover of the reprint, Clowes directly indicates that this is not only a typographical choice but how characters speak in Barnaby's world. The heavy black title, set in the same italicized Futura bold condensed but given larger space in the Fantagraphics reprint than in the 1943 edition, works not only as a way of underlining essential paratextual information but contributes important visual information: the large horizontal black title indeed fits within the graphic rationale of Johnson's style by "spotting blacks," giving its due weight to the distribution of solid black areas that systematically punctuate every *Barnaby* comic strip and shape its rhythm.[93] It also functions to separate Barnaby from his fairy godfather Mr. O'Mailley, drawing a line between reality and imagination that is the central thematic conceit of the comic strip.[94] By all means, the cover thus strengthens the relationship between text and image and underlines their graphic reciprocity: the minimalist style of *Barnaby* becomes as neutral and legible as the Futura typeface. In this way, it gives a narrative function to the cover as the characters running toward the left directly invite the reader to follow the movement. Clowes's design, then, is an ingenious reworking of the 1940s book design: if relatively sober and unassuming, and much less marked by Clowes's imprint, it nonetheless constitutes an important intervention in the framing and understanding of *Barnaby* as a historical work as well as an adaptation of the strip in a graphic novel where text and paratext are seamlessly tuned to the same visual tone.

FROM GASOLINE ALLEY TO WALT & SKEEZIX

In many ways, today's reprints – in their self-description as archival collections – tend to present themselves as authentic reference versions of an oeuvre. What is retrospectively assembled as an oeuvre often results from a long and messy serial history that complicated the canonizing process – a case that the reprinting of *Gasoline Alley* helps to understand in further detail. Although he is now frequently mentioned in the same breath with Winsor McCay and George Herriman,

Frank King was poorly remembered in comics culture until his rehabilitation in the twenty-first century. The works of McCay and Herriman had been repeatedly brought back in print and, in however haphazard or partly unsuccessful ways, they have remained shared visual references across generations of cartoonists. *Little Nemo* and *Krazy Kat* were integrated into a particular process of canonization early on that has sustained their persistence and cultural transmission. In the twenty-first century, they then became obvious candidates for extensive, near-complete chronological reprints (building on previous enterprises bringing their work into new formats). Frank King's *Gasoline Alley*, by contrast, had barely been reprinted over the course of the twentieth century, except for a handful of Sunday pages in anthologies of the 1970s. King's comic strip, even when *Gasoline Alley* is still running today, was nearly completely forgotten. Its contemporary resurgence – in the form of the *Walt & Skeezix* series edited by Chris Ware and Jeet Heer for Drawn & Quarterly since 2005 – constitutes a surprising return in the context of the graphic novel and presents a complex and fascinating case in the cultural transmission of old comics. It is not that *Gasoline Alley* was unpopular or at odds with its time, however. The recovery of his work is not the same as the fascination for neglected comics, short-lived titles, and other graphic curiosa embraced in anthologies such as Dan Nadel's impressive selection of "unknown comics visionaries" in *Art Out of Time*.[95] King's *Gasoline Alley* was a big success in its heyday in the 1920s and 1930s because it was well suited to the newspaper regime of popular seriality. This organic link to the format of the strip, however, has made it difficult to precisely remember and pass down across generations.

If we want to understand the challenges that anyone faces when setting out to reprint *Gasoline Alley* (and some of these challenges are common with any other comic strip with a long serial life), we need to take a closer look at its historical origins within a specific model of "open-ended seriality."[96] Debuting in 1918 in the cartoon pages of the *Chicago Tribune* as a series of recurring gags about cars, King's strip transformed into a family strip when an orphan – to be named Skeezix – was dropped on the doorstep of bachelor Walt Wallet in 1921, changing the course of the strip. The introduction of an orphan allowed King to depict Skeezix growing up, breaking off the usual convention and displaying characters aging: from then on, "each day in the lives of the readers matched a day in the lives of the characters, who aged in real time."[97] The shift was made under the impulse of an important change in newspaper comic strips. In the late 1910s, starting in the sports pages of the *San Francisco Chronicle*, Bud Fischer's *Mutt and Jeff* had already given a successful push toward stronger narrative continuity and the development of an open-ended seriality that relied on the active engagement and constant dialogue with their readers.[98] Following suit, *Chicago Tribune* editor Joseph Medill Patterson was looking to reposition newspaper comics by catering to the new serial pleasures of the decade and strengthening the syndication of comic strips, then increasingly distributed to local newspapers across the whole United States and synchronizing national audiences to the rhythm of the daily comic strip. The "Chicago School" of the *Tribune* would excel at this game by deliberately making strips about ordinary life, spawning some of the most widely read comics (Sidney Smith's *The Gumps* and indeed King's *Gasoline Alley*) and affording their top cartoonists extremely profitable careers.[99] Clearly, Patterson had understood the commercial gains of institutionalizing the family strip, which conjoined readerly habits and audience segmentation to the ritual publication schedule of the newspaper.

Accordingly, the habitual serial regime of King's comic strip (its aging characters, its chronicle of everyday life) was entirely dependent on its synchronization with the "real time" of newspaper publication and its particular "temporality of circulation."[100] King further made clever use of the distinctions between weekday and Sunday papers: the condensed, black-and-white space of the daily comic strip was mostly used to develop the ongoing narrative, which was then bracketed off on Sundays, where the full-color and full-page installments offered more room for reverie and visual experiments. Clocked in to the time of the newspaper, *Gasoline Alley* fully exploited the medium specificity of the syndicated strip. In this sense, its narrative effect was strongly "mediagenic," difficult to transfer or adapt to another medium – and this of course also includes its repackaging from newspaper strip to graphic novel.[101] If it did not hinder the successful merchandising of the strip's characters (which rocketed with an extremely popular oilcloth doll version of Skeezix) and a few film and radio adaptations, it does raise a number of issues when it comes to reprinting – some common to any long-length serial comic, others more specific to *Gasoline Alley* – that might explain the surprising lack of book collections of King's series.[102]

It is indeed telling that the few books printed in the heyday of the strip (by Reilly & Lee, a New York publisher notorious for Frank L. Baum's *Oz* books) were not reprints of selected comic strips but rather novelizations, condensing chosen narrative segments into illustrated children's books.[103] In a speech broadcast on the radio to publicize the first title, Frank King offers a perceptive commentary on the necessary ephemerality of his strip:

> The book was first suggested by people who wanted the story of Skeezix in some permanent form. The newspaper is a wonderful medium of distribution but it is probably the most perishable household product of the moment. . . . Eggs and meat grow old rapidly but a newspaper eight hours old is dead. Another fresh supply is on the street and will be in the home shortly. This is an aid to continuity – the carrying on of the story, because the time element is already established. Something happens today in the comic strip. The event of the following day is shown tomorrow and another the day after that. This is why the growth of Skeezix in the paper seems to be as natural and logical as in real life. . . . However, all this does not make for a permanent record.[104]

King clearly presents the book as a keepsake, a condensed version and record for the comic strip. In his eyes, the comic strip is organically related to the newspaper and would have little sense if it appeared in another format (King also develops the economic dimension of this everyday work, comparing the labor of the cartoonist to that of delivery workers: "What would become of the ice man if the ice didn't melt?"). All of this contributed to make *Gasoline Alley* a strip that is hard to reprint because its basic mechanism demands ephemerality and one that was impinged on its continuous obsolescence. That this speech by King is itself included in Ware and Heer's reprint further echoes the difficulties of their own reprinting enterprise, which precisely strives to reconstitute a permanent record for King's strip. Prior to that, it is interesting to look at an initial launch of the reprint project in the publisher's title magazine.

In April 2000, Drawn & Quarterly relaunched its anthological magazine, this time in a heavier glossy format, with a prominent place given to thirty *Gasoline Alley* Sunday pages culled from the collection of its cartoonist Joe Matt, with extra archival help by Daniel Clowes and Art Spiegelman (the latter provided King's original drawings and watercolors for an unpublished Sunday page).[105] The covers and endpapers of the anthology are designed by Chris Ware as a tribute to King's work and include a pastiche essay about *Gasoline Alley*, drawn in its Sunday style. The anthology was the first substantial reprinting of these early pages and would prepare the ground for the current interest in Frank King's work.

Ware's design of the paratext is effectively wrapping up the anthology and in itself contributing a clever reworking of King's *Gasoline Alley* that guides the reader's attention to certain aspects of the strip (Figure 3.4). The colors of the covers immediately produce a strong vintage look in their imitation of Sunday comics supplements. With the colors done digitally, Ware's emulation of Ben Day dots is not overplayed (the dots are visible only on closer inspection) and follows an emulation rather than a magnification of newspaper printing techniques. Moreover, this coloring replicates King's strategic use of the primary colors by keeping a solid yellow, setting its brightness off against the other screentoned colors, which also contributes to making the composition of the page more dynamic. Similarly, the paratextual information is completely integrated into the designs of the covers and their evocation of early-twentieth-century Sunday pages. The title is drawn in rounded letters, just as a regular *Gasoline Alley* title, while the contents and colophon fit in speech bubbles that seamlessly integrate with the general aesthetics. While these elements strengthen the intericonic connection to King's Sunday pages, the cover layout deviates from the usual composition of newspaper comics and is much more typical of Chris Ware's experimental page compositions.

The covers of the magazine indeed play up the architectural quality of the object (which is perfect bound, hence closer to a book in its printed format), weaving an analogy between the fold-out covers and the spatial representation of the various *Gasoline Alley* places. The reader moves

Figure 3.4 Inside covers by Chris Ware for *Drawn and Quarterly*, no. 3 (Montreal: Drawn & Quarterly, 2000). Source: Copyright © Ware. Courtesy of the artist.

from outside small-town Midwestern landscapes to a bird's-eye view of the "alley" – partially redrawn from the iconic May 1931 Sunday page discussed in Chapter 1 (Figure 1.3) – and an increasingly detailed picture of the inside of Walt Wallet's house. The process is rigidly segmented by a logic of incremental subdivisions of the page: the page is divided into four clusters that are each subsequently divided into two alongside a diagonal aspect ratio that follows the reading process from top right to bottom left. In this way, Ware gradually focuses the reader's attention from the large picture to the small detail, from a moonlit open landscape to the tip of Walt's cowlick. The background panels establish a consistent sense of place that is further segmented into particular details, which allows Ware to bring in a high degree of temporal variations in the image: it is not simply that each panel singles out a specific element but also that it singles out a different moment in time.

This juxtaposition of heterogeneous temporal moments is a recurring trope in Chris Ware's work, relying on a highly constrained grid to represent a specific space while juxtaposing wildly separate moments in time – a strategy he has explored and refined partly based on his continuation of Frank King's Sunday pages. In refocusing readers' attention on the space and place of *Gasoline Alley* rather than the characters – an approach that Seth has similarly adopted for the interior design of *The Complete Peanuts* – Chris Ware emphasizes the temporal everydayness of King's comic strip. Adopting a radically nonsequential approach to the grid, Ware crafts an unassuming comic within the confines of the non-narrative perigraphic space: these pages indeed read as a seemingly randomized selection of background moments in the long serial history of King's comic strip. This design approach runs in fact very close to some of Ware's own comics, drawn around the same time and sometimes done in a pastiche of King's style. It reframes the comic strip as an everyday life narrative, which is further bolstered up in Ware's comics essay for the anthology.

Ware's essay in comics form adopts the style of a typical *Gasoline Alley* Sunday page, using the same newsprint features as the covers but replicating the regular grid layout, title header, and reiterating one of King's favorite themes with characters walking across the space of the page. The essay further relies on a dissociation of text and image (already introduced in the design of the table of contents) as the characters are not speaking out the text of the speech bubbles tailed to them.[106] The text reads instead as a segmented but continuous commentary on Frank King's comic strip, recounting how it shifted from a gag-a-day strip about tinkering men and their cars to a narrative-driven family strip with aging characters, transforming into "a modest chronicle of every-day middle class American life."[107] Ware writes its history as one that reflects the decline of newspaper comics, due to the withering of their size from large full-color broadsheets to "the cocktail napkin-sized scraps that remain today." The page communicates an overall sense of loss against which the recovery of the Sunday pages becomes all the more important. The last piece of text replicates a 1929 citation from King: "Almost anyone would make a good comic character. There is no lack of raw material. Not only the woods, but the streets and houses, are full of it." The quote retro-spectively casts Ware's perigraphic design as an extension of that state-ment, with a literal focus on the rawest material that makes up *Gasoline Alley* just as much as its main cast of characters: the stones, the pipes, the cooking dishes, the household plants, the trees, the fences, the fire hydrant, the utility pole, the faucet, the curtains, the rain, and so on.

Around the same time, Chris Ware had also drawn a few pages in a pastiche style after King's *Gasoline Alley* as part of his *Quimby the Mouse* series, in which he explored a mode of covert autobiography related to the memory of places and particular objects. One strip is entirely told around a lamp, reproduced in about forty panels with speech bubbles tailing "outside." Another strip, "Every Morning," is an elegiac piece about Ware's childhood memories of his grandmother and her house, in the form of Quimby Mouse's exploration of her house. While Benjamin Widiss identifies the piece as an indication of Ware's more personal and mature style, as opposed to the heteroge-neous styles of *Quimby* strips and their dense references to comics history (presented as "apprentice work"), it remains that this personal style is here, too, infused with Ware's digging in the archives of newspaper comics.[108] These comics reveal how much Chris Ware's graphic experiments were intertwined with his appreciation of Frank King's *Gasoline Alley*. More than a question of influence and lineage, it is clearly through the appropriation, imitation, and continuation of some of King's iconic pages that Chris Ware devised some of his strategies for page compositions, his approach to temporality, and his aesthetics of everyday life. In turn, the way that Ware has reimagined the work of Frank King has strongly shaped its contemporary canonization. A subtler but nonetheless central part of this linkage also entails an indirect mode of autobiography that already appears clearly in Ware's pastiche of King's style as a way of exploring autobiographical concerns and that will move to the core of the extensive *Walt & Skeezix* reprint project, which can be read as a reinvention of King as an autobiographical cartoonist.

Published by Drawn & Quarterly, Jeet Heer and Chris Ware's reprint series was launched in 2005 and today counts eight chronological volumes of daily comic strips with an additional volume for Sunday pages, also designed by Ware but published at broadsheet scale through Peter Maresca's Sunday Press. The volumes tap extensively the collection of *Gasoline Alley* clippings assembled by Joe Matt, but they also draw from the extensive private family archives made available for the project by the granddaughter of the cartoonist Drewanna King. As an archival project, *Walt & Skeezix* converges with the rising vernacular interest in family genealogies and the opening of online photographic archives and newspaper repositories. In terms of book design, the volumes adopt a format with the exact same size as the hardback edition of Ware's *Jimmy Corrigan*, and with a similar rounded corner binding and dustjacket. For the rest, however, Ware's perigraphic design is less obviously marked by his own graphic style and selects, reorganizes, and colors relevant fragments from King's comic strip, emphasizing the strip's central conceit of aging characters: the spine of each volume, for instance, depicts the relevant years' version of Skeezix, immediately evidencing how the character grows up through the years.

By integrating a significant wealth of the family archives kept by Drewanna King, to whom the first volume is dedicated, *Walt & Skeezix* appears as a threefold enterprise, combining the chronological reprinting of the series (starting in 1921 with the arrival of Skeezix), carefully researched and detailed biographical essays written by Jeet Heer and accompanied by a rich amount of documents and iconography. The links between both the development of the comic strip and King's life are constantly stressed by the editors. From the get-go, Heer indeed writes in his introduction that "Frank King was among the most autobiographical of cartoonists."[109] His historical essays offer important insights into how King drew elements from his own life to build *Gasoline Alley*, while the photographs – replicating a family album – sustain this autobiographical reading. The main focus of Heer's essays is set on the father-and-son relationship that is at the center of *Walt & Skeezix*, as its title already indicates (this alternative title is further linked to copyright reasons as *Gasoline Alley* remains the property of the newspaper syndicate and the comic strip is still continued). Heer overlays Walt's relationship to Skeezix – a very close and loving relationship but one that is constantly threatened by external forces – with King's own troubled history of parenthood, presenting his characters' relationship as a kind of wishful, surrogate life-writing.

The reframing of *Gasoline Alley* as a covert autobiography can be read as a "distinctive device" to canonize Frank King as an *auteur* figure, perhaps framed from a retrospective lens.[110] This, however, would not be taking account of the celebrity status that some successful newspaper cartoonists took on in their own time, and among which Frank King is certainly a key example. Tapping into the clipping files from the King family, the reprints display the interaction between the comic strip and the paratext of the newspaper as both *Gasoline Alley* and the cartoonist's life were frequently the subject of short articles and headings in the newspaper in which the comic strip was syndicated. Newspaper articles would frequently underline that Walt was based on King's brother-in-law, sometimes playing up the parallel between the paper character and the flesh-and-blood person. Such examples show that the autobiographical reading of the strip is perhaps not as strongly shaped by a retrospective view as we might at first think. By contrast, it displays how much the comic strip could be read in conjunction with the creator's public life as part of this lively serial regime. In framing this regime primarily in terms of an attention to everyday life and as covert autobiography, however, the reprints do tend to play down other elements of the comic strip, such as its strong generic ties with the Chicago style of the family strip. The difference with *The Gumps* by Smith, also part of the *Tribune* staff, is stressed time and again to set out the melodramatic narrative suspense of the strip against what is presented as the quieter tone of *Gasoline Alley*. Nevertheless, King's strip certainly had its nail-biting moments, relying on well-worn narrative tricks of the trade: the kidnapping of Skeezix and the breach-of-promise trial are both long continuity sequences that drive a strong narrative into the strip and that intensely mobilized their historical readership's affective attachments to the strip. This means that other aspects of the strip, more tightly connected to its workings within the genre of the family strip, are downplayed by the reprints.

Writing on the development of the open-ended serial and *The Gumps*, Jared Gardner has shown the crucial role played by readers in co-defining the narrative development of the comic strip, notably through correspondence and readers' letters. The distinctive particularity of *Gasoline Alley* engaged in similar forms of audience participation, using moments of dramatic suspense to solicit readers and heighten its media circulation, but also more simply by playing up the "synchronic time" of the newspaper, developing a close relationship to its readership. In the *Walt & Skeezix* reprints, this larger cultural working of the comic strip and the connection between cartoonist and audience is superseded by the autobiographical connections between the creator and its work, between the father and his son. The everyday life that matters is that of Frank King more than that of his readers (one that is necessarily harder to reconstruct).

The reprints tend to privilege King's portrayal of ordinary everyday life in its small details. This is already the trait that Ware had emphasized in his comics essay and perigraphic designs for the *Drawn and Quarterly* anthological magazine. In the reprints, Heer further connects it to the diary form typical of contemporary comics autobiographies:

> In King's diary, we can see the real seeds of his achievement in *Gasoline Alley*. Diary-keeping, like drawing a newspaper comic strip, is a daily activity. Aside from King, many other cartoonists of his time used a daily diary as a planner, to keep track of extended narratives and tight deadlines. But King's strip was especially journal-like in its pacing and rhythm: every fresh *Gasoline* strip is a record of a new day, with the characters accumulating experience.[111]

Reimagining *Gasoline Alley* as a diary comic seems apt in the twenty-first century precisely because it runs parallel to online practices of

serialization that have embraced the diary form to present autobiographical or pseudo-autobiographical narratives, such as James
Kochalka's *American Elf.*[112] By emphasizing the diary form, Heer underlines the importance of the synchronic serial regime of King's comic
strip and its ties to the sense of an accumulated experience that built up
a habitual ritualistic relationship with its original audiences. The
reprints thus somewhat present themselves as the archival reconstruc-
tion of this daily newspaper strip, built around an expressive array of
documents and long essays that are to be read conjointly with the comic
strip. Tellingly, Heer hints, in his essay on Ware's book design, that they
had imagined the *Walt & Skeezix* series as a project akin to Nabokov's
Pale Fire, if only "more sober," just as "multilayered": the high-modernist
novel presents itself as a long epic poem with an extremely dense critical
apparatus, in which the notes system threatens to overwhelm the poem
itself.[113]

This overwhelming of archival material, both in the longevity of the
comic strip and in the wealth of documents that are reused in the reprint,
does attempt to redirect attention to King's contribution to comics
history beyond that of a handful of experimental Sunday pages. In
representing *Gasoline Alley* as a quietly incrementing diary of everyday
life, the *Walt & Skeezix* series reframes the comic strip as an interestingly
boring one. Gilbert Seldes, one of the earlier critics to celebrate comics in
The Seven Lively Arts and a particular fan of Herriman's *Krazy Kat*, had
little patience for the family strip:

> The Chicago School I have frankly never been able to understand . . .. The
> Gumps are common people and the residents of Gasoline Alley are just
> folks, but I have never been able to understand what they are doing;
> I suspect they do nothing. It seems to me I read columns of conversation
> daily, and have to continue to the next day to follow the story.[114]

Where everydayness is judged utterly boring by Seldes, it generates a clear
new interest within contemporary alternative comics.[115] It is precisely for
its portrayal of everyday life that Frank King's comic strip develops
a renewed interest in the early twenty-first century. *Walt & Skeezix*, in
this sense, tries to reposition the boring moments of King's strip as the
most interesting ones.

REPRINT RHYTHM

The reprinting of *Gasoline Alley* in book format, while the strip had never been republished before, thus presents a major intervention in the survival of the work. It recirculates the comic strip in a completely different way, with stakes that are underlined by Eddie Campbell in a perceptive comment that could apply to a great number of other archival collections: "*Gasoline Alley* is reprinted, but it's dressed up lovingly by graphic novelist Chris Ware. Now, the book has been assembled and produced within the sensibility of the graphic novel. ... You would take *Walt and Skeezix* and file it with the graphic novels because it belongs to that sensibility."[116] The linkage with Ware's work and the economic recontextualization of an old newspaper comic strip (now more likely to be shelved next to a graphic novel like *Jimmy Corrigan*) necessarily change how the work is going to be read today. Of course, as Daniel Stein and Lukas Etter point out, this also means that "much of what made them meaningful for their readers is lost in the republication," which cannot hope to recreate the lively and messy contexts of their popular serial reception.[117] Rather, as they suggest, reprinting consists in an intervention in comics history and in explicit canon formation. This view, however, tends to produce a picture of reprinting as akin to pinning a dead insect in a vitrine: lively popular serial culture anesthetized into a museum exhibit. Contemporary reprinters are undoubtedly aware of this inevitable dynamic and do participate in crafting reprints that somehow commemorate the disappearance of newspaper comics culture. As Baetens and Frey suggest in a critical survey of contemporary reprints:

> [R]eprints and their reframing of old comics does in the end consign that material to the past and hence clears a space for different work in the future – that is, products that look more like graphic novels and less like comics. It is an efficient operation because it is nuanced and seems to celebrate the historical, yet simultaneously forgets many products and frames the others as 'museum exhibits.'[118]

Nonetheless, these reprints do participate in contemporary archival pleasures that are not simply based on the retrospective reinvention of these old comic strips as literary graphic novels. The sheer fact that the coined term is "archival reprint" or "archival collection" suggests an understanding that these books aim less at producing an active canon than at commemorating works that largely belong to the past but are nevertheless important enough to save, preserve, recirculate, and potentially to generate new uses for – if only by the commercial logic that the sales and revenues that such reprints generate for their publishers allow them to put out new works. In the reprinting of old newspaper comics in lavish book editions, the careful attention to perigraphic design also suggests certain ways of reading. And the monumentalizing stake of these reprints cannot be separated from their further use, a dimension that Chapter 4 will contribute to bringing into a somewhat different light.

CHAPTER 4

Forging

That process of digging up the older artists was so integral to my experience as
a cartoonist in my twenties.[1]

– Seth

BY CONTRAST WITH ACTS OF CURATING AND REPRINTING,
which represent and reframe works from the past into the present by drawing from a range of archives between public library collections and private holdings, the contemporary fascination with comics
archives also revolves around imaginary collections of invented "forgotten" comics. Contemporary cartoonists have indeed become experts at
"forging" archives. This chapter, however, is not about forgeries of actual
cartoonists (adding to an oeuvre and monetizing its piracy – also a vibrant
phenomenon) but about imaginary constructions, fictive comics objects
and pseudo recoveries whose transmissive function can nevertheless be
very effective. Commenting on the long literary history of apocryphal and
pseudo works, of fake translations and forged pieces, Judith Schlanger
has underlined how "citations can have effects, old unearthed writings
can induce practical consequences, even when those are invented citations and ad hoc documents."[2]

Invoking imaginary pasts can be a very potent rhetoric argument, with
a practical intervention into contemporary stakes. It is perhaps not
surprising that some of the most noted works of graphic forgeries in
English-language comics originate at the peripheries of the United States,

as a way of affirming a knowledge of mainstream histories of comics and highlighting the shadow they cast on local traditions. Dylan Horrocks's *Hicksville* imagines a small town in New Zealand that is also a protected haven for comics, with a secret library holding "the *other* history of comics" (for Horrocks, it should be one untainted by commercial imperatives and "small-minded editors").[3] Sonny Liew's *The Art of Charlie Chan Hock Chye* crafts the intricate graphic biography of an invented Singaporean cartoonist as a way of retracing the postcolonial history of the Southeast Asian state.[4] The former is entirely drawn in a black-and-white brushwork, a typical example of the 1990s alternative comic book (*Hicksville* was serialized in Horrocks's *Pickle*). Liew's graphic novel, published in 2015, integrates a variety of pseudo-comics produced by Charlie Chan Hock Chye, presented as archival items, mimicking the wear-and-tear and yellowing paper of cheap print.

Liew's pastiches directly hint at the work of both American and Japanese "masters" of comics (Harvey Kurtzman, Carl Barks, Osamu Tezuka) to tackle troublesome episodes in Singapore's political history. For all its forgeries of graphic history, its political function was nevertheless concrete and with practical consequences, as Singapore's National Arts Council decided to pull the $8,000 it had granted Sonny Liew for the making of the graphic novel.[5] Sonny Liew's graphic novel also draws its effectiveness from its mimicry of the anthologies and reprints that present archival items in similar ways – a tendency that, by the end of the 2000s, was entrenched in the field in and outside of the United States. This also arguably contributes to making his graphic novel more relatable to North American (and global) audiences as it invokes a familiar canon of comics history to chart the postcolonial history of Singapore (and indeed Liew's graphic novel has been a successful volume in the United States).

The difference between Horrocks's *Hicksville* and Sonny Liew's *The Art of Charlie Chan Hock Chye* indirectly traces a profound transformation of how one engages with archives of comics history (even forged ones) between 1998 and 2015, which the foregoing pages have cast some light on. By the late 2000s, it had become common to reprint comics from the past in new ways that emphasized their original materiality, partly thanks to the digitization of production techniques. Moving to other examples, this chapter tries to understand how graphic forgeries, often playfully read as such, mirror this "moment of the archive," teasing out some of the ambiguities of its backward look.

CHICKEN FAT AND BEMUSED BIOLOGISTS

Graphic forgeries are not necessarily a twenty-first-century phenomenon in the world of comics, even if they appear as a lively subgenre of the graphic novel. According to Thierry Smolderen, "polygraphy" is a fundamental dynamic in the long and varied history of graphic humor. In Smolderen's view, the "stylization (and hybridization) of existing visual languages" makes for a more enduring feature of comics than their retrospective definition as sequential art.[6] Polygraphic humor embeds drawing within a dynamic graphic culture, as a dialogue with various visual idioms that it simultaneously adopts and reforms and which precisely sustains the permanent update and reinvention of the medium within a tradition: "a margin can always generate another margin" and cartoonists "who belong to this artistic family jealously reserve the right to add a double layer of irony every time their language runs the risk of stiffening or becoming established."[7] Not surprisingly, Smolderen iden-tified in the early *Mad* magazine examples of this "spirit of ironic viola-tion of the boundaries" perpetuated from the nineteenth-century graphic stories of Töpffer, Gustave Doré, Cham, and others.[8]

Founded and financed by *EC Comics* publisher William Gaines, *Mad* was creatively and editorially led by Harvey Kurtzman only for its first twenty-eight issues, from 1952 to 1956. This four-year window, however, covered a crucial turn as the periodical shifted from comic book to satirical magazine. With artists Will Elder, Wallace Wood, Jack Davis and other fine brushes from the EC masthead on board, *Mad* was a collection of parodies aimed at the entire gambit of popular culture: film, television, advertising, and of course comic books. The first issue, published as a four-color comic book, was a conscious exercise in self-mockery, sneering at EC's preferred genres of horror, crime, western, and science-fiction comics that were then at the center of an ongoing crusade against comics as juvenile delinquency. Subsequent issues would lampoon specific newspaper comic strips and comic books, from Milton

Caniff's *Terry and the Pirates* and George McManus's *Bringing Up Father* to DC's *Superman* and Fawcett's *Captain Marvel*. Through its brand of unrestrained satire, *Mad* thus developed a highly self-reflexive, always tongue-in-cheek discourse about comics that would have an important impact on further developments of the graphic novel – after all, as Spiegelman declared: Harvey Kurtman's *Mad* "is what doomed me to cartooning."[9]

Typical of these *Mad* parodies was a brand of ironic self-reflexivity that made fun of comics' own status as mass entertainment (including *Mad*'s) and of the evasive pleasures associated with it. Generally, a twin emphasis on escapism and childhood have tended to "keep comics away from real life, real history, and real time."[10] That is exactly the spot where Kurtzman and his peers would lay their ink-stained fingers. Their satirical humor disrupted familiar comic book characters by endowing them with a self-reflexive two-dimensionality, playing on the discrepancy between reality and comics conventions. This discrepancy is evident in "Bringing Back Father!," a take on George McManus's family strip that uses two different graphic styles to lampoon the visual workings of comic book slapstick.[11] Every other page oscillates between Will Elder's pastiche of the original comic strip and its new rendering in Bernard Krigstein's dark, expressionist style. The story alternates Jiggie getting beaten up by his wife (which involves rolling pins and entire cupboards of china) with cartoon slapstick and an address to the reader's complicit laughter: "I suppose you think it's funny getting bounced off the wall?" (which, of course, only adds an extra comical layer).

In the same strip, Jiggie also reckons with his long serial life (*Bringing Up Father* had, by then, already been running for forty-one years): "same routine . . . same story again and again . . . ." As with many *Mad* parodies, it eagerly follows the serial thread of repeated motifs that constitutes the pleasure of reading such comics in the first place. By doing so, these parodies disrupted the "immobile present" that, Umberto Eco argued, characterized many early superhero titles and popular serial narratives.[12] A 1962 issue, for instance, featured a "Yellowed Kids department" with Wood's parodies of aging comic book characters, condensing a recurring side-gag of many previous *Mad* parodies: "Everybody gets old! Everybody, that is, except most comic strip characters! These jokers have the uncanny ability to remain the same dull age year after year, getting into the same dull situations. So Mad's gonna break the monotony."[13] The irony, of course, is found in a playful inversion of the spectacular and the adventurous by the simple reintroduction of everyday matters, such as aging characters. "As *Mad* magazine discovered, the new audience found the scenes and themes of ordinary life as funny as anything," Marshall McLuhan astutely observed in the mid-1960s.[14]

While *Mad*'s editors were certainly not aiming for boring, its parodies worked by folding the extraordinary onto the ordinary, a theme that later underground and alternative comics would replay in a more serious tone.[15] This ironic confrontation with the everyday arguably brought back the "real life, real history, real time" that comic book reading was promising escape from. *Mad* devised, as Hillary Chute argues, "a mode of engaging in and reflecting reality. ... This is 'reality' not in terms of content but rather in terms of transparency, as the nontransparency of form: reality as attention to the narrative frame."[16] The thumbnail reading of the Elder/Krigstein collaboration on "Bringing Back Father!" makes this nontransparency of form immediately clear: how the story is drawn makes all the difference. And indeed, creators for *Mad* developed a particularly dense approach to cartooning that begged their readers to slow down and dissect the visual density on the page.

The early *Mad* implicitly developed an endogenous theory of intertextuality that contemporary cartoonists frequently have looked back on. As is fit for a magazine that perpetually derided itself, this theory is best encapsulated in Will Elder's "chicken fat," that is, "the part of the soup that is bad for you yet gives the soup its delicious flavor," and which is frequently used as an analogy for the side-gags and marginal jokes that crowded Elder's panels.[17] While Elder excelled in this graphic excess, the "chicken fat" approach came to embody the visual pleasures of *Mad*'s graphic humor. Art Spiegelman, perhaps unsurprisingly, elaborated a wordier definition, borrowing from Elder's and adding his own ingredients to the soup:

> Chicken fat is the guilty pleasure. It is the thing that will cause cardiac arrest eventually. It is that ladling onto an image all those extra images that slow it down. So you have to give the picture a lot of time. Even though we use the word "read comics" more than "look at comics," basically what *Mad* insisted on was that, like a Hogarth picture, you would have to reenter deeply and decode all of the little background stuff. It's a lot of images to decode.[18]

While Spiegelman insists on the background of the swarming image (in a reference to Hogarth that flatters Smolderen's polygraphic tradition), he also underlines the effect of this visual density on its readability and hence its temporal thickness. This thickening of time that results from such "ladling onto an image all those extra images" does not only slow down reading time, it often condenses an already dense image with an even denser web of references to other images. The borrowings, cameos, and other intertextual minutiae infuse the panel with a tightly packed cultural memory of comics that call on the reader to decipher a set of common references.[19] And this is not only a matter of panels crammed up with side details and background gags; this thickening is inseparable from the drawn line itself. As Daniel Clowes – an unabashed inheritor of Will Elder – remarks in a commentary of his work that is worth quoting at some length: "There is a very palpable sense of the history of comics flowing through his brush-line, implemented not with a fannish slaver, but with the engaged dispassion of a bemused biologist. It is this half-step of distance that makes him such a great (an understatement – he is the best ever) dismantler of his fellow cartoonists."[20]

That Clowes's interpretation of Elder's citational style distinguishes between "fannish slaver" and "bemused biologist" speaks volumes to the understanding of different ways of copying, reflecting the distinctive dynamics of alternative comics. Imitation, here, is not about learning to draw by the styles of the comics industry (which Elder knew equally well) but rather about a reflexive practice carried out with an "engaged dispassion" that combines criticism and attachment. This kind of reflexive gesture and its "half-step distance" marks a specific relationship to the history of comics, at once close and remote, that can be understood in parallel with the graphic novel's "self-knowing 'play with a purpose' of the traditional comic book form."[21] And indeed, the kind of playful mimicry of graphic styles is a recurrent trope of many graphic novels. Schooling its readers into seeing the narrative frame, *Mad*, through its parodies, was also teaching them to see comics historically. This is what makes them different, for instance, from the bare parody of the Tijuana Bibles which quite simply stripped famous comics characters down into porn scenarios. In contrast with the "immobile present" that defined the temporality of the original strips, *Mad* engaged with their long serial lives, as objects that had accumulated history. In the process, Kurtzman and his peers solicited readers' visual memory of comics as a common archive to engage with by imitation, parody, mockery, or else. The lesson would be well learned as Daniel Clowes's works, such as *Ice Haven*, which frequently imitate particular styles from the history of newspaper comics and comic books indeed show the same kind of half-step distance.[22] A somewhat similar example of graphic forgery, amalgamating different styles from similar periods, can also be found in Emil Ferris's *My Favorite Thing Is Monsters*, which relies on the print visual imagery of monster culture, forging "ghastly" magazine covers that compound the memory of pre-Code EC comic books with the horror magazines of the 1970s (such as those published by James Warren) and which were unrestrained by the Comics Code Authority.[23] Through her graphic forgeries, Ferris masters both the first-hand horror graphics of EC comics as well as the contemporary parodies that the same *Mad* cartoonists were producing, and reharnesses this visual idiom in a diary format and a growing-up narrative.[24]

IN SEARCH OF LOST CARTOONISTS

Where *Mad* cartoonists were operating parodies that presumed readers knew their references, forging "imagined" cartoons in the graphic novel engages a different relationship with one's readers. The issue lies at the core of Seth's *It's a Good Life, If You Don't Weaken*, as well as more recent works such as *The Great Northern Brotherhood of Canadian Cartoonists*.[25] These graphic novels commonly summon the knowledge of their readers by copiously referencing real creators – providing a glossary at hand – as well as forging imaginary comics from distant pasts, staging impossible recoveries, and inventing alleged cartoonists societies. *The Great Northern Brotherhood of Canadian Cartoonists* profusely cites well-known cartoonists whose work Seth has publicly endorsed, such as the comic strips of Doug Wright, but also invents a myriad of fake titles, sometimes directly echoing existing genres and figures and at other times engaging in more virtual speculations. Understandably, such works have fascinated comics scholars and there is a rich scholarship about Seth's engagement with comics history – in addition to Seth's own carefully wrought and always clear-headed insights shared in the interviews and talks that are also part of his public image.[26]

It's a Good Life, If You Don't Weaken, Seth's first long-length narrative serialized in his comic book *Palookaville*, presented a more ambiguous relationship to the past as it staged his own fascination for the assumingly long-forgotten cartoonist "Kalo." Seth shared his findings and the few cartoons he had tracked with his readers, forging a "Kalo" style in the paratext of his autofictional comic book (Figure 4.1). The fictional identity of "Kalo" is constructed from a handful of cartoonists from the 1930s, such as Peter Arno and Jack Markow who drew illustrations and cartoons for literary magazines like *The New Yorker* and *The Saturday Evening Post*, and which Seth has deliberately imitated in elaborating his personal style.[27] This "quest" for a singular voice through a close engagement with the past, through the prism of forged cartoons from the 1950s, is also a means for Seth to engage his audience. Even when many readers might have guessed the fictionality of Kalo, fact-checking at a time when the World Wide Web was still indexed by hand was not such a common thing to do. Letters to Seth, as reproduced in the dedicated page of *Palookaville* and often sent from fellow cartoonists, frequently mention Kalo and the proximity with his style. James Kochalka, for instance, writes "that Kalo illustration on the back of #5. You draw *a lot* like him. Did you purposely ape his style? Or do you like him 'cause you see yourself in him? The tiny hands and feet look so much like your drawing it's uncanny." To which Seth answers: "I'm definitely not apeing anyone's style. I've been influenced by a wide variety of old cartoonists ... but I do certainly fall into the school of 'little feet' artists (such as Irving Tripp, Sam Cobean, Hergé and Jack Markow."[28] Just as, in the autofictional narrative, "Seth" is frequently shown talking with his friends and fellow cartoonists Joe Matt and Chester Brown about cartoonists and about Seth's recent obsession with Kalo, the *Palookaville* comic book constructed a similar emulation around comics history, embodied in the forged "cartoonists' cartoonist" Kalo.[29]

The forgery of Kalo has often been read as a form of "historiographic metafiction," highlighting the constructedness of our engagement with the past.[30] Some have read this strategy as a way of unsettling traditional history and ironically interrogating its own nostalgia. As Daniel Marrone points out, "Seth's work fully accommodates the double meaning of the word 'forge' and in doing so points to the deliberate manipulation of material that even the most apparently

Figure 4.1 Inside cover of Seth's *Palookaville*, no. 6 (Montreal: Drawn & Quarterly, 1994). Source: Copyright © Seth. Courtesy of Drawn & Quarterly.

neutral history entails."[31] Such accounts also attempt to reframe the longing for the past that is overwhelming in Seth's work as a critical engagement that sometimes upholds positioning Seth's work as "anti-nostalgia."[32] To describe a work as nostalgic often carries with it a complex set of value judgments. Despite more positive views on nostalgia that have emerged recently, the term remains handily used to write off or dismiss an interest in the past, reaching back to the clinical and psychological history of the term.[33] In this context, it is often felt necessary to read graphic novels against the grain of their nostalgic impulse, and this is seen nowhere clearer than in the reception of Seth's work. In this context, presenting a work like *It's a Good Life, if You Don't Weaken* as "anti-nostalgia" functions as a way of rehabilitating its critical engagement with the past and distinguishing it from other assumingly nostalgic relationships to the past.

Taking a welcome counterpoint, Giorgio Busi Rizzi has suggested that we gain a more nuanced understanding of the work if we appreciate the nostalgic feelings that Seth is variously able to integrate and generate through a set of narratological and formal techniques.[34] In this view, nostalgia and self-reflexivity are not necessarily working against each other and the outcome that Busi Rizzi brings out is one that runs parallel to Richard Dyer's demonstration of pastiche as a genre where "self-consciousness and emotional expression can co-exist, ... allowing us to contemplate the possibility of feeling historically."[35] The forging of Kalo follows through: "despite being a fictional construct, Kalo is the epitome of a pastiche condensing Seth's love for the 1950s imaginary and illustration – a period that indeed he did not experience directly, but that exercises an irresistible attraction for him."[36] This attraction to the past is a communicative one, built with a community of readers. In turn, it might seem logical that this backward look evident in Seth's works, as well as in those of his peers, would also in part influence and shape how next generations approach the history of comics.

RETRODRAWING

Published in 2013, *Little Tommy Lost* is the debut graphic novel of Cole Closser, a younger cartoonist trained at the Center for Cartoon Studies.[37] Read as part of the Koyama Press catalog, *Little Tommy Lost* might come across as an antiquated oddball. Established in 2007, the small Toronto-based publishing house has been at the vanguard of alternative comics, offering a first publication platform to cartoonists such as Eleanor Davis, Michael DeForge, Aidan Koch, and Patrick Kyle, who have become main-stay names on the contemporary scene. At the crossroads of fanzines, contemporary art, and popular culture, Koyama Press reflects a cutting-edge trend within what is sometimes referred to as "art comics."[38] As diverse as it is, Annie Koyama's publishing venue stays far away from the nostalgia corner and rather represents what is hip and cool on today's alternative comics scene, putting in print cartoonists who regularly serial-ize their work online and have contributed to expanding the breadth of the alternative comics genres.[39] But even though the relationship to comics history is not a conspicuous drive, it does crop up in its catalog through citations of recognizable characters and through a cartoon aes-thetics that cuts across various media, sometimes blended in with refer-ences to science-fiction, manga, or punk, as in the comics of Ryan Cecil Smith, Mickey Zacchilli, or Alex Schubert. The work of Michael DeForge, one of Koyama's lead authors, is a perfect example of this aesthetic. It displays a recognizable cartoony style, one that cuts across comics and animation (DeForge has worked for the *Adventure Time* cartoon series), and mixes the cute and the grotesque with a discomfortingly graphic attention to bodily surfaces.[40] When DeForge invokes familiar characters in his short stories, he leans on a familiar parodic take that confronts popular comics characters with everyday problems (going back to the *Mad* parodies). DeForge also plays up grotesque situations, often in a close investigation of psychological and bodily matters: Peter Parker telling his shrink about a weird sexual dream in a short story that could pass off as a weird slash fan fiction (Peter's aunt/Dr. Octopus), or the familiar outline of Snoopy recurring in a cross-species teenager narrative of angst, high-school bullying, and therapy (again). Less transgressive and more deferring in its citationality, and above all rigorously retro, Cole Closser's *Little Tommy Lost* clearly upholds a tone and mood that contrast with other, more eclectic ways of redrawing older comics in the Koyama Press catalog. The consistently retro aesthetics of Closser's comics also extends the historically self-reflexive works of Seth, Daniel Clowes, Chris Ware, and others. The references that Closser weaves into the fabric of his graphic novels are also those that the previous generation has contributed to unearthing and making available. But where Seth finds in past cartoonists models for the elaboration of a personal style, the project of *Little Tommy Lost* expresses another form of retro.

What is at work in Closser's *Little Tommy Lost* is something that within game studies is often referred to as "retro reflexivity," a concept coined by Brett Camper in his analysis of the 8-bit video game *La-Mulana*, developed with newer digital technologies but mimicking or emulating all the visual dimensions of a 1980s MSX console game.[41] Camper observed how the fast turnover pace of video games cultural industries, strongly driven by technological innovation, simultaneously generated a "platform nostalgia," a fascination for obsolete techniques that further developed into a dense web of cultural practices known as "retrogaming." For Camper, a video game like *La-Mulana* opens up a self-reflexive take on video game history that unfolds through local remediation:

> Remediation also happens "locally": as a medium evolves, its earlier stages begin to be remediated within it. The emphasis on legitimization or realism fades, and remediation drifts from a fallback to a conscious stylistic choice, a tactic for evoking and re-interpreting the medium's past, an expert vehicle for the homage, the parody, or the genre revival. This is where remediation meets retro.[42]

The same lines could easily apply to describe *Little Tommy Lost*, which functions in quite similar ways to a game like *La-Mulana* in its attempt to produce a new work by rigorously emulating past works. While comics history is arguably not as strongly paced by the fast obsolescence of platform updates and technological innovation as video games might be, the importance of its material formats and heterogeneity make it a medium that is similarly prone to the local and retro-reflexive remediation of its own pasts in a tight interplay among genre, aesthetics, and technology. And, as Baetens and Frey note, "the break that the graphic novel established (if even only symbolically achieved) has prompted much fascination with comic book history, literal and metaphorical."[43] This is less the comic book that Closser returns to, however, but the early newspaper strip that, as we have seen in previous pages, has been at the center of the post-2000 graphic novel's archival impulse.

Little Tommy Lost indeed reads like an explicit tribute to the early-twentieth-century comic strip that clearly builds upon the reprint work done by publishers such as Fantagraphics, IDW, and Sunday Press Books. The attempt leads to an ambivalent object. It is an oblong softcover booklet, relatively thin in paginations, but printed on thick glossy paper; at the same time, it visually alludes to anachronistic design values and presents each strip as if it was a collection that had been long forgotten and simply rediscovered (Figure 4.2). *Little Tommy Lost* plays up the contrast between the solid and time-enduring materiality of the book and the ephemeral quality of the newspaper comic strips it mimics. While the contemporary comic strip, after being allocated ever-shrinking space in the newspapers, has arguably undergone a revival on online platforms, Closser advances a remediation of the graphic novel that meshes together the graphic novel and archival reprints.[44] At this crucial moment when the identity of the comic strip is being replayed, including in the strategies of reprinting, Cole Closser's *Little Tommy Lost* proposes a form of local remediation of the history of the comic strip that is particularly attentive to its materiality but also to its cultural memory. This form of remediation qualifies the resurgence and reinvention of older identities of the medium in a present where the medium is crossed by multiple temporalities.

The retro reflexivity of *Little Tommy Lost* can be found in the "as if" character of its intramedial references, which establishes a playful relationship with the reader: while being fully aware that what we hold in our hands is a contemporary product, we are confronted with a work that mobilizes all the conventions of an anachronistic comic strip.[45] It is as if *Little Tommy Lost* actually was an old strip, published in North American newspapers in the 1920s. The book tells the story of a young lost child, Little Tommy, who finds himself interned in an orphanage, then stands up to the bullies of the institution and tries to go looking for his parents. With this Dickensian substrate and its narrative framework based on the abuse of an innocent victim, emotional pathos, and the moral polarization of the characters, this story is entirely in line with the melodrama that flourished in the comic strips of the 1920s and 1930s. With his distinctive blank eyes and companion animal, *Little Tommy Lost* is a boyish reincarnation of Harold Gray's comic strip *Little Orphan Annie,*

Figure 4.2 Typical page from Cole Closser's *Little Tommy Lost* (Toronto: Koyama Press, 2013), n.p.

Source: Copyright © Closser. Courtesy of the artist.

Figure 4.3 Harold Gray, "Little Orphan Annie – Wants to Leave Her Home," *Daily News*, August 5, 1924.

which debuted in American newspapers in 1924 as a serialized account of the adventures of a determined orphan girl in a constant struggle with a corrupt society (Figure 4.3). *Little Tommy Lost* is not a rewriting of *Little Orphan Annie*, despite the fact that the strip would have offered a lot to deal with, such as tension between the conservative and anti-communist leanings of its original author and the more progressive reading that can be made of its title character.[46]

Besides *Little Orphan Annie*, Closser integrates a range of references from the classics of newspaper comics that reprint initiatives have sporadically kept alive since the 1970s. Part of the pleasure also activates an encyclopedic reading and an invitation to recognize the various shared references. Among them are the autumn walks from the Sunday pages of King's *Gasoline Alley*, the weirdly defaced characters from Gould's *Dick Tracy*, the final waking-up panel from McCay's *Little Nemo in Slumberland*, the uppercuts and other fistfights from Segar's *Thimble Theatre*, the distracted and turbulent child from Swinnerton's *Little Jimmy*, and Forbell's *Naughty Pete*. All these references, however, remain homogeneous in their graphic treatment, which arguably also makes Closser's line stand out as slightly technically less confident than the drawing hand of the "masters" he sets out to imitate. In this use of pastiche, Closser's *Little Tommy Lost* runs along the same lines as Seth's works, at least in part. Simon Grennan has argued that Seth's *Clyde Fans* can be described as resulting from a constrained rule of "nothing un-North American, nothing after 1960." The recourse to "types of past expression" necessarily "takes place in terms of our contemporary relationship with them" and thus our ideas about the past and our ability to see them as belonging to that past.[47] While Closser's *Little Tommy Lost* is perhaps less defined by a specific place and time in terms of the fictional world it depicts (although it would meet a "nothing un-North American, nothing after 1940" constraint), the process of creating a convincingly anachronistic object remains similar to that goal.

Through a thorough imitation of various newspaper strips, Closser engages in a particular retro-reflexive approach, distinct from other approaches that pay tribute to the same period in comics history. The Belgian cartoonist Olivier Schrauwen, for example, in 2006 delivered *My Boy*, a pastiche of the comics of Winsor McCay, but readapted to another context and introducing an irony that contrasts with its borrowed style.[48] Another example would be Tony Millionaire, author of *Maakies*, a comic strip published from 1994 to 2016 in the alternative press; its outdated graphic style is very much inspired by adventure comic strips such as those of Roy Crane, but it updates these with an extra ladle of raw, cynical humor. Such an ironic dimension is completely absent from Cole Closser, for whom make-believe is crucial, which brings *Little Tommy Lost* closer to the tradition of pastiche and retro reflexivity. Beyond the melodramatic genre and its encyclopedic character, Closser gives the impression that the strips he offers for us to look at have been published in newspapers, in a serial mode. He therefore does not appropriate texts as a disembodied genre; rather, he proposes a remediation of the material forms of circulation and transmission of comic strips, thus underlining their dynamics of memory and oblivion.

NEWSPRINT NOSTALGIA

Key to this reflection on the materiality of *Little Tommy Lost* and its retro-reflexive gesture are of course the very paradoxes that come with mimicking a serial genre while adopting the literary format of the graphic novel by including a chapter structure. Relatively thin, totaling seventy-two pages, *Little Tommy Lost* is a graphic novel with an ambiguous serial regime: the work is presented as a first volume, with no sequel planned for the moment (and it is quite possible to think that none was ever planned). It is therefore a one-shot that leaves its narrative in suspense. Closser's graphic novel, moreover, has not been serialized beforehand, but plays as if it has been. Closser thus completely avoids serial publication, but reintroduces within *Little Tommy Lost* all the tropes that make up the serial imaginary of the interwar newspaper comic strip. In doing so, Closser develops what could be called a strategy of pseudo-seriality. Closser indeed segments the narrative in a way typical of the open-ended seriality of 1920s and 1930s comic strips – the kind of serial regime that Frank King's *Gasoline Alley* was tied to, but with a sense of suspense closer to the mix of melodrama and adventure of titles such as Harold Gray's *Little Orphan Annie* or Roy Crane's *Wash Tubbs*. The necessarily unfinished character of *Little Tommy Lost*, remaining open to a possible continuation, already marks this imitation of an open seriality. But this form of seriality peculiar to the comic strip of the interwar period can also be found in the alternation between dailies – strips of three to four black-and-white panels published with each weekday newspaper – and Sunday pages – as part of the full-color comics supplement. *Little Tommy Lost* resumes this weekly distribution by segmenting the story into six consecutive dailies followed by a half-page in color.

The contradictory nature of this pseudo-seriality is that it is obviously disconnected from the newspaper, its particular rhythm, the varied paratexts, the practices and rituals bound with daily reading. The crucial role that readers play in the serial development, the emotional investment in the strip's life, the narrative dynamics of suspense and anticipation: all these fundamental characteristics that make up the indefinitely open-ended regime of 1920s comic strips are completely lost on us.[49] This return of the comic strip under the guise of a graphic novel produces something of a paradox that is wittily described in the blurb on the back cover of *Little Tommy Lost* signed by Tony Millionaire: "Cole Closser noticed a drip in the mouth of an old man in a comics shop and created a whole new encyclopedia of newspaper comics. These comics are the freshest I've seen since my grampop showed me his collection of Roy Crane clippings. Amazing work and it doesn't even need a newspaper."[50] A newspaper strip without the newspaper: that neatly sums up the situation of *Little Tommy Lost*. As the creator of *Maakies*, a long-length comic strip that ran in alternative weeklies from 1994 to 2014, drawn in a classic cartooning style, Tony Millionaire is well aware of the stakes of seriality in both old newspaper comics and their present-day heirs. In his blurb, the cartoonist also partly hints at how much his own style owes to his discovery of Depression-era comic strips, pointing to a collection of Roy Crane clippings assembled by his grandmother. His strip *Maakies* is indeed drawn in a traditional cartooning style, with heavy cross-hatching, and is filled with specific nods to comics from the first half of the twentieth-century, including the sea-faring adventures of Roy Crane's *Wash Tubbs* (a comic strip that was given a privileged spot in *The Smithsonian Collection of Newspaper Comics*) and the repetitive antics of anthropomorphized animals in George Herriman's *Krazy Kat*. Most importantly, however, by comparing *Little Tommy Lost* to a collection of clippings, Millionaire stresses an archival pleasure in the "fresh" discovery of something that looks resolutely old and forgotten, while stressing the paradoxes of reading a comic strip outside of its original publication context, as curated by someone else.

Millionaire's quote underlines not only the references to old comic strips in themselves but also the way they have been kept by common readers (one's grandmother) – practices that Closser clearly hints at in the design of his work. *Little Tommy Lost* combines two design strategies that frame his pseudo-serial narrative. At first, it explicitly alludes to Cupples & Leons's thin book collections of famous comic strips in the late 1920s and 1930s, Cupples & Leons being one of the rare publishers to have attempted to republish comic strips in book form at the height of their serial existence (Figure 4.4). That counts for the perigraphic design of *Little Tommy Lost*. Inside the book, Closser adopts another strategy, which is to mimic the look of a scrapbook or album in the way that each strip is isolated against a white background from which it is detached by a slight shadow zone, as if it had been glued to it. In addition, Closser takes great care to imitate the texture of the newspaper, as well as its transparency and traces of degradation. For example, the transparency effect is suggested by the inclusion of a layer of text that can be seen behind the lines and traces drawn on the strip. For the color Sunday pages, the author also uses a raster effect reminiscent of the Ben Day dots used for the color printing of newspaper pages. These aspects of texture, transparency, and raster are the result of meticulous digital work on the original drawings, enriched by the multilayered work

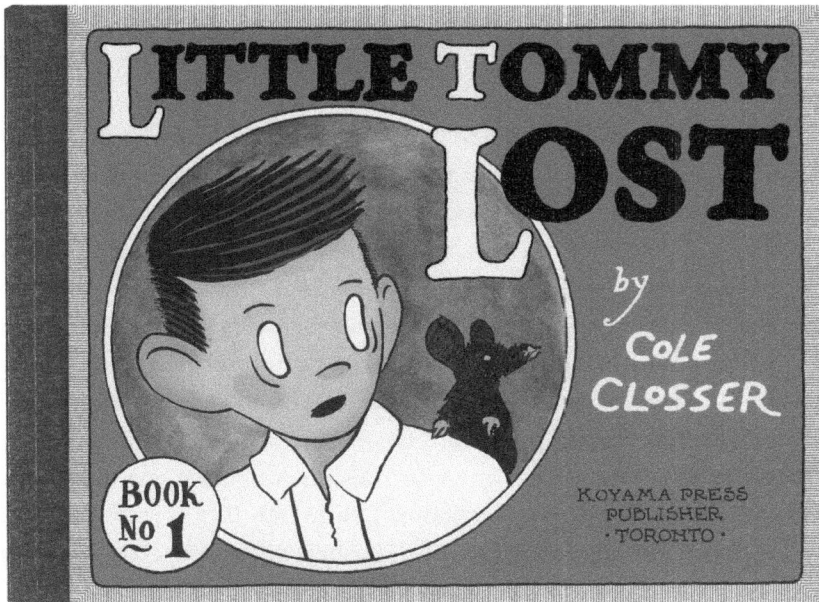

Figure 4.4 Comparison of two covers: (a) Sidney Smith, *The Gumps: Book 3* (New York: Cupples & Leon, 1926); (b) Cole Closser, *Little Tommy Lost* (Toronto: Koyama Press, 2013). Source: (a) courtesy of Heritage Auctions (HA.com); (b) copyright © Closser. Courtesy of the artist.

characteristic of digital image–processing software. Closser also includes numerous traces of degradation, wear and tear, and yellowing, as a reminder of the poor quality of the paper on which the comic strips were printed.

This kind of digital simulation of time's chemistry with its process of degradation and decay displays an "analog nostalgia" that has grown to be particularly strong within different types of digital culture, from photography to retrogaming.[51] Writing about video and cinema, Laura Marks has coined the term "analog nostalgia" to describe a "desire for indexicality" and "a retrospective fondness for the 'problems' of decay and generational loss."[52] By presenting itself as a forgotten and rediscovered scrapbook, whose strips are marked by the passage of time, *Little Tommy Lost* expresses nostalgia for the ephemerality of newspaper comics, even though its own pages are made of thick, glossy paper, more capable of withstanding the test of time than the comic strips they mimic, which are now falling apart. This is a contrast that is familiar in the reprints discussed in Chapter 3 and particularly played up by Chip Kidd's designs in collaboration with the photographer Geoff Spear, which often overemphasize the yellowed and damaged aspect of the degraded paper and the various material forms of past comics: original plates, pages published on poor-quality paper, merchandising objects.

A similar approach is applied to the reproductions of comics pages in Dan Nadel's anthologies such as *Art Out of Time*, which mainly collect newspaper comics.[53] While Chip Kidd plays up his design compositions by means of blown-up details and juxtaposed images, Nadel is more concerned with reproducing longer examples, although the anthologized comics are reproduced emphasizing their original material conditions, distinguished against a white background and printed on glossy paper. Moreover, with a subtitle such as "Unknown Comics Visionaries," anthologies like Nadel's pursue an "objective of rediscovery" that tends to "broaden the comic strip canon by making 'unknown' or 'forgotten' authors visible and accessible again."[54] Although this objective testifies to a commitment on the part of the publisher, this approach is also more globally characteristic of the dynamics of cultural memory within the contemporary reprint market.

PARADOXES OF PSEUDO-SERIALITY

By adopting the visual presentation of contemporary archival reprints, *Little Tommy Lost* tends to pass itself off as one of them, like a collection of forgotten and then rediscovered adventure comic strips. The fact that a young comic book author is dedicating his own practice to the creation of a fake anthology of forgotten comic strips, in a retro-reflexive gesture rarely so advanced, also shows not only that this "retro-mania" is the result of nostalgic marketing strategies but that they do have a positive impact on new generations. Closser knows these comic strips perhaps first of all through their re-editions, whose mediating action led him to pay a faithful tribute to this comic strip from the beginning of the twentieth century. The retro reflexivity evidenced in *Little Tommy Lost* is a recursive take on the memory dynamics of preservation and recirculation that have shaped the twenty-first-century market of archival reprinting in comics. In the process, it also demonstrates the ambiguities that shape the graphic novel's remediation of its serial origins and spotlights some of the practical challenges posed for contemporary archival reprints. By producing a pseudo-serial narrative in the mode of a 1930s comic strip in the format of a 2000s graphic novel, Closser highlights some of the ambiguities of contemporary reprints, while also exemplifying that these reprints are generative and productive in casting a light on forgotten comic strips.

The retro reflexivity of *Little Tommy Lost* highlights the memory dynamics of preservation and recirculation in comics, suggesting that a nostalgia for the past may be the site of a vivid, rather than ossified, memory of the medium. Its playful reliance on a form of pseudo-seriality, however, precisely embodies the limitations of the post-2000 graphic novel's fascination for newspaper comics: while paying homage to the serial imaginary, particularly in relation to the syndicated comic strips of the 1920s and 1930s, the retro-reflexive strategy breaks with a long tradition of comic strips by merely simulating this serialization within the form of a one-shot graphic novel. While serial comics are resurfacing in the digital age through webcomics and other serial online forms, Closser's retro-reflexive approach can be contrasted with a different track put forward by cartoonist Frank Santoro in a short essay. Prompted by an article on early-twentieth-century sports cartoons and the origins of serial comic strips, Santoro invited his peers to study the history of comics in order to find new ways of navigating the contemporary: in a gesture closer to media archeology, he sees the context of early newspaper comics publication as an inspiration for navigating the diffuse paratext of the Internet, in a way similar to the early cartoonists' uses of the raucous newspaper (indeed, the same historical moment that Eddie Campbell turned to in *The Goat Getters*), and cites a range of cartoonists – Kate Beaton, Ed Piskor, Jesse Moynihan, Meredith Gran – "who have found a way to make 'being in the [digital] newspaper' payoff [*sic*] in some manner or another."[55] What makes seriality interesting as a terrain for formal experimentation and readerly engagement runs the risk of being obscured by the mimicking of its strategies. What *Little Tommy Lost* effectively draws attention to is the multiple archiving practices – from scrapbooks to various types of reprint – that have allowed for newspaper comic strips to survive as a heritage to reexplore: by contrast, the very possibilities for such rediscoveries in the context of digital comics are of a completely different order, as webcomics appear to be an even more fragile and easily forgotten medium than their century-old ancestors.

CHAPTER 5

Swiping

Unoriginal sins. The act of repetition and copying of other cartoonists. That is plenty of sin for us.[1]

– Art Spiegelman

O NE OF CHARLES BURNS'S "MOST PRIZED POSSESSIONS," AS displayed in Todd Hignite's *In the Studio*, is a scrapbook of comic strip clippings put together by his cartoonist-dilettante father.[2] The scrapbook contains a collection of comic strips which he used for reference when drawing: it assembles panels and details clipped out from various newspaper comic strips from the 1940s, such as Frank Robbins's *Johnny Hazard*, collecting material that could then be copied and imitated (Figure 5.1). The cut-out elements are organized according to topic, gender, angles, perspectives, body framing: the scrapbook produces a repertoire of drawing elements meant to be reused in specific situations. As such, it is the model definition of a *swipe file*, a collection of images cut out from other comics that can then be redrawn into the cartoonist's own work. Burns's father's scrapbook is not an odd piece in comics history.

Going back to the nineteenth century, newspaper readers have assembled scrapbooks archiving their favorite comic strips, following a tradition of "writing with scissors" in which the pleasures of rereading and sharing favorite strips resulted in the widespread saving and collating of such material.[3] These scrapbooks often palliated for the lack of

Figure 5.1 Double pages from a scrapbook of comics clippings, c. 1950.
The clippings were assembled by Charles Burns's father from various newspaper comic strips, with many panels clipped from Frank Robbins's adventure comic strip *Johnny* Hazard (King Features Syndicate). The bottom page reveals how the panels were ordered according to angles, perspectives, and body framing.
Source: Reproduced from Todd Hignite, *In the Studio*. Courtesy of Charles Burns.

reprints and allowed repeated readings; but scrapbooks of comics clippings were also an important source of apprenticeship. For artists, these self-curated archives of comics could then be reused, repurposed, and redrawn.[4] Michael Chabon describes this phenomenon somewhat romantically in his novel *The Amazing Adventures of Kavalier and Clay* when he writes of Sam Clay, a young, aspiring cartoonist who keeps a stack of clipped comics in the closet of his Brooklyn bedroom:

> He clipped favorite pages and panels out of newspapers and comic books and pasted them into a fat notebook: a thousand different exemplary poses and styles. He had made extensive use of his bible of clippings in concocting a counterfeit *Terry and the Pirates* strip called *South China Sea*, drawn in faithful imitation of the great Caniff. ... He had tried swiping from Hogarth and Lee Falk, from George Herriman, Harold Gray, and Elzie Segar.[5]

A pervasive practice in the comic book industry, *swiping* is the common term used by makers, readers, and fans to refer to the long-standing practice of "stealing" or "borrowing" fragments from other comics to reuse in one's own work. Charles Burns unashamedly commits to the practice, confessing to having swiped images from his father's scrapbook for his own comics.[6] This confession to swiping, however, is not a dirty secret, only revealed by an insider's visit to the cartoonist's studio: Burns has repeatedly embraced swiping and displayed his own "swipe files" in various contexts and formats, from his online Tumblr blog *Johnny 23* to small-press books and zines such as *Swipe File, Close Your Eyes,* and *Love Nest.*[7] These small editions collect Burns's swipes, sometimes alongside their sources, foregrounding how his work is not merely tapping into an abstracted "familiar iconography" of "comic book clichés" but actually based on diligent acts of retracing and refashioning images selected from a mass of comic books.[8]

These swipe files highlight a practice of redrawing that pervades Burns's entire body of work, but which has remained overlooked by a critical research heavily focused on *Black Hole*. This blind spot in approaches to Burns's work is related to the format of the graphic novel and the institutionalization of comics studies around single "plausible" texts, which make smaller, dispersed objects less fit for close-reading and teaching.[9] Yet, these small experimental swipe files are not simply peripheral to Burns's graphic novels, of mere interest for the behind-the-scenes of comics production. By tracing networks between his own work and a curated collection of older comics, Burns's swipe files highlight how redrawing informs Burns's entire oeuvre. This chapter reads these swipe files alongside Burns's graphic novel *Last Look*, in which he extensively redraws images from comics as diverse as American romance comic books and *Tintin* albums. More broadly, Burns's citational practice invites us to consider swiping as a complex economy of mark-making, touching on the consumption, reproduction, and circulation of comics images. It is not only that Burns "copies" or "appropriates" images but above all that he constructs and shares archives of reusable images (including his own) that are constantly redistributed in his work. This means understanding swiping alongside swipe files or, in other words, citational practices alongside the process of collecting. In this sense, Burns brings together very closely the dimensions of archive and repertoire that play such a key role in the construction of comics memory.[10]

Approaching Burns's references to older comics as swiping not only explicates the cartoonist's own fascination for the practice but more fundamentally complicates questions about how copy and quotation operate in comics on medium-specific terms. That Burns hangs onto redrawing as *swiping* foregrounds the continued relevance of the specific cultural practice that the term delineates. In a context where transmedia storytelling arguably blurs boundaries between media, swiping confronts us with a localized practice of citation situated within the history of American comic books.[11] To a large extent, swiping shares characteristics with digital remix culture – fragmentation, reuse, a lax relationship toward copyright – but it also points to an analog, "low" practice of remix embedded within comic book culture.[12] Swiping relies more on craft than on technology, as it often involves cut-and-paste in a more literal than metaphorical way, and relies on a material process of selecting, assembling, and redrawing images. What Burns's swipe files suggest is precisely the continued relevance of internal and vernacular citational practices, even when the very practice of swiping seems at odds with the *auteur* model of the graphic novel. Based on imitation and repetition, flirting with plagiarism, swiping indeed contrasts with the emphasis on personal style and the opposition to industrial models that characterize graphic novel. Yet, the declared swipe files highlight a medium-specific way of citing that inscribes the graphic novelist's practice into a multilayered memory of comics. This chapter inquires into the various valences of swiping and copying in the contemporary graphic novel; this will also lead us to trace a longer historical framework for the practice of swiping as a necessary prerequisite to understanding the more particular case of Charles Burns's swipe files.

SECONDHAND AND SHORTHAND

Swiping mobilizes a set of medium-specific concerns about the ways in which graphic style works in comics and how repetition and copying are negotiated in their situated contexts. As many have argued, following Philippe Marion's seminal theory of graphiation, comics always self-reflexively exhibit the mark of their maker.[13] According to Jared Gardner, this is fundamental to comics storytelling: "The physical labor of storytelling is always visible in graphic narrative, whether the visible marks themselves remain, in a way unique to any mechanically reproduced narrative medium."[14] If graphic narratives are defined by the labor of a "visible hand," swiping makes visible the labor of a "*second* hand."[15] The "physical, bodily encounter with an imagined scene of embodied enunciation" that comics compel is doubled over in the act of redrawing.[16] When redrawing, the cartoonist embodies, so to speak, someone else's act of graphiation, re-performing this imagined scene, and displacing it into another context. Considering that drawn lines are often indexical of a cartoonist's distinct graphic style, the kind of embodiment afforded by swiping calls for a dialogic reading. Charles Hatfield's discussion of Jack Kirby's graphic style is enlightening on the fascinations, pleasures, and ambiguities that pervade the practice of narrative drawing in the comic book industry, more sensitive to heteronomous regulations, intensive collaborations, and hence prone to reproduction and imitation: "any slavish imitation of an artist's style, once recognized as such, takes on a certain ideological value as a perceived rip-off, homage, or parody. Such imitation is, if you think about it, an odd thing: the result of an artist apprenticing his own eye and hand to another artist's peculiar and hard-won style, a style born of personal experience and struggle."[17] Hatfield importantly underlines graphic style as "hard-won," a dimension that matters beyond its particular meaning for Kirby's biography (a self-taught kid growing up in the tough streets of the Lower East Side) as it more generally describes the time and labor that go into acquiring a graphic style and that makes it uncommon for professional cartoonists to radically change their way of drawing (especially so in a context where speed of execution and efficiency strongly matter).

Practicing redrawing as an experimental demonstration of his theory of narrative drawing, Simon Grennan likewise comments, after reading his own attempts at pastiching Mike Mignola's graphic style: "I read a doubling of motives in the drawings themselves, compared with the existing bodies of work to which they contribute. It is not possible for me to be someone else, to make someone else's trace or to be in someone else's situation."[18] That situation, as Grennan further demonstrates, is tightly linked to a complex ecology that binds together body, intersubjects, and their social institutions.[19] Drawing and redrawing negotiate constructions of authorship and graphic style in which readers are always necessarily implicated: in this, swiping gets at the core of graphiation as "a socialized act involving many codes and constraints."[20] The secondhand work associated with swiping precisely frames this socialized dimension of drawing insofar as the term is used to distribute authorship and discuss the workings of imitation and influence in comics.

Swiping is perhaps not best understood through typological theories of intertextuality: as insightful as they may be for understanding particular cases, swipes are perhaps too close to copy or plagiarism to fare well under a model that privileges analysis of the transformative relationships between two texts.[21] Nor does it seem to be marked by an "anxiety of influence" and the "swerve" or "misprision" it entails: repetition is rarely something to get anxious about in comics culture, unless it comes to its legal liabilities, and the field is arguably more easily aligned on an "ecstasy of influence" that embraces repetition.[22] The recursive logic of swipes and its roots in lowbrow popular culture make it more readable against the backdrop of intericonicity and image circulation that scholars of visual culture have been particularly interested in.[23] Yet, what is properly interesting in swiping is arguably less found in how it might fit into well-known imitative processes rather than in the term in itself: the need to coin a particular usage highlights a vernacular about the medium's derivative practices, which implicitly produces an endogenous theory of intericonicity. Thinking of swiping as a medium-specific term for conceptualizing patterns of imitation and citation in comics helps us complement graphiation theory – by inviting a closer look at the role of derivative processes that have been out of its conceptual focus – as much as it entails grounding that specificity within a historical and cultural perspective, that is, a constantly moving and renegotiated medium-specificity. The heuristic value of swiping, then, has less to do with its being a hermeneutic tool for analyzing the dialogic relationship between two images than with its capacity to designate the medium-specific proto-cols that organize the very process of copying and its evaluation. Looking at swiping as a discursive object in its own right invites us to historicize "the material processes of copy routines" in comics culture.[24]

Drawing comics is in most cases a matter of redrawing, if only because its production process generally relies on various stages: sketching and refining, repeating the same panels over and over, drawing after various types of reference, imitating and reproducing defined graphic styles. According to comics theorist and scriptwriter Benoît Peeters, cartooning is strongly based on an "iterative principle" that makes redrawing a fundamental feature of the medium "from the sketch to the rough, then from inking in to the coloring, but also from panel to panel, page to page, and often from album to album."[25] The necessary process of redrawing, in this sense, can make the making of comics a particularly slow, painstaking, and labor-intensive enterprise – especially for "complete authors" that take on most if not all of the production process.[26] This also implies that redrawing is all the more organized in profit-driven publishing companies where the production process is more likely to be distinguished in successive phases and to engage a wider set of collaborators.[27] As an industry term, then, swiping is strongly associated with redrawing practices from the comic book world and the deadline-driven "hackwork" that cartoonists have to carry out. Wallace Wood, a comic book artist renowned for cranking out pages at remarkable speed, famously went by the motto: "Never draw anything you can copy, never copy anything you can trace, never trace anything you can cut out and paste up."[28] While the motto has a playful tongue-in-cheek character, it speaks to the working conditions and was meant as a guide for Wood's assistants. Keeping a swipe file at hand allowed professionals to draw from a collection of panels that could be reused in various graphic contexts and narrative opportunities. Swiping worked as a shorthand and a trick of the trade developed to meet tight deadlines. Wood kept a large swipe file, composed of photographs, pictures, selected images from comics he admired, and including also his own drawings[29]. He famously made a selection of his own sketched panels to be reused in a variety of narrative settings, as a handy tool for a creative labor regulated by fast-paced production demands. Later xeroxed and pasted up on a poster by his assistant Larry Hama, "Wally Wood's Panels That Always Work" has since been widely reused and recirculated in different formats and in diverse settings, continuing to influence various generations of cartoonists (Figure 5.2).

GRAPHIC POACHING

Many aspiring cartoonists partly taught themselves how to draw comics by copying their favorite strips.[30] That might partly explain why the term has taken on a particular importance in comic book culture specifically, as the burgeoning industry in the 1930s tapped into the cheap workforce of aspiring teenage cartoonists, organized in sweatshops, and often trained to imitate and draw in a specific style – an account somewhat romantically portrayed in Will Eisner's *The Dreamer*.[31] In the hyper-competitive comic book publishing context of the 1930s and 1940s, swiping was common because the main goal of the emerging publishers was precisely to imitate the successful products and to do so as fast as possible.[32] This competition not only encouraged copying but also enabled the expositive discourse around swiping by latching it onto battles over copyright ownership, intellectual property, authorship, and plagiarism. The ambiguities surrounding definitions of originality appear clear in the case of the comic book industry, which produced collaborative and derivative works but had to rely, in court, on "a living and breathing author" to testify to originality and hence defend the "copyrightability" of its products so as to ensure further licensing and merchandising, as Shiamin Kwa has remarkably unpacked.[33] Swipes can indeed be marshaled to the construction of material proofs in claims of copyright infringement: there have been several court cases where the competing parties assembled

Figure 5.2 Wally Wood, *22 Panels That Always Work*, 1980.
Source: TM & © 1980 & 2012 Wallace Wood Properties, LLC, ARR. Used by permission.

swipe files as evidence, juxtaposing images as visual proof of a clear and direct imitation.[34] Even then, though, "swipe" is anything but a legal term and as such holds no value in a court case.

The term itself is more properly embedded into the vernaculars of the comic book industry and of its fandom. If swiping is tightly connected with the comic book world, it shows residual meanings from the early-twentieth-century seedbed of newspaper culture, commercial illustration, and advertising. According to the Oxford English Dictionary, "swiping" had become, by the end of the nineteenth century, slang for "appropriating" or "stealing." In turn, it seems that the slang was quickly adopted into the professional jargon of the mass print industry: in 1910, *Printers' Ink*, the main trade magazine for advertising, presented "swipe" as "the term applied to advertisements whose design, or copy, or both, have been stolen or clumsily adapted from other advertisements."[35] Responding to their readers' letters and enclosing them in the pages of their magazines, the editors indicted the practice as a form of stealing. The exposition of the swipe in itself was meant as a "remedy" against blatant copying. As we will see, *The Comics Journal* (*TCJ*) would adopt a similar model of internal evaluation and exposition.

As panels get copied and recirculated, swipes crop up and turn into recognizable icons that become knowingly cited. The most stereotypical images and pictorial tropes defining certain comics genres (the close-up kiss panel of romance comics – an example we will return to) often rely on the more or less close tracing or redrawing of existing images, whose circulation gives further weight to the scene they depict. This process is clearly evidenced in *Polyepoxy*, a small booklet that collects, compiles, and documents the proliferation of a single image (a woman in a classical nude pose) through forty of its various copies found in the cheaply produced *fumetti per adulti*.[36] The book displays the fast rhythm under which cartoonists were often compelled to draw and which fostered any shorthand that could be used. Even more importantly, it demonstrates that genre comics do not simply rely on existing transmedial tropes (free-flowing "content") but often materially recirculate the same handful of iconic images. Resulting from a nearly forensic investigation into private archives of the most lowbrow comics, an object like *Polyepoxy* clearly derives from "fannish epistemologies" that have always developed an interest in identifying and collecting repeated images, borrowings, and citations.[37] The vocabulary of swiping in comic book culture has clearly emerged as a way of discussing the practice among makers and fans, who frequently invoke it to express a particular value judgment; to demonstrate an encyclopedic knowledge of the comics they read; to identify, distinguish, and authorize specific graphic styles; and, accordingly, to denounce plagiarism and copying.

From the very start, swiping not only was about the single act of copying a panel but involved material processes of managing and storing visual information. The swipe is inseparable from its filing media, including scrapbooks, albums, folders, and furniture: material technologies responding to increasing demands to preserve and organize images and documents for future use. In the context of instant access to large online databases of images, where much of that work is handed over to server farms and search algorithms, it is evident that swipe files are a thing of the past. It is perhaps harder to grasp how much the process of copying was itself tied to a repertoire of ordinary archival gestures: handling and sifting, identifying and retrieving images, preserving these items in a way that facilitates their reuse. Although the term "swiping" does not seem to appear in early discussions of newspaper comic strips, the process of assembling swipe files ran similar to the "morgue files" of journalism and cartooning. Long before the emergence of pre-cut catalogs of copyright-free images or today's digital image databases, newspapers often kept their own morgues with shared clippings used for reference material, while individual cartoonists frequently assembled their own files or visited public iconographic archives such as the New York Public Library's Picture Collection. How-to-cartoon manuals and correspondence courses frequently advised aspiring cartoonists to build up their own morgue or swipe files – while also precisely cautioning them not to commit plagiarism.[38]

Swiping was intertwined with an array of archival gestures: researching, selecting, organizing, storing images to facilitate their future use. Makers selecting and collecting panels and images, saving and storing them to facilitate their future use; publishers clipping panels and pasting them side by side in notebooks to exhibit as evidence; readers, likewise, collecting and arranging panels to map out particular idiographic qualities and expose copies. All of these are "gestures of archivalness" that run tangentially across the production and reception of comics, but which have been fundamental to the practice of swiping and to the recirculation of a visual memory of comics.[39]

The writerly and readerly pleasures of swiping, the archival gestures they require, and their role in the context of an emergent comic book culture have been best described by Jules Feiffer in the mid-1960s in his preface to *The Great Comic Book Heroes*, which consigns a chapter on the subject.[40] The first in a wave of nostalgia books on comics, Feiffer's book reprinted some of the first issues of *Superman, Batman,* and other superhero titles, bookended by a substantial memoir-like preface about his comics youth and a shorter critical afterword on the fannish resurgence of comic book interest. Looking back at the emergence of the comic book industry in the early forties, Feiffer highlights the importance of newspaper comic strips for his generation, while emphasizing that the term "swiping" is distinctively used in comic book culture: "Swiping was and is a trade term in comic books for appropriating that which is Alex Raymond's, Milton Caniff's, Hal Foster's or any one of a number of other sources and making it one's own."[41] Citing the most influential adventure comic strip artists, Feiffer presents comics as part of a culture of sharing, constituted by practices like swiping – which is not merely a synonym for copying but rather spans a whole array of gestures that range from clipping and collecting to redrawing and recirculating the swipes:

> Swipes, if noticed, were accepted as part of comic book folklore. I have never heard a complaint. Rather, I have heard swipe artists vigorously defended, one compared to another: who did the best Caniff, the closest Raymond? ... I often preferred the swipe to the original ... and paid his swipes the final compliment of clipping and swiping them. ... I not only clipped swipes, I traced and managed to get hold of their sources. ... I swiped diligently from the swipers, drew sixty-four pages in two days, sometimes one day, stapled the product together, and took it out on the street where kids my age sat behind orange crates selling and trading comic books. Mine went for less because they weren't real.[42]

Feiffer's appreciation of swiping casts redrawing other comics as part of a participatory network of reading, sharing, and creating that, as Jared

Gardner has shown, characterized the "creative agency" of early comic book readers, who were often encouraged to "pick up a brush and try it themselves."[43] Clipping, copying, stapling: swiping triggers a chain of activities intimately related to engaging with print ephemera. Whether in newsprint or in comic books proper, the comics text was an open invitation to destruction and repurposing, the inclusion of paper dolls and other cut-out elements calling out for scissors and glue. In this sense, comics culture rehearsed the "repertoire of gestures of archivalness and cutting and pasting" typical of nineteenth-century scrapbooks, fore-shadowing contemporary remix culture.[44]

Writing at a point where fandom was leveling up, with soaring prices for vintage comic books that made news headlines, Feiffer nostalgically identifies early traces of this participatory culture in the "graphic poaching" of swipers, to reformulate a lasting metaphor used by Michel de Certeau to describe the readerly appropriations of texts.[45] The acts of swiping, stapling, and recirculating that Feiffer describes for the 1940s are just as much those of the fanzine makers of the sixties, who often engaged in "reproductions, imitations, copying, redrawing, tracing" – a set of derivative techniques that, as Fredric Wertham notes in *The World of Fanzines*, are discussed and debated as swiping.[46]

SWIPING BACK

Originally emanating from fanzine culture, *TCJ* would mark a new epi-sode in this definition of swiping, as the magazine, published by Fantagraphics, became a critical weapon rallying against the comic book industry and valorizing an *auteur* ideology. *TCJ* indeed took on the issue of swiping through a regular column called "Swipe File," which explicitly invited its readers not only to propose swipes but also to pass judgments on swipes that appeared in contemporary cartoonists' work. As Robert Boyd noted in the column's introductory installment, "Swipe File" intended to simply lay out next to each other images that could be read as swipes, without necessarily implying plagiarism: "Each installment of Swipe File will feature two images, carefully identified and dated, which bear some similarity to one another. Being included in Swipe File is not necessarily a condemnation; these 'swipes' will include homages, parodies, ironic appropriations and bizarre coincidences, as well as outright rip-offs. You, the reader, can decide what kind of swipe you're looking at."[47] This shared dialogue with the reader connects the practice of swiping to a communal belonging in the spirit of a (counter) public debate. The framing of the editorial column as a simple juxtaposition defers the judgment to the readers, a position that remains important in today's online fan communities who continue to share and discuss swipes in a way that always calls for evaluation ("homage or plagiarism?" is the standard question) but always leaves its negotiation up for grabs.[48] Straddling the line between ethical and epistemic positions, swiping is rarely fixed to a single value and more often entails a deferral of judgment, or at least an invitation to assess the status of the copy and its work within a particular narrative economy. In particular cases, however, and before it started dedicating a column to the issue, *TCJ* sometimes took on a more explicitly militant position toward swiping as plagiarism, directly condemning certain creators for obvious and repeated swipes. In the late 1980s in particular, at the time when the magazine was starting to explicitly champion alternative comics while keeping up with mainstream comic books,[49] *TCJ* spotlighted two particularly problematic cases of swiping: Rich Buckler's swipes from Jack Kirby and Keith Giffen's swipes from Argentinian cartoonist José Muñoz.[50]

Buckler's case highlights the importance that "house style" had taken in mainstream comic book publishing, with Kirby's 1960s work for Marvel forming "the visual template from which much subsequent superhero work has derived."[51] *TCJ*'s intervention in that debate is part of its struggle alongside Kirby's tensed relationships with Marvel (over ownership of original art, notably), and directly intervenes in debates over graphic authorship and ownership in the legal battlefield of comic book production. The Giffen/Muñoz case shares similar issues but, rather than replaying a tug-of-war that is internal to the American comic book, it entails a more complicated appropriation of material that reflects how asymmetric power relationships can come to bear on the economy of swiping.

Keith Giffen's successful DC miniseries *Ambush Bug*, for instance, marked a stylistic change in the artist's career, with an influx of heavily inked blacks and jagged graphic lines strongly inspired by José Muñoz's distinct graphic style. More than simply an inspiration, though, Muñoz's work turned out to provide the American cartoonist with nearly ready-made images: in a 1986 *TCJ* article titled "The Trouble with Keith Giffen," Mark Burbey laid out a surprising number of evident swipes by Giffen, directly pilfered from Muñoz and Carlos Sampayo's *Alack Sinner* series.[52] *TCJ* further fed the controversy in its columns and letters pages: the journal railing against Giffen as a plagiarist while some readers stood up for him, both sides recognizing the weight of his debt owed to Muñoz.[53] While Giffen himself denied swiping at all, insisting that "he never traced a panel, or even drew with Muñoz's work in front of him," the Argentinian cartoonist felt bitter at the appropriation but could not afford the financial costs of a suit against DC that would probably have been a battle lost in advance.[54] Instead, together with writer Sampayo, Muñoz responded to Giffen in an installment of their *Alack Sinner* series titled "Por unos dibujos ..." ("Over Some Drawings").[55]

In the flexible structure of the *Alack Sinner* series, which allows for digressions and tangent narratives, "Over Some Drawings" marks such a cluster story.[56] The opportunity to briefly change the course of the main narrative comes with the eponymous character's chance encounter, on a Greyhound bus, with a cartoonist named José Martínez (whose face is drawn after Muñoz's own) who immediately shares his story: he is going to "make things clear with another cartoonist" who has copied his work and "make sure he stops copying me" – "I will break his hands."[57] As Sinner falls into slumber, an embedded dream story indeed casts a brutal confrontation between a disenfranchised South-American cartoonist José Martínez and the rich and successful American comic book artist going by the not-so-subtle name of K.K. Kitten (Figure 5.3). The arguments used as excuse by Kitten seem directly lifted from the columns of *TCJ*, as both Kitten and Giffen refuse to recognize any direct swiping and invoke an inspirational use, while highlighting how their "new" style has had little success with their followers.[58] Arguments escalate and Martínez and Kitten engage in a duel – umbrella against fire iron, drawn in a parody of the graphic style of American comic books, multiplying speed lines and disproportioning bodies for rhetorical effect – which ends with another outcome than the one announced earlier in the story.

Figure 5.3 José Muñoz and Carlos Sampayo, "Pour quelques dessins" *(À Suivre),* no. 159 (1991), 27.
Source: Muñoz and Sampayo © Casterman. Courtesy of Editions Casterman.

As Sinner wakes up at the final stop (his neighboring traveler has disappeared) and comes off the bus, he is stricken by the newspaper headlines: "South American cartoonist José Martínez died yesterday from a gunshot wound to the head." The news article invokes the good reputation of Kitten and his right of self-defense, which allows him to rewrite the story and inverse the roles: "his attacker used to plagiarize his drawings which, in his view, was a sign of mental illness."[59] The voice of the South-American migrant cartoonist is silenced and his version of the story left unheard. By redrawing this narrative of plagiarism into the larger critique of American imperialism found in *Alack Sinner,* the Argentinian duo effectively aligns swiping-as-stealing as part of a larger power struggle, symbolically writing back to the swiper.[60]

Where swiping often serves as homage to and the expression of a shared culture, the Giffen/Muñoz case highlights the extent to which market and legal forces can regulate the economy of redrawing. Muñoz and Sampayo point out the asymmetrical relationship between the swiped and the swipers that leaves few resources for culturally marginalized artists. "Like any legal code," Paul Saint-Amour reminds us, "copyright can replicate dominant power relationships as much in what it permits as in what it prohibits."[61] Swiping is not a level playing field and, for better or worse, copyright restrictions and economic forces can establish what gets recognized as plagiarism or homage. Similarly, a "signature style" is also an institutional concept that cultural industries trademark: redrawing is a key part of the mainstream comic book artist's formation as they often need to conform to a "house style," which conversely implies that the "graphic poaching" of that publisher's territory is strictly prohibited. The most famous case here is the legal battle that opposed Disney to *Air Pirates*, a group of underground cartoonists who had extensively copied from Disney comics, especially Floyd Gottfredson's comic strip, for satirical purposes.[62]

The graphic novel has partly emerged in contradistinction to this relative dissociation of graphic style and individual artist that commands the mainstream comic book industry.[63] As Jan Baetens and Hugo Frey put it, "it is part of the graphic novelist self-construction as a serious author to oppose the industrial principles underlying the production of comics."[64] This distinctive emphasis on personal graphic style is in part a heritage of the underground comix culture and its dissent against the main production practices in the comic book industry. In such a framework, swiping often becomes a shorthand for the most fast-paced and derivative work in comic book culture and hence a model that the graphic novelist will consciously oppose as part of an authorial strategy. At a moment where the underground comix scene was losing momentum, Bill Griffith, Art Spiegelman, and Joe Schenkman's 1973 "Centerfold Manifesto" lampooned the clichés of mainstream comic books as much as the by-then-established clichés of underground comix and advanced a vision of comics as "experimental personal statements crafted by artists," a lesson that many cartoonists would live by in the years to come with the emergence of so-called post-underground and alternative comics.[65] In the manifesto's attack against unoriginality, swiping becomes a catchphrase for all the repetitions and commonplaces that crowd the field, distinguished against a process of "experimentation" that allegedly encompasses more personal forms of appropriation. The contrast is made visually clear by having a famous scene from James Whale's *Frankenstein* (1931) interrupted with a honking car and a "Keep on Trucking" label, hinting at Robert Crumb's most copied and reused phrase.

Of course, this also has its own economic reasons, as it indeed becomes important for the cartoonist to develop a specific and recognizable graphic style that will distinguish their work in an otherwise crowded field. As a result, "[d]rawing style becomes an absolutely central notion in the structure of the graphic novel. It is supposed to be one of the signatures or trademarks of the author, and one can easily observe that personality and individuality really matter in the field."[66] While this intimate connection between graphic style and authorship is quintessential to the graphic novel, it does not mean that graphic novelists simply do away with forms of redrawing, quotation, references, parody, and pastiche – as should be quite clear by now.

To cite Baetens and Frey again, "graphic novels are especially capable of making meta-commentary and reflexive references to existing titles, creators, and even whole genres."[67] Graphic novelists often express their indebtedness to the history of comics and rely on or tease out their readers' knowledge of that past in their graphic strategies. Few, however, explicitly ground these referential practices within the "copy routines" of the comic book world, and quite often the reference to comics history might also reinforce a certain sense of distinction from that very history: an iconic example would be the contrast in Daniel Clowes's *David Boring* between the black-and-white lines that make the main narrative and the recurring full-color visual quotations from a forged comic book, *The Yellow Streak*.[68] While Clowes imitates the style of a range of comic books in a retro-reflexive fashion, the process is not itself evidenced as swiping. And indeed, Clowes's preparatory sketches and notes indicate that his stylistic references are based on identifiable genres or period-bound styles: his notes for *Ice Haven*, a book drawn in different graphic registers, feature drawing indications for the various storylines such as "draw in Gasoline Alley/Hergé 'clear line' style, w/ no modeling, etc. correct proportions," "Possibly somewhat comic? Drawn in 20s Mutt & Jeff style?" or, more simply and precisely, "Peanuts/Barnaby."[69]

By contrast, in a parallel series published in his comic book *Eightball*, Clowes directly tackles swiping as a prime example in his unbridled satire of the comic book world. In one of the last *Pussey!* stories ("The Death of Dan Pussey"), Clowes indeed pictures a comics artist veteran visiting the rich estate of the Pussey studios: embittered by his own lack of financial success, the older cartoonist angrily accuses Pussey of swiping from him, before crumbling into an apology about how that panel was swiped from another guy who had probably just swiped it from yet another comic (Figure 5.4). The swipe appears, nearly by definition, as a recursive object, accumulating copies of copies of the same images. Clowes's biting satire, however, cuts across the entire spectrum (including a hilarious parody of Spiegelman and of *RAW* magazine). Another instalment of *Pussey!* in fact draws a parallel between Pussey's swipes (a quick means to meet a tight deadline) and the appropriation of his drawings by the

Figure 5.4 Panel excerpted from Daniel Clowes, *Pussey!* (Seattle, WA: Fantagraphics, 2000), 50.
Source: Copyright © Daniel Clowes. Courtesy of Fantagraphics Books (www.fantagraphics.com).

gallery artist "Slugger Onions," in a thinly veiled caricature of the art world and easy pop-art-like appropriations of comic book images. In so doing, Clowes speaks out about a resentment toward the art world typical of alternative comics, stressing the contrast between two types of laying claim to an influence: the unassuming, noncitational swipes internal to comic book culture clashing with the careless, flagrant, "make-it-art" appropriations of popular culture by the art world.[70]

It further contains an implicit and common critique of Roy Lichtenstein's appropriation of comic book images, mostly lifted from romance and war comics, that is widespread in the comics world. As Clowes's publisher Kim Thompson once said of pop art, "one of its unfortunate side-effects has been to relegate comics art to the same cultural compost heap as urinals, bricks, and Campbell's soup cans."[71] Nevertheless, as Frey and Baetens recently argued, the relationship between comics and pop art was more of a feedback loop and Roy Lichtenstein's appropriation and transformation of comic book panels also brought the logic of reframing into a very different realm and gave it a wider public outreach: "Lichtenstein was another kind of comics historian, clipping and selecting the images that his eye was drawn to for potential reimagination, and thus also a different kind of preservation for posterity."[72] While some contemporary cartoonists have openly voiced criticism against Lichtenstein and the art world's appropriation of comic books, others have shown less resentment and have instead embraced this kind of practice, reinventing it for their own approach to cartooning. In this sense, it is not surprising that Charles Burns, who frequently draws from romance comic books, declared his interest in Lichtenstein's work in an interview with *TCJ*, precisely at a moment when the magazine was debating the legacy of the pop artist for the comics world.[73] The practices of identifying, clipping, and reusing comic book images were common for creators and readers, and Charles Burns's swipe files specifically assert a continuity with such gestures.

TRACING THE SWIPERS

In his introduction to *The Best American Comics 2009*, Burns aligns his editorial choices with a search for "'what's good' in the world of comics."[74] "What's good," to Burns, is often intertwined with imitation and copying, a theme that runs throughout the introduction. Burns notes: "'Flash Gordon' by Alex Raymond is pretty good, but 'Flesh Garden' by Harvey Kurtzman and Wally Wood is better," alluding to the *Mad* parody of the classic superhero comic, of which he found three redrawn panels in his father's swipe file. To Burns, this was an "early epiphany": "Even though I recognized the fact that it looked like a slightly distorted version of Wally Wood's artwork, it was amazingly precise – especially the lettering. It was at that moment I realized comic books were actually drawn by human hands."[75] In a medium simultaneously marked by the handmade mark and mechanical reproduction, the swipe does not take away the indexical function of the drawing but makes it all the more salient.

Tracing a genealogy of swiping from Alex Raymond to his father, Burns places his practice in the sign of the copy. Years later, Burns would himself swipe the same three panels from "Flesh Garden" in his self-published giveaway zine *Free Shit* #15, suggesting that copying is not simply a kid's thing or a developmental stage.[76] Growing from this fascination with "what's good" as a process of copying, Burns's embrace of swiping appears clearest in the various swipe files that he has constructed and shared on the web or published as zines and small-press books. This act of collecting, reframing, and redrawing swiped comics panels explores a residual conception of swiping that conflicts with the *auteur* model associated with the graphic novel.

Pointing out the handwritten/mechanical nature of cartooning and counteracting the idea of a teleological development, Charles Burns's discussion of redrawing follows Christopher Pizzino's important reading of his style as "autoclasm" in *Arresting Development.* Pizzino describes autoclasm as "a formal tendency specific to conditions where the act of making comics is not considered legitimate" that makes the medium's disenfranchised status visible through a self-destructive dynamic: autoclasm is indeed "present when an image effects a kind of self-breaking, as if it is designed to work against itself."[77] It is precisely this self-canceling dynamic that makes Burns's graphic style autoclastic, as it is marked by aesthetics familiar to comic books – repeating and reproducing familiar tropes from pre-Code genre comics, for instance – combined with a highly idiosyncratic approach to inking: strong black-and-white contrasts rendered by thick to thin brushstrokes. In this way, as Pizzino argues, "Burns's images evoke artisanal and mechanical production in a way that seems at once to emphasize and to obviate the distinction between them," playing the two economies of the image against each other: the mechanically reproduced narrative line of traditional cartooning and the expressive mark of the fine arts.[78]

Burns's swipes articulate both these dimensions, bringing these two economies together in the very act of redrawing: by making another cartoonist's lines his own, Burns literally draws attention to the expressive, mark-making function of reproduction by means of drawing. This dual facet, however, is not necessarily self-canceling. In autoclastic fashion, I believe that Burns's practice of swiping corroborates Pizzino's reading while also suggesting that his images simultaneously operate in different narrative economies of power and desire. The production and circulation of Burns's swipe files within a transnational context of small-press experimental comics, often through European publishers, entails a more relaxed relationship to cultural status. The question of legitimacy is much less pressing, especially as the small-press scene upholds a subcultural ethos that does not make cultural recognition its central concern, but also because comics reading in Europe is now increasingly inscribed in a "post-legitimate" context.[79] Accordingly, while they are often issued on limited print runs and get close to the realm of artists' books, Burns's small-press books remain cheap and affordable publications, with no extravagant display of refined printing techniques, in keeping with a punk ethos.[80]

Even while Burns swipes from the "lowest" genres in comics history, his practice of swiping expresses a different relationship to the marginalized status of comics, eschewing autoclasm. The very practice of swiping expresses an attachment to comic book culture and an iconophilic collecting, gathering, and redrawing of visually striking images. In this way, Burns's swipe files resist the *Bildungsroman* discourse – which aligns comics history with a teleological coming-of-age narrative from juvenile comics to mature graphic novels – without necessarily relying on a self-breaking tactic.[81] Tapping into childhood gestures of redrawing and a culture of graphic poaching, Burns exhibits his influences and inspirations in a way that contrasts with the emphasis on originality and personal style in the graphic novel. As a result, his swipe files present a comingling of consumption and reproduction of comics images, highlighting an "intimate process of comics reading" that is not necessarily marked by disruption and delinquency.[82]

Indeed, Burns foregrounds swiping as a set of gestures – reading, selecting, clipping, collecting, reproducing – that very concretely participate in an economy of desire between comics and their readers. This economy is relatively free from regulatory tendencies, keeping in mind that such an economy always runs the risk of asymmetric power relationships. In constituting his various swipe files, Burns reiterates a "repertoire" of actions that transmit an active memory of comics (collecting, clipping, copying).[83] The way Burns engages with the swipe file format spans a wide degree of reproduction, from the scanning or xeroxing of cut-out comics panels to more creative reworking and collages. His Tumblr blog *Johnny 23* works as a digital scrapbook featuring drawings, photographs, and panels selected and sometimes collaged from various comics.[84] These swipes often alternate with Burns's own quotation of these comics in his own work. Alongside this online swipe file, Burns's various small-press booklets *Close Your Eyes, Swipe File,* and *Love Nest* invest the "swipe file" format in more creative ways.[85]

Relying on different swiping strategies, these three booklets display an increasing fascination for the (non)narrative potential of the swipe: the fragmentation and dislocation of an image from its original context. *Close Your Eyes* presents a swipe file that records Burns's practice of redrawing. It prints each original panel alongside its copy in double-page spreads that force the reader to notice the slight differences and additions, foregrounding the act of redrawing as a complex embodied process of copying. The sketchbook style adopted by the short introduction presents these swipes both as an exercise – practiced while waiting during his daughters' piano lessons – and as a nearly physical response to visually striking images. The act of copying itself is uncovered in a confessional tone: "It's true. I *copied* every single drawing in this book. I copied the work of artists I admired – I even copied my *own* work. . . . [E]very once in a while I'll come across an amazing image in some book or magazine I'm reading and get the uncontrollable urge to copy it."[86] In response to his urge to copy, *Close Your Eyes* is framed as a collection of favorites, weird but fascinating images clipped from other comics, pasted in a sketchbook and redrawn in Burns's signature style.

Copying as much from his contemporaries – Daniel Clowes, Julie Doucet, and Gary Panter, to name but a few – as from anonymous artists and debased comic books, Burns credits, whenever possible, each swiped artist, expressing his swipe as a homage to their work. There is, moreover, an explicit fascination for images that are themselves swiped or drawn from somewhere else. Burns copies a romance comic book artist who "has the Milton Caniff style down cold," or adds his own image to "two disturbing images . . . taken from the same romance comics" and "showing that the artist obviously had an extensive 'swipe file'" (Figure 5.5).[87] The "second hand" holds an extra attraction: connecting his own collection of swipes with the swipe file of some romance comic book artist, Burns follows Feiffer in "swiping from the swipers," tracing recurring single images, abstracted from their narrative sequences and repurposed within the context of a small-press anthology, or "weird" images he encountered and their redrawn twins.[88]

Figure 5.5 Charles Burns, *Close Your Eyes* (Marseille: Le Dernier Cri, 2001), 80–81.
Source: Copyright © Charles Burns. Courtesy of the artist.

Swiping, here, expresses a desire to own or possess an image singled out from its original context in a way that parallels what film scholar Laura Mulvey has called the "possessive spectator," who fixates on a particular image torn away from the filmic sequence and who, in doing so, "commits an act of violence against the cohesion of a story, the aesthetic integrity that holds it together, and the vision of its creator."[89] As a still medium, and despite the "iconic solidarity" of its images, comics have arguably always held the potential for this kind of disruptive reading: allowing the reader to "hold" a sequence of images, fixate on a single image, and revel in the pleasures of pure graphiation.[90] This desire to "possess" an image is clearly expressed in the clipping and scrapbooking that often precedes swiping, which can then be seen as a way of taking ownership of the image through the act of redrawing. The panels collected and redrawn by Burns, as presented in *Close Your Eyes*, form a catalog of images that the cartoonist has recirculated in various contexts, as background details in his illustration or comics work, for instance.

While Close Your Eyes is closer to an actual swipe file, documenting Burns's personal collection of favorite panels, his two subsequent small-press books, *Swipe File* and *Love Nest*, compile and assemble swipes in a way that puts the original sources at a greater distance from Burns's own. This increasingly confuses the reader about the nature of the swiped images, while reactivating their narrative potential in the form of Burns's multipanel comics. While repurposing the swiped images, Burns does not, however, seamlessly camouflage them into another narrative. The fragmented gesture of cutting up disrupts the swiped panel from its original sequence, while retaining a visual and narrative unity. As a result, the sequences that Burns assembles from various swipes are extremely discontinuous and minimally narrative: with no conventional plots or clear cause-and-effect linearity, the wordless sequences refocus the reader's attention onto the graphiation.

In *Swipe File*, Burns pays homage to five major cartoonists, which he credits at the end of the booklet: "The 'swipes' in this book are taken from existing images by artists I have a deep admiration for: Johnny Craig, Bruno Premiani, Jack Cole, Jack Kirby and Chester Gould."[91] Each double-page spread draws from the work of one artist, meticulously redrawing that artist's images into four-panel strips. The whole work displays a consistent treatment that unifies the separate strips: not only through Burns's redrawing of the original images using his own inking style but also in the way they stage a visual metamorphosis through recurring motifs of circles, mirror images, burning backgrounds, gazes, and monstrous faces. The graphic trace appears here as fundamentally ambivalent, as one recognizes the strange comingling of Burns's signature style with that of the admired cartoonists, who all have their recognizable graphic style: Burns redraws many of their idiographic signs, such as the "Kirby krackle," while lightly transforming the panels, adding small graphic details that are indexical for his own style. The panels drawn after Chester Gould's *Dick Tracy*, based on an April 29, 1965 four-panel strip, index many of Gould's graphic idiosyncrasies (Figure 5.6): the strong black-and-white contrast, the thin cross-hatching, the grotesquely caricatured faces, "compounded of folds and sinister deformities" – even the flames have a Gould flourish.[92]

At the same time, the swipes are also classically Burns: details such as the finely detailed dirt ground and the broken trees – recurring visual motifs in Burns's comics – and his easily identifiable inking and shading technique, which, as Pizzino argues, "arrests the narrative flow" to point the reader's eye to its function as an expressive mark.[93] This swipe file thus emphasizes the same gestures as *Close Your Eyes* – selecting visually striking images and redrawing them – without displaying the originals alongside their copy, blurring the lines between imitation and transformation. The swipes are

Figure 5.6 Charles Burns, *Swipe File* (Philadelphia, PA: Common Press, 2008), n.p.
Source: Special collections of the Penn Libraries at the University of Pennsylvania. Burns lifts and recomposes panels from an April 1965 comic strip from Chester Gould's *Dick Tracy* Both versions were exhibited in the 2012 *Cent pour Cent* show at the Centre international de la bande dessinée in Angoulême.

not meant to be compared to their sources, and yet they do not gain an autonomous status, nor are they inconspicuously integrated into a narrative economy: the appropriative gesture of redrawing remains central to the book as a way of defamiliarizing the style of the swiped artists, while appropriating their work to constitute nearly abstract, collage-like sequences.

Love Nest further extends this logic, putting the original sources at yet more distance, as no credits appear in its paratext. It quickly becomes apparent that the book is mainly constituted of swipes from romance and other genre comic books, but, given Burns's fascination for some of the most debased examples of the genre and his recurrent swipes from swipers and anonymous artists, the sources are hard to locate. Yet, some dedicated fans of Burns's work are spurred to source some of the original comic books. It turns out, for instance, that the anonymous short story "Marked Woman," with drawings attributed to Bill Draut and published in 1945 in the Harvey romance comic *True Love Problems and Advice Illustrated*, provided Burns with several striking panels to redraw.[94] The short five-page narrative – a love story about a woman with a scarred face – is a concentration of many tropes that have been recurring fascinations in Burns's works, particularly around body horror and skin-bristling images of suburban America.[95] The example not only substantiates the suggestion that *Love Nest* is entirely made of actual swipes; it also highlights how the images are taken out of their context and of their original narrative sequences (indeed, the six images lifted from "Marked Woman" are redistributed across Burns's whole book; they do not form a sequence in themselves).

As such, they primarily make up a set of images selected for their striking visual effect, enhanced by stripping away the heavy text and dialogues, as well as a more or less substantial transformation of the source images (Figure 5.7). All images are evidently redrawn and reinked in Burns's hand, even when they are extremely closely retraced. The panels are also rescaled to the one panel per page rhythm of *Love Nest*, which, at 15 cm × 17 cm, presents altogether larger individual images than the original comic book would have. The black-and-white lines make the inking work (one of Burns's most distinguished trademarks) all the more salient, while also implying something of a shift from comic

Figure 5.7 Comparison of selected panels: (a) Bill Draut, "Marked Woman," *True Love Problems and Advice Illustrated*, no. 29 (New York: Harvey Comics, 1954); (b) Charles Burns, *Love Nest* (Bordeaux: Cornélius, 2016).

book to graphic novel (where black and white is often a distinctive choice from the strategic importance of color in comic books).[96] More substantial changes might also include mirroring, adaptations, new backgrounds, the addition of grotesque details, or minute changes that reflect the process of drawing (tellingly, one swipe replaces the broken mirror with a comic book page and inking tools). For all these transformations, however, what is most striking is the faithfulness with which the images are redrawn, evidencing a clear attempt at preserving the qualities that make them recognizable as romance comics images.

In *Love Nest*, the swiped (or not swiped) images are thus assembled into a collection of single panels that offer no explicit plot or narrative. In this way, the book stretches out the "abstract piece" that Burns had composed early on for *RAW* magazine with his one-page comic "And I Pressed My Hand against His Face, Feeling His Thick Massive Lips, And ...."[97] *Love Nest* starts out with the exact same words as the aforementioned strip, facing the same image of a woman in bed, engrossed in her reading. This opening panel stages a stereotypical scene of passionate reading and, although no title or other explanatory information appears on the covers, we could easily imagine the woman reading a romance comic book given the size and leaflet quality of the object in her hands. *Love Nest*, then, recirculates familiar tropes and stereotypes typical for Burns's entire oeuvre: the uncanny repetition performed by the act of swiping extends to the way Burns nearly exactly reproduces stereotypes as a way of confronting his readers with them. As Pizzino argues, "Burns seeks to dwell on familiar tropes, but not serve their usual ends."[98]

Repurposing the swiped panels leads Burns down a path similar to *Swipe File*, as *Love Nest* does not recreate a consistent, linear narrative from the collected fragments. Rather, while the swiped panels are highly figurative and often suggest a strong narrative effect with moments of tension, fear, anger, surprise, the book unbinds them from their original sequences by stressing fragmentation and discontinuity rather than linear sequentiality. *Love Nest* encourages readers to flip through the text in order to identify recurring elements, although this braided network of panels does not coalesce into a clear narrative: the images ask to be looked at, contemplated, rather than just inserted into a plot, even as the door to narrativize these separate images always remains ajar. *Love Nest* thus brings us back to the aesthetics of the scrapbook, weaving together the various swipe files that Burns has been carefully assembling as part of his creative practice, while also giving a greater autonomy to the swipes. In this way, *Love Nest* epitomizes a dynamic that is also at work in Burns's long-form, more conventionally narrative graphic novel *Last Look*, which not only swipes from old comics but also spreads these swipes across a variety of formats situated between the hardcover graphic novel and the small-press zine.

SWIPE SWARM AND TAINTED LOVE

Originally published in three separate volumes, Charles Burns's *Last Look* presents a highly fragmented narrative, moving us through the life of Doug as a young and not-so-young artist in the punk scene and his complex relationship with Sarah, whom he abandons while she is pregnant with his child after her brutal, abusive ex-boyfriend beats him up.[99] Through constant flashbacks and flash-forwards, alternating with another narrative thread that relates the adventures of Doug's alter-ego Nitnit in a parallel, weird dream-world, *Last Look* articulates Doug's troubled memories, desires, fears, and failures. The assault itself, if only the trigger for Doug to leave Sarah, is made explicit in the last volume of the series and functions as a node around which the dispersed fragments of narrative articulate themselves. Even collected into a single book, *Last Look* remains a strictly nonlinear graphic novel, based on a large stock of recurring images.[100] Those repeated pictures are themselves compulsively gathered, collected, circulated, and produced by the characters: photographs, Polaroids, posters, comics, and drawings made by the characters saturate the comics grid, creating frames within frames. In the process, Charles Burns draws heavily on the history of comics, directly borrowing a significant number of panels from sixties American romance comics and from Hergé's *Tintin*. The swipes make up a significant part of the braided network that *Last Look* traces in a highly fragmented, disjointed, and seemingly random logic that evokes William S. Burroughs's cut-up technique.

Burns makes multiple references to the fictional universe of some of Burroughs's texts, notably through the "NitNit/Johnny 23" performance that Doug puts on at a punk show, reading aloud some cut-ups over a tape of random sounds.[101] Yet the relationships between comics and literature are not articulated here following the usual logic of adaptation. Rather, on the grounds of what Irina O. Rajewsky has termed an "intermedial reference" or a case of intermediality based on the thematization, evocation or imitation of another medium "through the use of its own media-specific means," Burns cites Burroughs's cut-up in the very form of his own graphic novel.[102] The cut-up itself is already, at its very core, an intermedial concept, given that it was coined by Burroughs in collaboration with visual artist Brion Gysin, and Burroughs himself went on to adapt the technique to filmmaking.[103] Burns's citation of Burroughs could itself be seen as an adaptation of the cut-up technique in comics, except that, at the level of production, he does not actually try to reproduce the aleatory and method of cutting up fragments at random. Rather, Burns elaborates on the cut-up as a narrative effect rather than an artistic method, following what Rajewsky describes as the "as if" character proper to intermedial reference.[104] The result is a graphic novel that *looks* like it was cut up, except it was not. As Burns has explained, "some of the writing or the structure imitates collage or cut-up. What William Burroughs was doing was cutting up a page of existing writing and then collaging it. I wasn't doing that at all, I was doing something that maybe visually imitates that, but was very controlled. There was nothing random about the structure at all."[105] This quote pinpoints an apparent paradox at the core of Burns's whole trilogy. Burns is not relying on Burroughs's method of random composition, but, through this very controlled approach to storytelling, strengthened by a rigid page layout, he nonetheless succeeds in evoking and visually imitating the idea of "cutting up" physical materials by constantly alternating between various temporalities, destabilizing sequential panel-to-panel transitions and thus disorienting the reader.[106]

This evocation of the cut-up method is reinforced by the many quotations that Burns disseminates in a seemingly random way throughout the trilogy: they make up the vast network of recurring images and motifs that slowly coalesce into a relatively intelligible narrative of fear, violence, opiates, pollution, sickness, pregnancy, and abortion. But if a centripetal force brings the elements together, there is simultaneously a centripetal tangent to Burns's approach that is apparent in the fragmented materiality of the project. Not only did Burns publish the books in three separate installments, not the obvious choice in the context of the graphic novel, but he also published countless extra images and small-press versions that expand on the original trilogy.[107] These dispersed materials include a "Cut-Up" piece realized for Geneva-based small-press publisher B.ü.L.b. comix, a regular "Random Access" comic strip in *The Believer*, numerous spoof covers of the *Nitnit* and romance comic books eventually gathered together in a single volume as *Vortex*, and, last but not least, the faux bootleg version of *X'ed Out* printed by Le Dernier Cri under the title *Johnny 23*.[108]

Johnny 23 explicitly plays out the cut-up idea by suggesting that the graphic material composing Burns's graphic novels can be rearranged and recirculated in different ways, reinforcing the nonlinear structure of the original as a collection of discrete items that can be reassembled. *Johnny 23* indeed reuses the exact same images as *X'ed Out*, but reorganizes them in new sequences, mixed up with new images, and changes the text to an imaginary alphabet that, if decoded, is close to the Burroughs-like literary cut-ups that the title character of *X'ed Out* performs under the pseudonym Johnny 23. The book itself, then, appears as a kind of cut-up version of *X'ed Out*, as if composed by hands foreign to their original creation. With its abstract sequencing of images, *Johnny 23* is very similar to Burns's infra-narrative experiments with *Swipe File* and *Love Nest*, strengthening a processual approach to comics based on the redrawing and rearranging of existing, past material. The horizontal Leporello format further evokes *lianhuanhua*, the Chinese format for popular picture books, strengthened by the fake graphic alphabet used by Burns for the entire text. It connects the process of cutting and rearranging the panels not only with avant-garde traditions of the cut-up method but also with the changing formats of globally circulated comics, which can require substantial changes and adaptations, changing the sizes of the panels, redrawing missing parts, and so on.

Spreading its network of recurring images across a body of alternate texts, *Last Look* creates a dense swipe file of sorts that connects its various fragments without arranging them into a linear narrative sequence. Moreover, a large part of the trilogy, and particularly the Nitnit storyline, is composed of panels swiped from Burns's preferred canon of *Tintin* and romance comic books, as many of these borrowed panels intersect with Burns's swipe files. With *Last Look*, the swipes here are embedded within a longer narrative form and become objects in the fictional universe: the "crappy romance comics from the sixties" that Sarah finds at a yard sale, and which appear throughout the *Hive* episode, and the *Nitnit* comic books and their share of panels and images redrawn from *Tintin*.[109]

While the swipes take on a greater narrative function than in Burns's small-press experiments, they also resist any smooth narrative integration; nor does their recognition as swipes elicit a code with which to decipher the images. As Jan Baetens and Hugo Frey argue in their clever reading of Burns's "remake" of Tintin, Burns offers a modern "stylization" of Hergé's character based on a reversal of the clear line ideology, which is rooted in "clarity, transparency, health, order," on the level of content and form.[110] The swiped panels contribute to this defamiliarization of the clear line, as Burns

> relies on the insertion of small capsules of Tintin-like material that proliferate as dangerous cells through the work that hosts them. ... The meaning of such a 'quotation' does not stop once its source has been identified: quite the contrary. Even if the source of the quotation escapes the reader's memory or expertise, the very readability of their internal networking forces the reader to permanently put into question what she is reading.[111]

The ambivalence of the quotation that Baetens and Frey describe is fully aligned with Burns's practice of swiping and sharing swipe files, honing an ambivalence that the disclosure of the sourced images does not help to clarify or ease. The ceaseless process of selection, reframing, and internal reorganization creates proliferating links that unsettle the origins of the image. And, indeed, it is also the case that swipes, especially in romance comic books, were quasi meant to be recirculated and reused, making the question of originality irrelevant to the process.

Accordingly, the same disquieting treatment of comics images also applies to Burns's swipes from romance comics, as *Last Look* offers a narrative of romantic relationships that is strikingly different from traditional romance plots as it is marked by failure, rape, self-delusion, trauma, abandonment, and male guilt. This alternative to romance, however, is not simply a debunking in the style of underground comix such as *Young Lust*, but integrates romance comics as key objects within both storylines. In this aspect, Burns's swiping strategy is similar to, yet slightly different from, his use of *Tintin* panels as "dangerous cells": the swipes are often clearly identified as images from the romance comics that Doug and Sarah are reading and, as Burns is swiping from a large variety of romance comics, often drawn by anonymous artists, it becomes less important to identify panels as quotations than as reiterations of visual tropes typical for the romance comics genre, such as the kissing scene. Like the proliferating cells of *Tintin* swipes, the romance comics material resists interpretation and further embodies the characters' inability to connect the bits and pieces together, their failed romance underlining the fragmentation of the book.

A significant part of the second chapter thus revolves around the characters Doug and Nitnit's quest for missing issues of romance comics. Doug comes to share Sarah's excitement and fascination for the "crappy" romance comics they find at a garage sale: the way they read and contemplate them lying in bed, half-laughingly, half-seriously, is similar to their consumption of other types of image that recur throughout the book, as Lucas Samaras's Polaroids or Louise Bourgeois's sketches. In the parallel storyline, Nitnit reads a very different kind of romance comics, complete with "creepy, violent guys" and multiple abortions, which indirectly invokes Doug and Sarah's story, abruptly terminating upon the return of "her old boyfriend who got thrown in jail for beating up a cop" only to jump a couple of issues in which everything has changed as "Danny's all messed up .... His head's all bandaged up and he's taking a whole bunch of heavy-duty narcotics."[112] Those missing issues are also and above all the gaps that the readers of *Last Look* are confronted with, embodying their sense of disorientation and the inability to connect the various fragments.

Midway through the graphic novel, the recursive retelling of its own narrative through romance comic swipes does not elicit a clearer picture. Later on, Doug comes across a stack of romance comics that his girlfriend, Sarah, had been eagerly looking for. As he starts leafing through the comic books, however, their frames begin to mingle, doubling up their gutters and blanked-out speech bubbles, metamorphosing into explicit images only to finally burn away. The narrative voice accompanying this collage of redrawn romance comics states: "As I look I realize the image won't hold ... it has a life of its own. There's nothing I can do about it. Nothing to hold on to."[113] This short sequence illustrates the slippery status of the swipes as they are disseminated across Burns's various works: not only their resistance to a clear interpretive framework in *Last Look* but also their own lifelike agency mobilizing an iconophilic desire that cannot be met by the character. By invoking the Code-era plague of comic book burnings in America, the image of the burnt-out panels is typically autoclastic and draws attention to the comics medium's troubled economy of desire. As in his previous work, Burns subtly aligns the violence in the narrative with the cultural memory of the violence done to comics. However, *Last Look* simultaneously draws attention to the circulation and reproduction of comics, both in the panels and through the swiping of existing panels, highlighting the particular gestures that draw productive, affective relationships between comics and their readers. The agency attributed to the image is thus not only the overwhelming, haunting violence of images that Philippe Maupeu identifies in Burns's graphic novel as "tyrannical revenants," "ghost images" that leave us in "a state of stupefaction."[114] On the contrary, Burns's fascination for swiping expresses a sense of being overwhelmed by the image that does not end with an obsessive reproduction.

Swiping becomes a key vector of cultural memory, showcasing a deep entanglement with the history of comics. As Ken Parille suggests in an illuminating analysis of Burns's reuse of the famous kissing scene, Burns "encourag[es] us to rethink the visual/narrative power of romance comics and arrive at a new understanding of the medium's history: he gives us a new origin story for contemporary comics. *The Hive* argues that we should take girl's [*sic*] comics seriously – a case this strong could never be made in prose."[115] Indeed, the romance comic books that Sarah and Doug describe as "crappy," and read with slight mockery, are not simply presented as kitsch or sheer parody; rather, they provide heartfelt material. The whole trilogy speaks of an intimate knowledge of, indeed love for, these romance comic books that is not necessarily an ingenuous embrace of their heteronormative narratives and gender stereotypes and that can include an internal critique. While engaging with a complex story of abuse, mishandling, and male guilt, *Last Look* also integrates swipes of romance comics in the most literal ways, such as the conspicuous reuse of the kissing scene without any ironical distance. Through humble and silent acts of redrawing, *Last Look* reclaims a deeper connection between romance comics, comics for girls, and the contemporary graphic novel. Burns's reappraisal of romance comics not only unfolds in generic terms but also entails a relationship to the image that frames originality and copying in a different dynamic: copying romance comics is also embracing images that have been copied and copied again, swiping from swipers in a way that entails a somewhat different relationship to originality, graphic style, and authorship than the economy of the graphic novel in which Charles Burns nevertheless fully operates. Romance comics, in Burns's works, are not mere stuff for appropriation; they have lives of their own.

VERNACULAR GESTURES

Where many of his peers are engaged in curatorial, canon-building activities that explicitly reframe the past of comics through essays, exhibitions, and reprints, Charles Burns has been less explicitly committed to canonizing masters of comics. His cartooning practice is nonetheless embedded in a deep knowledge of comics history. Swiping precisely appears as a memory-making gesture, part of a "repertoire" of creative gestures that constitutes the narrative economy of comics-making. As Diana Taylor notes, the repertoire "enacts embodied memory: performances, gestures, orality,movement, dance, singing – in short, all those acts usually thought of as ephemeral, nonreproducible knowledge."[116] While it might be not evident to think about transmission in comics in embodied terms, cartooning practices and the graphic trace that remain somehow present in the drawing also index a physical process. While mechanically reproduced, drawing in comics functions as a "voiceprint – ... in a way necessarily effaced by print," bringing the physical labor of comics close to "the human voice of oral storytelling, song, or performance."[117] In this sense, swiping is always a partial reproduction, an embodied interpretation of someone else's graphiation: in this way, it is a performative gesture and a literally appropriative process. While its appropriative tendency can also flout the ethical reach of such a gesture, giving in to power asymmetries, swiping can also express a culture of sharing.

By describing his practice of redrawing as swiping, Burns taps into a long tradition of copying as an embodied gesture within a repertoire of comics memory. In the close attention needed to redraw existing panels, and in the concomitant gestures of assembling and sharing swipe files, Burns expresses a strong commitment to the preservation and recirculation of selected comics images that yield a visual memory of the form. The recirculation of those images taps into a history of swiping as a vernacular practice of copying, gathering readers, fans, creators, as well as publishers, even censors and lawyers. As a narrative art of fragments, printed on cheap paper, comic books were always matter ripe for manipulation, tearing, cutting up. For Thierry Groensteen, one of the pleasures in reading comics lies in their accumulation of small, isolated images, "memorable" because potentially visually striking but also specifically linked to a particular place on the page. Dedicated comics readers, Groensteen suggests, all have in mind a "*vignettothèque*," a mental library of preferred comics images that are mnemonically connected to the reading experience but also "retrievable" because of the spatialized nature of comics narrative (which allows one to find a remembered panel fairly easily by flipping through).[118] As we have seen throughout this chapter, this mental "*vignettothèque*" finds its extension in material ones: the swipe files assembled by readers, creators, and others are ways of managing the accumulation of images, the "visual archive" that comics compose in themselves.[119] Comics images might be tied to a particular space; they can also just as easily be taken out of context, reused and recirculated in new ones.

Swiping thus refers to a way of copying and talking about copying that is both amplified and made obsolete by digital remix culture. The practices around swiping, clipping, and collecting panels have partly made way for new ways of sharing and recirculating comics alongside digital networks. Swiping might still be the subject of passionate expositions and more lighthearted debates taking place in online discussion groups, mostly gathering older fans. What today's comics readers might first think of when it comes to the term proper is indeed the swift, sweeping move of their finger on the touchscreen of their digital devices – "swiping" from one panel to the next. By contrast, swiping appears as a medium-specific way of copying that has been tied to ephemeral print culture, the fragmented structure of comics, and readerly practices of sifting through a visual mass. Against an overly metaphorical usage of the term remix that privileges digital forms of networked recombination, Margie Borschke has proposed an "analog history of remix" that retrieves the importance of material gestures and users' agency prior to the emergence of digital technologies.[120] Burns's swipe files participate in revisiting that history in times of digital culture, hinting at the "analog" redrawing and archival activities linked with swiping. Sharing his own "*vignettothèque*," he draws attention to the material practices that come along with the use and reuse of preferred comics images.

CHAPTER 6

Undrawing

The future of comics is in the trash can.[1]

– Zou Luoyang

I N 2019, CALLS FOR FUTURES OF COMICS ARE STILL IN THE AIR.
At least, this is what is suggested in the title of the online platform
"Futures of Comics," meant to support new initiatives in the making and
sharing of comics, launched by Ilan Manouach – a multidisciplinary artist
best known for his radical comics *détournements* and for producing
a tactile system of communication for persons with visual disabilities
called *Shapereader*. The website page opens onto an image of Felix the
Cat melancholically dragging his feet around towering racks of blade
servers. This opening image encapsulates the ambiguities of digital cultural memory: it serves as a reminder of the very concrete reality of the
hardware and energy-demanding material infrastructures needed to sustain new ways of storing, sharing, and accumulating information.

The Internet has not concretized older hopes for a memory machine
or a mode of automatic archiving as its users have grown accustomed to
its shutdowns, dead URLs, general link rot, decaying hardware, and
digital obsolescence.[2] Online archives effectively require constant maintenance work, human labor, and repeated actions and contributions – as
indeed do libraries and archives in bricks-and-mortar buildings. But
online archives also unsettle the professional forms of archiving by prioritizing other issues and unsettling the chronology of their uses. As De

Kosnik notes in her conceptual description of these "rogue archives," modeled on fan fiction archives, "memory has gone rogue in another sense: where it used to mean the *record* of cultural production, memory is now the *basis* of a great deal of cultural production."[3] In the digital environment, the membrane between archiving and making becomes thinner than ever: "At present, each media commodity becomes, at the instant of its release, an archive to be plundered, an original to be memorized, copied, manipulated – a starting point or springboard for receivers' creativity rather than an end unto itself."[4]

The recirculation and the manipulation of comics archives have a long history in a comics culture that largely had to develop its own modes of preservation and transmission, moving between Bill Blackbeard's files of newspaper comic strips and the different swipe files kept by cartoonists. In both cases, archiving was always considered less an end unto itself than a means to different ends. Bill Blackbeard wore on his sleeve the pirate imaginary of his family name, as played up in the portrait included in his *Destroy All Comics* interview, which depicts him handling old newspaper volumes clad in pirate gear.[5] The swipe files of Chapter 5 also reflect archival gestures as they result from the process of clipping and collecting images, organizing them according to particular processes, and facilitating their reuse. Swiped images are often selected and preserved on the basis of their direct utility, so as to be easily reused in specific circumstances, but they also constitute a reader's memory and a repertoire of visually striking images. Digital networks, however, do make a difference in that they increase the speed, scale, and scope of such processes, which also means that contemporary readers are faced with an overabundance of material to sift through. This prospect returns us to one of the more complex arguments made by Jared Gardner in his inquiry into the puzzling ubiquity of archives and collectors at the turn of the millennium, as it overlaps with the spread of the personal computer and digital networks. As much as graphic novels have resisted a wholesale digital transition more steadfastly than their competitor media, Gardner argues, comics "ha[ve] been navigating the database of modernity for over a century," training their readers for what Lev Manovich described as the "database logic" that new media are pushing as the unmarked symbolic form of our digital times.[6]

As comics become digital files, and as comics are increasingly used as visual archives to draw from, sample, and remix, the feedback loop between archiving and making yields particular gestures of transmission and raises new questions – a prospect embraced by the Futures of Comics website:

> In an age where public libraries are an endangered institution, collections run by amateur librarians emerge as new, vital topographies of sharing. Confronted with an unprecedented amount of texts and images, contemporary comics artists are consistently expected to challenge conventional notions of creativity and authorship by engaging with archival research, appropriation, iterative and sampling techniques and other practices of mediation.[7]

Manouach's call for the contemporary comics artist is evocative of and alludes to the conceptual poet Kenneth Goldsmith's proposition of "uncreative writing": "faced with an unprecedented amount of available text, the problem is not needing to write more of it; instead, we must learn to negotiate the vast quantity that exists."[8] The mission of the "uncreative poet" in the digital age requalifies a series of gestures that have otherwise been thought of as belonging to the peripheries of traditional creative work: organizing, distributing, disseminating, archiving, curating, framing, copying, displacing, and other acts that prioritize handling existing material rather than creating from scratch. An important lesson that comes from managing this thicket of available matter is the realization that a mere change of context raises unanticipated issues, foregrounds unthought-of possibilities, and hence generally speaks volumes about the text it transforms as much as its inseparability from a host of social, cultural, and material assumptions. Manouach's experiments with comics, as we will see, bring to bear different "uncreative" gestures that reconceptualize comics archives.

Placed under the general act of "undrawing," this last chapter delves into self-knowingly "uncreative" practices that problematize notions of drawing in the graphic novel, engage with extensive forms of redrawing, or circumvent the activity of drawing in favor of the multitudinous handling of existing graphic matter.[9] This chapter thus offers a limit case in this inquiry in terms of the objects and gestures it charts, broadening the scope of the corpus and pushing against its chronological and geographical boundaries. It expands the scope to include some

European cartoonists as a comparative counterpoint; and, in terms of period, it principally focuses on works of the last decade (say, 2012–19). It also bears on a younger generation of cartoonists, even if there are crossovers with the generation at the core of this book. As such, it helps put the 2000s into perspective as a distinct moment in the history of the graphic novel, while trying to identify and delineate more recent trends. The institutions of the book trade, the university library, and classrooms are not the main settings for this chapter, which shifts focus to practices more in line with the art world or with the medley of digital culture. It gathers a flurry of sources and objects, published either online and/or as small-press editions, as a way of illustrating the variety of the contemporary field: such comics objects are often looking more toward poetry than the novel, and substantiate a significant trend in art comics and graphic poetry that has grown from the kernel of the contemporary graphic novel.

"THAT'S STEALING"

The application of "uncreative" protocols to comics does not take place on a *tabula rasa*: comics are already saturated with practices of reproduction, imitation, continuation, appropriation, pastiche, and other iterative acts. The sheer predominance of swiping in comic book culture shows how much comics making relies on repetition and copying. It is part of its working as a cultural industry to systematize production processes in such a way that it indefectibly involves a large segment of supposedly "unoriginal" labor, if we understand originality to be a relevant shifting criterion of aesthetic evaluation and appreciation in comics history.[10] At the same time, it is also the history of comics' industrial production and collaborative authorship that becomes of renewed interest to contemporary cartoonists interested in forms of appropriation and remixing.

At the same time, and as much as the graphic novel is rife with explicit references to comics history and consciously evocative of past graphic traditions, it has also been extremely wary of "appropriation" as a procedure derived from the visual arts, especially when imbued with the resentment against pop appropriations of comics images. Originality, personal expression, individualized graphic style are cornerstones of the graphic novel that are not always easy to reconcile with the logics of appropriation and strategic unoriginality found in digital culture today. A small anecdote told by Chris Ware about his art school years at the Art Institute of Chicago is revealing of these tensions:

> I actually had a teacher tell me to 'appropriate' Lyonel Feininger's work. I was just showing the work to him because I thought Feininger's cartoons were incredible, and he said, 'You should use them.' I said, 'What do you mean *use* them?' He said, 'You should put them in your work to make it art. Appropriate them. Everyone is doing it.' I said, 'That's stealing.' I got really mad at the guy. I didn't get as mad as I should have. It was just stunning![11]

The anecdote expresses a shared resentment in comics culture toward the art world, here specifically aimed at art trends in the 1980s in the United States, where it became common to reuse images from the massive stockpile of low media, advertising, magazines, celebrity images, and of course comics in order to carry out an explicit ideological critique of the so-called American way of life.

Even while there was a certain outspoken resistance to remixes, collage and sampling were not completely out of order before the spread of personal computers as we can find uses that foreshadow uncreative practices in the 1970s and 1980s, facilitated by the wider availability of Xerox machines, and that will find a particular echo in the United States through the avant-garde magazine *RAW* edited by Françoise Mouly and Art Spiegelman. Setting the tone, Spiegelman had already experimented with cut-and-paste in his famous two-page story "The Malpractice Suite," published in *Arcade* in 1976, the post-underground magazine he coedited with Bill Griffith.[12] The two pages offer a self-reflexive play on the *hors-cadre* of the newspaper comic strip *Nervous Rex*, as Spiegelman photocopies panels into larger drawn frames, offering a grotesque extension to the original drawings. As of 1980, the Italian cartoonist Stefano Tamburini serialized in the pages of the Milanese periodical *Frigidaire* a similar but longer intervention, completely based on the manipulation of an existing comic by means of xeroxing: *Snake Agent* is a reworking of Mel Graff's *Secret Agent X-9* that proceeds by sliding the originals as the Xerox machine duplicates the image, using the reproduction technology to distort the drawings and rework the process into a different narrative.[13] *Snake Agent* is a landmark in the repurposing of reproduction technologies, precisely one that was used to share and circulate older comics, for creating a completely different work.

Similar exercises in remixing would take place in *RAW*, whose editors were turned to Europe and undoubtedly aware of Tamburini's experiment, with the influx of Robert Sikoryak and Mark Newgarden, two cartoonists emerging from the School of Visual Arts where Spiegelman was lecturing.[14] Practitioners of the traditional short form and experts of the cartooning gag, they drew many short contributions to the magazine in the mid-1980s. Mark Newgarden's three-page "Love's Savage Fury," for instance, proposed a mash-up of two famous comic strip characters – Ernie Bushmiller's *Nancy* and Topps company's *Joe Bazooka* – in a highly formal design that visually recounts the story of a brief subway encounter.[15] The short comic was drawn in a strict graphic style that made both comics converge in their unabashed minimalism and the diagrammatic simplicity of their drawing: this made *Nancy* suited to widespread syndication and shrinking newspaper space, just as *Joe Bazooka* was from the start meant to be read on the tiny formatting of bubble-gum packaging. Intuitively drawn for rescaling, they become suitable matter for reuse and appropriation, which can in part explain why Bushmiller's characters Nancy and Sluggo have such a record history of being appropriated both in and outside the comics world. A trainee at *RAW* magazine, Robert Sikoryak similarly worked to conceive comics mash-ups, based on the contrasted juxtaposition of rigorous visual imitations of comics styles and the appropriation of existing texts. "Good ol' Gregor Brown," one of his first and most famous examples, crosses Franz Kafka's *The Metamorphosis* with Charles Schulz's *Peanuts*.[16] Juxtaposed in word and image, the modernist angst of Kafka's canonical novella and the mellow melancholia of *Peanuts* reflect on each other – a process that Sikoryak has extended in several combinations yielding *Masterpiece Comics*, offering a general parody of the 1950s literary adaptations in comics in the style of *Classics Illustrated*.[17] In these cases, the drawings are handmade, but they abandon the idea of a "personal style" in favor of the conspicuous citation of recognizable graphic styles. Or, rather, Sikoryak's distinct style and author profile on the graphic novel scene lie in this specific mobilization of quoted graphic styles and genres that juxtapose text lifted from other contexts – positioning him as the "master of the comic book mash-up" in the comics world.[18]

SHARING REDRAWING

Sikoryak's approach proved successful in the digital environment and his more recent work precisely honed in on a form of uncreative writing that works with digital platforms and textual materials copied from online sources. *Terms and Conditions: The Graphic Novel* offers a take on the iTunes Terms and Conditions contract: Sikoryak's intervention refits the text of the legal document into the speech bubbles of various pages redrawn from all periods of comics history.[19] The copied pages are precisely redrawn in their original cartoonists' styles with, as the only alteration, the integration of electronic devices and a recurring Steve Jobs figure as the main character. Before being published by Drawn & Quarterly, the pages of Sikoryak's *Terms and Conditions* were posted on a regular basis through a dedicated Tumblr, where readers could suggest potential pages or titles for redrawing, co-constructing the archive that Sikoryak ultimately used as a graphic basis: this led to a wildly varied and disparate trajectory through comics history, jump-cutting through periods, genres, and traditions and spanning a chronology that stretches from a 1905 *Little Nemo* Sunday newspaper page to a 2014 page from Raina Telgemeier's young-adult graphic novel *Sisters*.

While comics history is reused and cited at a one-page ratio, the uncreative dimension of Sikoryak's intervention holds in the dissociation of text and image and in the complete and "unabridged" reuse of a legal contract: where graphic adaptations such as *Classics Illustrated* were based on the idea of offering more readable versions of classics that no one otherwise read, as suggested in the "abridged" versions of the long literary masterpieces, Sikoryak reversed the process and tried to have his readers read, in full, a text and contract they consent to and sign every day but rarely ever read. By contrast with previous experiments, the type of document chosen, the amount of text that is reused, and the number of images that are redrawn are what align the project with the principles of exhaustivity that guide exercises of uncreative writing. Mimicking the layout and format of traditional comic books and the logo colors of *Classics Illustrated*, Sikoryak's *Terms and Conditions* presents itself as the "complete & unabridged," "unauthorized adaptation," making its iterative dimension very clear and questioning the reader on the very legibility of such documents.

That Sikoryak chose to first publish his pages for *Terms and Conditions* on a Tumblr platform and to produce zine versions not only is telling about the tentative nature of the enterprise, especially as it possibly borders on copyright infringement (although the transformative nature of the work appears quite clear), but also suggests that such practices have become a common part of networks of reading, sharing, and drawing in online comics communities. Sikoryak's trajectory thus illustrates how such practice of redrawing, remixing, and mash-up have become part of the "practice of everyday (media) life," as Lev Manovich argues, as cultural industries have integrated the tactical modes of bricolage and customization as part of their strategies.[20] A telling example is the "Redrawn" Tumblr curated by Charles Forsman and Melissa Mendes, which calls its followers to "Pick a random page of comic. Redraw it. Post it here," suggesting that the page-based redrawing protocol used by Sikoryak is one that is common in the online community of comics makers and readers and that, furthermore, tends to diminish the separation between professional and amateur productions.[21]

If old comics shared on digital platforms might sometimes appear as sheer graphic fodder for mash-ups, severed from their historical productions and circulations, redrawing is also found to be used as a way of expressing attachment and admiration, casting new light on forgotten works. The cartoonist Kevin Huizenga, for instance, has redrawn an entire story from the Dell comic book series *Kona, Monarch of Monster Isle*, a monster comic drawn by Sam Glanzman and written by Lionel Ziprin.[22] The pages are drawn faithfully, respective of layouts and reproducing the same dialogues, but they are done in Huizenga's personal drawing style, adapting the genre constraints to his own capacities, character styles, and shifting it to black-and-white with added gray-tones. By redrawing the comic without altering the story, Huizenga makes this older work function simultaneously in its original monster genre (a real craze in the 1960s) and in the contemporary domain of alternative comics.[23] The comic is done with overt admiration for the original artist; its main functions are presented as a drawing exercise, an explicit expression of admiration, and a means of sharing a forgotten comic book with a contemporary audience that is unlikely to otherwise encounter or go to such types of production. Tagged as "fan art" on his blog, the act of redrawing paradoxically obscures the style of the original cartoonist while otherwise valorizing his work and career.[24] Within an economy of digital reproduction, the amount of time and care invested in the physical redrawing of pages, applied at an entire story length, enacts a specific way of sharing an older comic book, bearing the stamp of its reader.[25]

This is also telling in a different exercise of redrawing by Derik Badman, which selects another Dell comic book: turning to a *Gene Autry* western comic title from 1948 drawn by Jesse Marsh, he redraws the entire story but uses redrawing as a way of selecting and erasing parts of the document, effacing all traces of human presence in the comic book and implementing a new narrative. Stripped to zones of black-and-white and abstract backgrounds, Badman reworks the popular comic book into an abstract comic and a piece of graphic poetry.[26] If Badman's intervention is more transformative, he similarly shares an online version of the original comic book that serves as the basis for his contribution. Through the cases of Sikoryak, Huizenga, and Badman, figures emerging from the alternative comics scene, the popularity of redrawing as an exercise on microblogging platforms and zines appears to manifest a continued attachment to drawing as individual expression and craft within practices of extended redrawing and a digital economy of sharing past comics.

British cartoonist Simon Grennan has also relied on redrawing as a form of representing old, forgotten works to new readers – but his practice of redrawing serves as a useful counterexample to the previous cases. Linked to a large project of recovery of the graphic work of Marie Duval, a "maverick Victorian cartoonist" who drew in the pages of the London comics serial *Judy* and who was practically forgotten in histories of British comics, Grennan has indeed produced a series of redrawn images that dialogue with this collective archival project.[27] With his work titled *Drawing in Drag by Marie Duval*, Grennan proposes to update the comics not by redrawing them in a more contemporary and personal style but, on the contrary, by performing drawing as Marie Duval in the twenty-first century.[28] The project evolves both from the careful study of Marie Duval's work and its archival recovery – Grennan and his peers Roger Sabin and Julian Waite created a publicly accessible online repository of her drawings, *The Marie Duval Archive* – and from the cartoonist's previous experiments with redrawing. As part of his research on narrative drawing, Grennan has indeed practiced various forms of "drawing impersonations," trying to embody other socialized practices of drawing, whether individual styles or genres, as an attempt to work through complex theoretical questions and engage with problems of appropriation.[29] From this background, Grennan plays with the situation of Marie Duval as a "vulgar" cartoonist and stage performer on the British Victorian scene, which involved acts of gender-swapping (both on stage and on paper, as she did sign on a few occasions as "Ambrose Clark") in *Drawing in Drag by Marie Duval*. A kind of companion piece to the reprint of Duval's drawings, the book adopts her loose drawing style, her page compositions, and the humor of her work – which focused on the familiar lives of lower-class readers and the newly accessible urban leisures – and reproduces specific pages to adapt them to twenty-first-century British urban pleasures and fashion trends (another of Duval's favorite targets). In "Pull, Pull Together," for instance, Grennan portrays the performance of working-class masculinity through a series of details in clothing and behavior (Figure 6.1). The humor relies on the recognizability and familiarity of the situation: in this, contemporary readers are arguably meant to partake in the shared humor that Marie Duval's drawing style would have occasioned with its intended readers. By contrast with the aforementioned practices of redrawing, Grennan thus attempts drawing as Marie Duval would have today.

COMICS SAMPLES

While Sikoryak, Huizenga, and Badman practice systematic redrawing, they remain close to an emphasis on the act of drawing as expression of a personalized style (even in the case of Sikoryak, whose pastiches gradually coalesce into a recognizable drawing style). Other cartoonists have adopted different gestures of making that put at a remove the practice of drawing itself, based on the sampling of existing comics works and the selection and manipulation of comics fragments. A good example of this raising of the stakes is provided by Canadian cartoonist Mark Laliberte, whose comics poetry book *BRICKBRICKBRICK* assembles a set of bricks, retraced and recomposed from the backgrounds of comics history.[30] The book is a collection of single panels filled with bricks as drawn by an

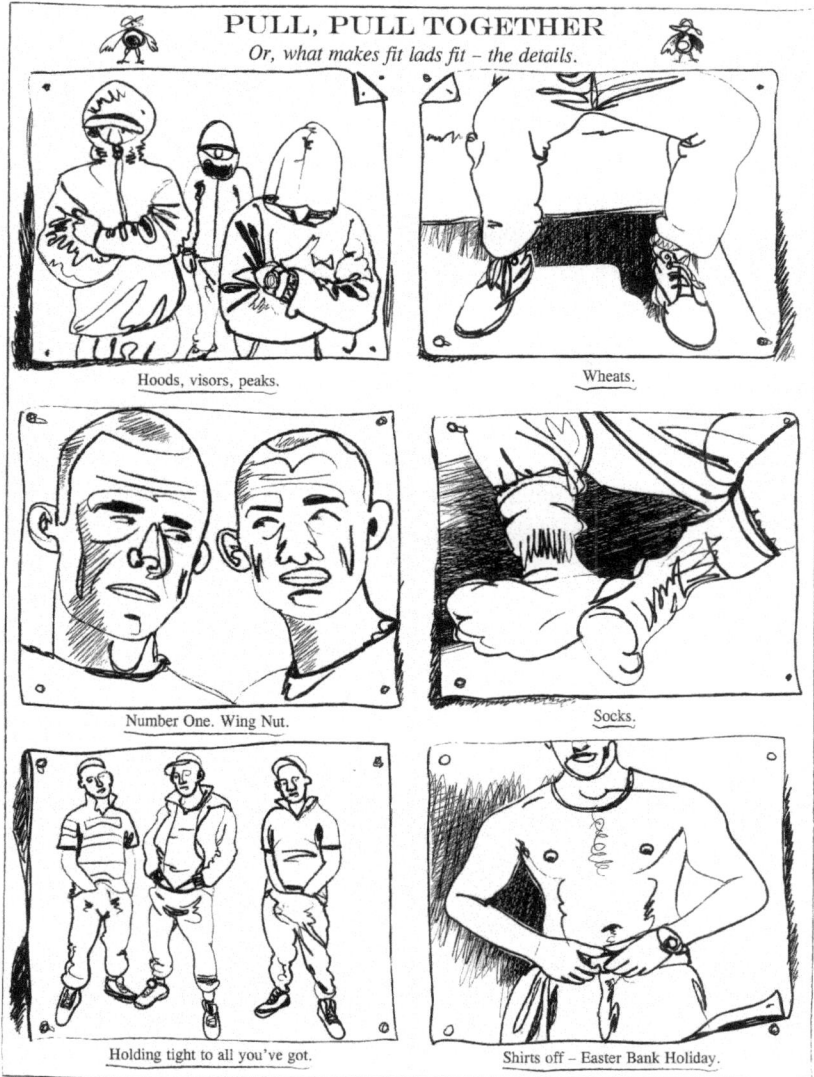

Figure 6.1 Simon Grennan, *Drawing in Drag by Marie Duval* (London: Book Works, 2018), n.p.
Source: Copyright © Simon Grennan. Courtesy of the artist.

impressively wide variety of cartoonists. The square panels condense
a graphic element that is often glanced over as mere backdrop and blows
it up as a peculiar index of its artist's style. Emerging from intense research
and rereading with particular attention, the building of these various brick

walls follows a strange drawing process: part scanning, part digital reworking, part original copying. By manipulating samples taken from a wide range of comics works and refitting them as measurable data – unified in their size, scale, and graphic presentation – Laliberte's graphic intervention allows an *auteur*ist reading of brick details, as evincing idiosyncratic ways of drawing brought about by their contrastive presentation, while anthologizing those brick poems according to narrative or thematic criteria (Figure 6.2). Each comics poem paradoxically appears, in a way, as testament to the individuality of graphic style. The collection demonstrates the many different ways of drawing such a seemingly simple background detail, which becomes an index of personalized drawing styles attributed to a range of comics creators working in very different contexts: Laliberte focuses both on recognizable graphic styles and major artists in the field – from newspaper comics legend Charles Schulz to alternative comics idol Julie Doucet – and on lesser-known figures in the field, such as Colin

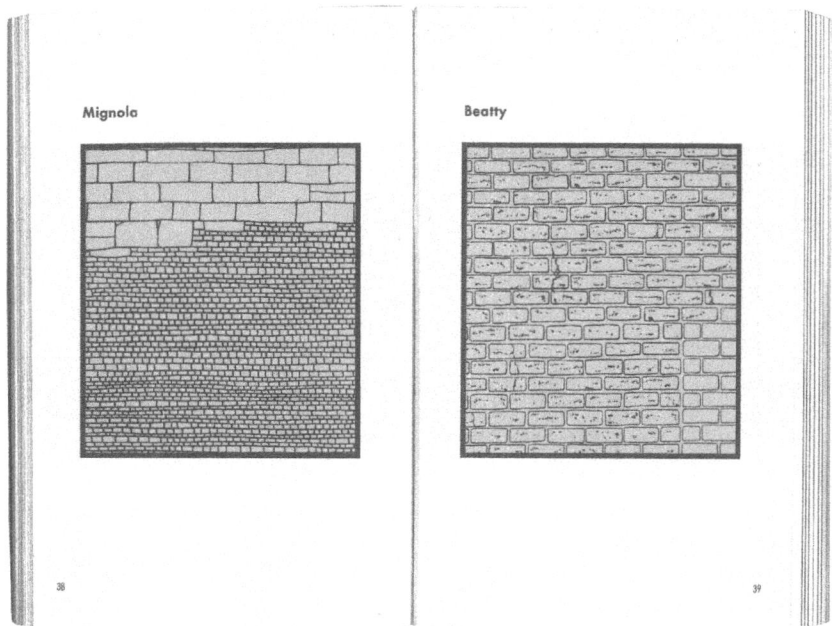

Figure 6.2 Double-page spread from Mark Laliberte's *BRICKBRICKBRICK* (Toronto: BookThug, 2010), 38–39.
Source: Copyright © Mark Laliberte. Courtesy of the artist.

Upton, from the Canadian mini-comics scene, or John Beatty, who has worked as an inker for Marvel and DC.

A striking example of "poetry by other means," *BRICKBRICKBRICK* exposes the literal bricks of comic book architecture, drawing the background to the foreground and presenting brick-drawing as an inventive variation of a theme within a constrained narrative form.[31] A well-practiced collagist, Laliberte describes his creative process as one of "drawing without drawing."[32] Laliberte's *BRICKBRICKBRICK* immediately foregrounds some of the tensions that run through such questions. It adopts an *auteur*ist approach, echoing fans' construction of individual genius in the industry (sometimes resulting from quasi-forensic investigation of graphic details) but recasting that attention on creators who have been frequently unheard of – only to undercut the same rhetoric of originality by its very reliance on an ambiguous citationality.[33] Laliberte here assumes a tactical role as curator, compiler, sampler.

Such practices of sampling are further facilitated online by the publicly available material repositories. Online repositories of public domain comic books such as the Digital Comics Museum, which provides its subscribers with access to a range of comic books from publishers that were driven out of business by competition, censorship, or general media change in the 1950s, provide material that is easily reused. As Kalervo Sinervo reckons, comic book scanning in the United States has been specifically constructed as a participative fan activity, largely removed from profit motives and with a particular preservationist dedication; as a result, "comics piracy catalyzed the formation of a creative commons in a niche online public," apparent in the open-sourced digital formats of comic book scans, such as CBR or CBZ, which directly allow, if not call for, such appropriations and remixing.[34] This is exactly what the French cartoonist Samplerman does, assembling cropped details from the files available online to constitute a repertoire of forms – the digital equivalent to a swipe file – that he can rework in his digital collage compositions (Figure 6.3). In transforming scans made available by fan archivists, Samplerman draws attention in his work to the circulation of comic books in digital contexts. Indeed, the visual aesthetics of his collages play up repetition effects that are not available in traditional print collage, limited by the relative scarcity of materials to cut from. Many of Samplerman's collages use mirror effects, duplication, and layering that

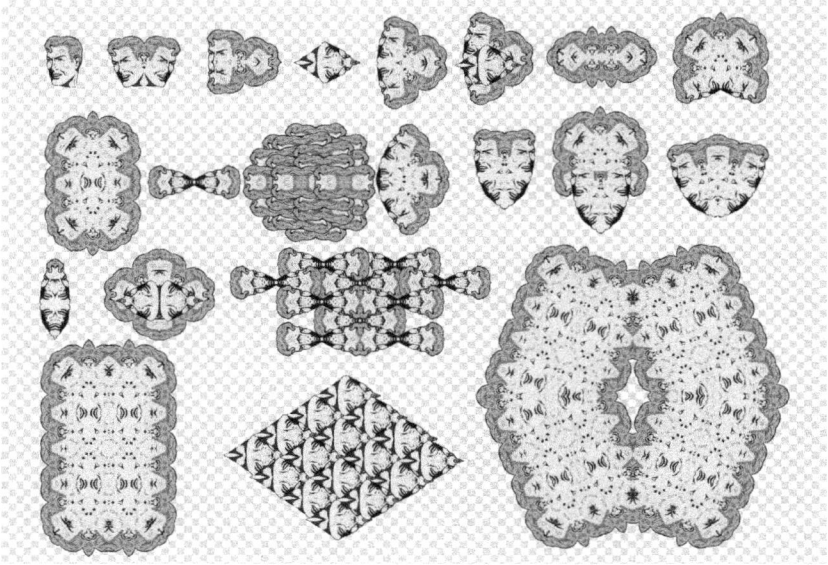

Figure 6.3 Several pattern transformations of a comic's detail against a transparent background, from Samplerman's database.
Source: Courtesy of the artist.

foreground the particular affordances of digital image editing software. By keeping the aesthetics of comic book scans, with their faded colors and newsprint backgrounds, these collages play up the recognition of familiar images against their distortion. Samplerman's work alternates between absurd but narrative-driven collages – unfolding over several pages and integrating speech bubbles – and single-page collages – prioritizing abstract layouts that defamiliarize the conventional structure of the comics page.

DISTRIBUTING DRAWING

The work of Ilan Manouach, to some extent, can be read as a return to Tamburini's *Snake Agent* and to the use and hijacking of technological infrastructures as a meaningful gesture in itself. Cutting through disciplinary practices, merging conceptual critique with praxeological experimentation, Manouach's work undercuts the usual trajectories in comics as well as the *auteur* model of the graphic novel. A cartoonist's path is often traced as a particular and often difficult relationship to graphic style: developing an individually recognizable drawing style is key in the graphic novel, but is also a hard-won enterprise. Trained to that very approach at the Saint-Luc art school in Brussels, and certainly endowed with the technical craftmanship to develop such a style, Manouach rapidly turned to exploring radical modes of making comics without drawing. His line of work is perhaps better described as a continuous process of *withdrawing*, of disengaging himself from the stylistic singularity that usually shapes the making and reading of graphic narratives.[35]

Throughout a diverse set of comics works he defines as "conceptual comics," Manouach has relied on a myriad of appropriative techniques, applied to a range of works that is as diverse. One of his first uncreative works opened onto an erasurist gesture: he selected a title of the Danish children's comic series *Rasmus Klump* and withdrew all its characters save for the one, lone-standing Riki the pelican, a relatively minor figure in the fixed cast of characters.[36] The narrative becomes a strange story of a funny animal talking to himself while passively observing how a farm seems to build itself, how fields are plowed by an invisible workforce, and of course ending with the traditional but now strangely superlative pancake banquet. The pages of the comics have been carefully photoshopped so as to leave as little visible trace as possible of the graphic intervention. And, indeed, the book itself is faithfully reproduced in the editorial style of the Casterman albums. This first experiment settled a set of ground rules for Manouach's next projects, often published with La Cinquième Couche: the appropriation is minimal and carefully focused; it bears on a complete work that is reproduced in facsimile; it leads to a generative displacement of the work and its surrounds. The most famously controversial piece in this series of works was *Katz*, in which Manouach and his peers reproduce Art Spiegelman's canonical graphic novel *Maus*, only replacing all animal characters with cat heads, blurring the ethnic codes of representation that the graphic novel installs. The book ended in a litigation with the French publisher, which led to the legally performative destruction of the entire stock of *Katz* copies, including its digital files. The case, amply documented in *MetaKatz*, reflects back on what makes a work canonical, the complicated intricacies of Holocaust literature and book destruction, and copyright issues in appropriation.[37]

While the case of *Katz* ended up driving most attention to the terms of the debates (reopening the discussions around the animal conventions set up in *Maus*) rather than its material outcomes (few copies of which survived), Manouach's *Noirs* opened up new avenues for a more conscientious reflection on materiality proper. *Noirs* is a reprint of Peyo's 1963 *Les Schtroumpfs noirs*, an album in which a black fly wreaks havoc in the Smurfs' village by biting the tails of the little blue cartoon characters, infecting them, turning them into mad black smurfs whose only obsession is to further spread the contamination: the obscuring of these color differentiations is used to bring the racist undertone into sharp focus. Manouach's intervention here again proceeds in an erasure, this time stretching further into the impersonality of the process by relying completely on the printing technology, filling in the ink toners of the four-color CMYK with but one single color, CCCC. Cyan takes over, eats all the other colors, and makes the comics partly illegible (Figure 6.4). In doing this, as Pedro Moura brilliantly argues, Manouach is not only launching a direct attack against the racist underpinnings of comics heritage, as they can be found in Peyo's *Les Schtroumpfs noirs*; he is also making a statement about or against expression, presenting an object that steps "out of the realm of authorial expression, and even of human expression, in order to discharge lines of depersonalized expression, as it were. In this case, the expressivity of the very materiality of the album's four-color printing."[38] As Moura notes, the fabrication of this reprint nevertheless takes a series of preparational gestures to produce a printable file: in this sense, *Noirs* is not simply a blue-only print; it also bears some marks of the assembling process. The flatbed scanning of the original album, which projects a bright light source on relatively thin paper, produces effects of transparency in the lighter zones of the image, partly imprinting the verso onto the recto page. Each page of *Noirs* thus bears traces of both sides of the paper as a kind of surplus excess resulting from the copying process.

This kind of material specificity is further put to work by Manouach in his *Compendium of Franco-Belgian Comics*, a broader book that compounds forty-eight albums typical of the Franco-Belgian comics production, gleaned in Brussels' secondhand stores.[39] This stockpile totaled 2,304 pages that the artist scanned and detoured to establish a large set of

Figure 6.4 Ilan Manouach, *Noirs* (Brussels: La Cinquième Couche, 2014), 9.
Source: Courtesy of the artist.

samples of the most typical units that make the "language" of Franco-Belgian comics. These samples are then layered in situ, according to the same spatial coordinates on the page. The result yields a compendium of prototypical fragments, each one evocative of its original context and yet reframed in a collage-like composition that disrupts their narrative function. The ensemble highlights the relative uniformity of Franco-Belgian comics, while advancing an implicit material critique of the semiotic perspective on comics as a grammatical language.

In mapping the vernaculars of Franco-Belgian comics, Manouach's *Compendium* is a sort of companion volume to his *Blanco*, which "merely" consists in a completely blankforty-eight-page hardcover album, save for the removable sticker that functions as the caption to this conceptual artwork.[40] "Blanco" in French means "dummy," the print jargon for the blank prototype used by printers as a mock-up for testing the result beforehand, getting a sense of what the book will look and feel like, whether the binding will hold. A dummy is generally needed for books that deviate from standard publishing norms: this is precisely what the comics album in France is not, given the level of format standardization in the comics industry. In producing a dummy for what Jean-Christophe Menu famously dubbed the 48CC (*quarante-huit pages cartonnées couleur*), Manouach puts on the market an object that reflexively calls our attention to the invisibility of material formats in comics culture.[41] Even while *Blanco* displays none of the visible signs of comics, its sheer materiality is enough to immediately tell us we are dealing with a *bande dessinée*. Through its circulation in the various contexts and settings of the social world of comics, the blank object contrastingly becomes a sounding board and echoes everything we would otherwise pay little attention to: distribution platforms, book tables, online retailing paratexts, reviews, festival participants – all become meaning-making agents imbuing *Blanco* with a particular function. The dummy, in this sense, performs knowledge work, accruing its meanings in the ways that it circulates and is used.

This series of conceptual books shares a genealogy with a long avant-garde history of blank objects, illegible texts, appropriations, and found objects. While sharing affinities with the erasurist techniques common in the realm of artists' books, these bookworks do not participate in the speculative logics of planned scarcity, unique editions, and limited runs – nor does Manouach pursue the artisanal techniques, handicraft, and specialized printing processes that are so present on the European alternative comics scene. Rather, his reflexive use of materiality is one that highlights the multiple agencies at work, human and nonhuman, by staging the withdrawal of the loudest of voices. The extensive logic here also bears on the technological uses, establishing productive overlaps with post-print and post-digital thinking – two notions that concur in a less binary narrative of technological change and that prioritize an understanding of mediality across the board.[42] De facto, Manouach's works trump the faultline between print and paper that has been continuously driving the debates around digital comics over the past decades. His printed books arise from micro-gestures of digital composition and collation required for the purpose of appropriation, processes that are mundane in the digital age. At the same time, Manouach has also extended this line of thought by increasingly relying on machinic processes (coding and programming are the contemporary cartoonists' required tools), maneuvering globalized digital networks to produce works reflective of these widespread changes in terms of readerships, circulations, and labor.

In doing all of this, Manouach continues to inquire into what it means to read comics, who or what performs the work of "reading," and how that activity plays out in the digital age. His latest projects involve the micro-reworking of comics by online laborers: compiling and assembling collections of images that are distributed to digital micro-workers through a crowdsourcing platform. This global cast of workers are remunerated on the basis of the very small tasks that they perform online. Manouach thus breaks down existing corpora of comics into more or less minimal units that are then subjected to specific appropriation and transformation depending on the task assigned to workers across the globe, from Malaysia to Uganda. *The Cubicle Island* is an inquiry into this new form of digital labor, an attempt at catching its office culture, and an ode to the tactical behaviors of online workers: it is a heavyweight, 1,000-plus-page collection of *New Yorker* desert island cartoons that have been uncaptioned and sent to thousands of micro-workers, expected to "provide a funny text between 50–70 words for each of these cartoons."[43] The mammoth volume binds together all of the results, juxtaposing the good puns alongside the spam (indeed, micro-workers, to try to increase efficiency, program bots to perform some very specific tasks). What emerges from this sea-wave of unsorted recaptioned cartoons is the messiness of a digital marketplace where human laborers and automatized machinic surrogates cooperate in ways that are sometimes hard to tell apart. Some cartoon captions are actual jokes; others vary between YouTube links, illegible series of letters, found texts, extensive fragments excerpted from public domain novels, misunderstood guidelines, accurate descriptions of the cartoon image, social media profiles, and many other types of writing. *The Cubicle Island* is thus a collection that updates the kind of "Xerox-lore" that was found in the office culture of the 1970s and 1980s, when employers would deviate the photocopying machines to other uses.[44] Equally, it is a reflection on the anomie of this kind of labor, where the cubicle becomes an ever more solitary and isolated one, where work hours extend into the twenty-four/seven regime of late capitalist production and where tactical behaviors are all that is left within an extremely precarious form of immaterial labor.[45]

Peanuts Minus Schulz, published by Jean Boîte éditions as part of its "uncreative writings" series, extends these interests and distributes the large corpus of Charles Schulz's *Peanuts* comic strip to a range of micro-workers from around the world. The book documents the protocols, which requests online workers to read a specific comic strip then, "On a white piece of paper, get ready to copy the comic strip by hand, as precisely as possible" – adding a range of more specific campaigns that are possible: "A2. Insert yourself in one of the panels" or "F6. Make a manga version of the strip." In doing this, Manouach scales up the practice of redrawing to a wide collective body of online workers, usually commissioned to perform small and precise tasks. Relying on the largely unregulated platforms of crowdsourcing labor, Manouach aims not to upscale comics publishing industries or to construct an entirely stream-lined comic book. Rather, he turns to *Peanuts* as an immensely popular and heavily merchandised comic strip, embodying the tension between the mark of a single cartoonist – Charles Schulz – and the commercial derivatives that his work led to. As already broached before, Schulz's graphic heritage is also posthumously managed by a series of creatives responsible for adapting the comic strip to a variety of commercial occasions, under strict guidelines of franchising management. Manouach seeks to play out these tensions by having worldwide readers of the comic strip, caught in a precarious labor condition, perform a striking task: redraw a few panels, "as precisely possible," adding their own signature to the comic strip.

Effectively relying on common notions of drawing as trace, drawing here becomes a paid task that makes visible the workers as they perform it: the variety of drawing capacities and talents, of creative misunderstanding and self-proposed additions, the rewriting of dialogues in different languages – all of these aspects highlight individual approaches and affective responses to the performed task, with some regular contributors returning across the pages. One worker consistently draws himself into the strip, adding short autobiographical comments in the margins of the redrawn *Peanuts* gags. The 700-page book thus assembles a sundry assortment of redrawn strips outside of the usual circulations of comics; the submissions that arise from this request, as Manouach declares, "radically reconfigure the assumptions made about the individual role different agents can have in a production chain. They underline the very nature of comics as an eternal score subjected to vagaries and contextual instantiations."[46]

As he underlines the multifarious potentials for comics as archives to be revisited, reread, and redistributed in constant new forms, Manouach both perpetuates familiar gestures of transmission while flouting traditional practices and professional virtues in the comics world. At the same time, he has also engaged in building a context for such practices of undrawing – often published through extremely ephemeral formats, whether online or in print – by organizing their archival curation and integrating them to existing rogue archives. Manouach's comics are hosted on online alternative archives such as UbuWeb – a groundbreaking database of avant-garde works founded in 1996 by Kenneth Goldsmith in the spirit of free culture – and he has collaborated to curate an archival collection of "conceptual comics" on Monoskop – an online collaborative wiki and archive for media, the humanities, and the arts founded by Dušan Barok in 2004. Both archives answer to De Kosnik's description of "alternative archives" (contrasting with "universal" or "community" styles of rogue archiving), which strive to assemble "diverse and robust collections of nonmainstream cultural genres," while operating in a similar commitment to free and complete access independent of copyright restrictions.[47] The conceptual comics made available through these online archives include a wide range of works, all shared in full high-resolution PDF, assembled from photographed reproduction of the flattened books, which emphasizes their material properties, and including an explanatory notice and extra metadata. In some ways, the "Conceptual Comics" collection available at Monoskop can be seen as an updated version of Chris Ware's *McSweeney's* anthology, establishing links and relationship between creators in the present and in the past, and showcasing comics in their specific materiality. The statement of the opening page presents the online collection as "a springboard for establishing the conditions for an affective lineage between similarly minded practitioners."[48] But while Ware's *McSweeney's* anthology tended to foreground a range of original voices expressed in the personality of their graphic style, Manouach's online collection deviates from the emphasis on *auteurs* to embrace a wide range of works, many of them based on uncreative processes of appropriation, republishing, sampling, recontextualization, and redrawing.

Conclusion

There is a pleasure in finding large pleasure in small things.[1]

– Jim Woodring

IDDEN WITHIN THE DUST JACKET OF AN ANTHOLOGY, Panter's poster image itself appears as an anthology of sorts: a personal selection of images that visually teases out a collective memory (Figure 7.1). In this, it echoes the program of the *McSweeney's* comics anthology, which by assembling sample contributions from contemporary cartoonists built a sense of generational connectedness, while also tracing its own genealogy by including archival features on comics history. The various paths and frames map out a visual history of comics by means of other images copied and redrawn from a wide array of graphic works, mixing art history, film, pulp magazines, cartoons, newspaper comics, comic books, graphic novels, and more. It is one big *pêle-mêle* of various images, brought together within a more homogeneous frame by Gary Panter's ragged lines. The sprawl of citations invites readers to a game of who's-who, inciting them to spot common references in a mixed bag of century-old paintings, modernist artworks, and cartoonists of all times.

The general concentric organization of the panels suggests a temporal concatenation: on the outside, a frame of cartoon faces and expressions in boxes, at the center a golden sticker, and surrounding it drawings copied from alternative cartoonists of the time (Julie Doucet Peter

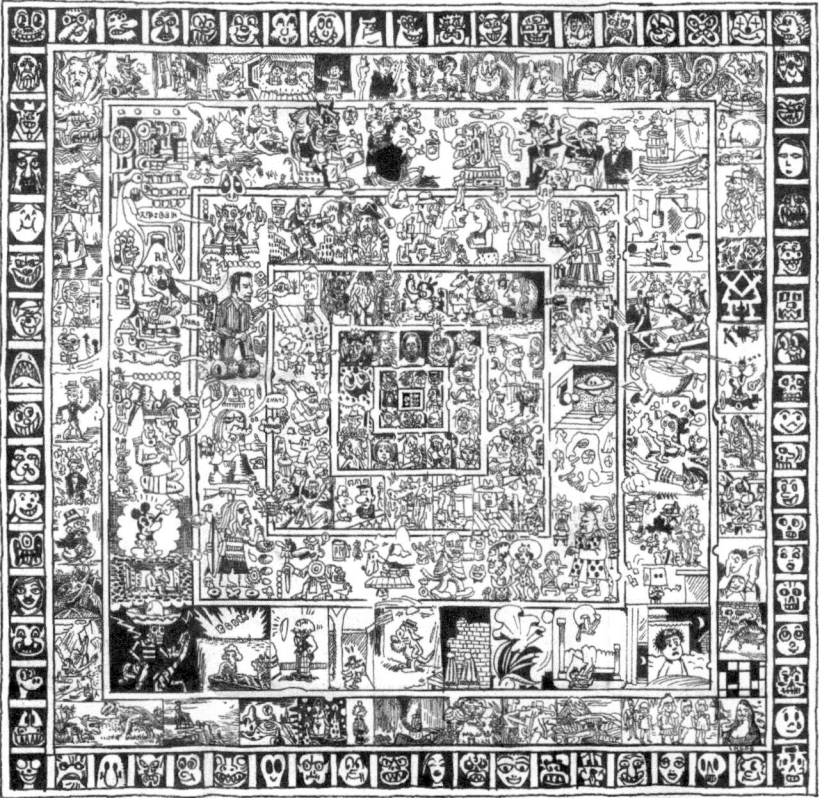

Figure 7.1 Gary Panter, "Some Drawers," 2001.
Source: Reproduced on the dustjacket of Chris Ware (ed.), *McSweeney's Quarterly Concern*, no. 13 (2004). Copyright © Gary Panter. Courtesy of the artist.

Bagge, Chris Ware, . . .). Moving away from the center, the concentric square holds *RAW*-generation cartoonists, further down underground, and progressively a mixed bag of newspaper strips, pulp comic books, art history, B movies, slapstick, modernist painting, old masters. The frames are not airtight and they overlap; messiness prevails more than chronological order. Panter's use of the nonsequential grid to display a personal history of comics made of visual fragments is not unlike the visual historiographies popular among the avant-garde. In forms such as the *pêle-mêle*, the avant-garde used the grid as a way of presenting their predecessors, upholding a sense of continuity while historicizing "their own novelty and originality."[2]

The title "Some Drawers" is further intriguing because it compounds two meanings that have been central to this book. "Drawer" can be taken as an alternative professional designation, emphasizing "drawing" as the driving logic behind this community of creators and graphic works. It highlights a history of comics that is understood as a stock of drawn images. Even as he copies and redraws characters or motifs, Panter's borrowed images remain surprisingly readable or recognizable, depending on a particular visual literacy. The determiner "some" evinces the selective scope of this visual history: the square image, even a large one, can only contain so much – just as it is likely that readers will only recognize *some* figures. The fragments offer a kind of "metonymic canonization," as Antoine Compagnon wrote of quotations; and their claim to representation can be only partial; they nevertheless summon a shared cultural memory.[3] Finally, "drawer" also simply designates the furniture item, a drawer. Drawers, in this sense, evidence the material availability of a history that can be touched only through what has been kept. It emphasizes the archival dimension that sustains this kind of historical self-reflexivity. Such drawers can designate those in the climate-controlled rooms of special collections, where original art and newspaper tearsheets might find a durable preservation and where their access and handling usually demand precautions and care, the kind of treatment that comics have only recently received in university libraries. Alternatively, the same drawers could also refer to the ones where cartoonists have often kept their clippings and what they call their swipe files: fragments selected and archived on the basis of their future use and reuse, images that cartoonists keep as inspiration, model, and reference for their own work – and on which Panter certainly had to rely to compose his panoramic history of comics.

The image condenses the key questions crisscrossing this book. It is a convenient example of the way cartoonists are prone to trace and construct their own genealogy through gestures that situate a relationship to drawing as the core matter of comics history. As is clear from Panter's graphic citations, only a few lines are enough to summon a sense of historicity. Panter's visualization also undoes the notion of a progressive movement even as it suggests that those at the center are necessarily enclosed and enframed by their predecessors. Its form and titles are further evocative of the boxes, furniture, and files that make up the archives of comics history. As a panorama of comics history, Panter's fresco returns us to our own methods of historiography: How do historians of the form approach the past and its archives? What structuring forms and patterns do we choose to order those narratives? How do we articulate the various temporal moments, rhythms, and genealogies that make up the course of comics history? What do we see at what scale? How do we redraw pictures of the past into the present?

The backward look of contemporary graphic novelists inevitably confronts us with our own practices as comics scholars and the extent to which we are indebted to a range of vernacular archivists and historians of the form. History is not limited to the confines of its scientific discipline; between that and other forms of history lies only a "difference in degree, not in nature."[4] Comics studies, as a field, has largely been shaped by fan historiographies and, more recently, by the reworkings and curations of contemporary cartoonists, indirectly enticing interests and defining priorities about comics history.[5] That also means that comics studies has sometimes tended to reproduce some of its hagiographies and romanticisms, as well as exclusions and erasures. This book, for instance, has amplified voices that already have a strong outreach: Seth, Art Spiegelman, Chris Ware are not only excellent and talented creators but also well-read historians of their chosen medium, which makes them adequate diplomats in comics scholarship. Their voices are easily amplified in their second careers as curators, designers, essayists, and all-round comics historians, which makes their narratives appreciable to the traditional modes of historiography.

At the same time, I have foregrounded other ways of engaging with the past, less evidently historiographic, but which nonetheless operate as important gestures of transmission in comics culture: scrapbooks, swipe files, rogue archives are all ways of constructing memories of comics and organizing their transmission. Such mundane gestures of transmission should warrant further inquiry as they engage with the practical specificities of comics as visual material culture. As comics move into institutional archives, giving attention to such vernacular forms of archiving and making space for the rogue archives of the present might appear as a key matter of concern for the future of comics studies.

Comics scholars can further find inspiration in and learn from these different gestures of transmission to renovate the traditional forms of scholarship, which remain so heavily and comfortably reliant on text. James Elkins has argued for a closer engagement of visual studies with the work of images in its forms of scholarly practice, "showing how images already work as arguments, resisting, speeding, slowing, affirming, contradicting, and sometimes partly ruining the arguments that surround them."[6] This is a lesson that we learn from the objects that contemporary cartoonists and other actors in the field produce when they recirculate, reproduce, redraw, reframe comics from the past: they result from a close engagement with comics as material visual culture, and pass on to readers visual archives that always hold the potential of affecting, changing, undermining their own framework of display. Contemporary cartoonists rarely shy away from this multiplicity and instability of images, and in the process invite us to be more aware of our own material engagement with historical images, what we do with them, and how we share the knowledge that results from these processes. The recent historical endeavors of Mark Newgarden and Paul Karasik, Simon Grennan, and Ilan Manouach already pave the way for such engagements and imagining of new modes of writing comics history, and making that work accessible and shareable without compromising rigor and method.

As comics studies is taking stock of the limited canon it has come to rely on, archives become all the more important to broaden the scope of our inquiries. As Margaret Galvan recently suggested, archives are primordial in interrogating the limitations of our histories of comics, and "we must be cognizant of how these archives operate to facilitate the discovery of these materials."[7] Attending to the self-curated archives of comics readers and creators is to become an important part of this process, as we might also find inspiration in the gestures of transmission that have shaped comics' relationship to their own past. Lisa Gitelman, in a compelling reflection on the historiography of media, reminds us of the complex historicity of media and our dependence on them: "Inquiring into the history of a medium that helped to construct that inquiring itself is sort of like attempting to stand in the same river twice: impossible, but it is important to try, at least so the (historicity of the) grounds of inquiry become clear."[8] It is hard to completely avoid an

anachronistic and retrospective reading of comics history, which is necessarily shaped by present perspectives and priorities; it is even more so
when the aim is to analyze contemporary historiographic gestures that
themselves direct our understanding of comics history in the first place.
In this light, it is not only important to understand how comics history is
reframed in the graphic novel in a retrospective fashion. It is just as
important to be able to grasp how much this backward look itself results
from historical practices of inscription, preservation, and transmission. If
there is one task that this book was taking on, it was this one: trying to
track the material processes and protocols that allow for the circulation
of past comics across time, trying to account for gestures of transmission
by which historical knowledge is made and remade in the contemporary
graphic novel.

Notes

INTRODUCTION

1. Daniel K. Raeburn, *Chris Ware* (New Haven, CT: Yale University Press, 2004), 9. As a source for the aphorism, Raeburn indicates: "Telephone conversation between Chris Ware and Art Spiegelman, 2001, reported by Ware." The aphorism reappears in other publications – such as Art Spiegelman, *Co-Mix: A Retrospective of Comics, Graphics, and Scraps* (Montreal: Drawn and Quarterly, 2013) – and is frequently headlined by journalists. The *Chris Ware* monograph is the oldest appearance I could retrace.
2. *Jimmy Corrigan* was awarded two literary prizes in 2001, the American Book Award and the Guardian First Book Award.
3. Raeburn, *Chris Ware*, 9.
4. Charles McGrath, "Not Funnies," *The New York Times Magazine*, July 11, 2004, 24.
5. One should nevertheless signal at least two important contributions which this book relies on and seeks to expand: Jeet Heer, "Inventing Cartooning Ancestors: Ware and the Comics Canon," in *The Comics of Chris Ware: Drawing Is a Way of Thinking*, ed. David M. Ball and Martha B. Kuhlman (Jackson: University Press of Mississippi, 2010), 3–13; Jan Baetens and Hugo Frey, *The Graphic Novel: An Introduction* (New York: Cambridge University Press, 2015), chapter 9.
6. Baetens and Frey, *The Graphic Novel*, 222.
7. For a concise and up-to-date guide to authorship in comics, see Maaheen Ahmed, "Comics and Authorship: An Introduction," *Authorship* 6, no. 2 (2017): 1–13.
8. On the blind spots of the recent canonization processes in comics studies, see Bart Beaty and Benjamin Woo, *The Greatest Comic Book of All Time: Symbolic Capital and the Field of American Comic Books* (New York: Palgrave Macmillan, 2016).
9. Chris Ware, ed., *McSweeney's Quarterly Concern, Issue Number 13* (San Francisco, CA: McSweeney's, 2004).
10. Astrid Erll, "Generation in Literary History: Three Constellations of Generationality, Genealogy, and Memory," *New Literary History* 45, no. 3 (2014): 385–409.
11. See Pascal Lefèvre and Charles Dierick, eds., *Forging a New Medium: The Comic Strip in the Nineteenth Century* (Brussels: VUB University Press, 1998); David Kunzle, *Father of the Comic Strip: Rodolphe Töpffer* (Jackson: University Press of Mississippi, 2007).

12. Thierry Smolderen, "A Chapter on Methodology," *SIGNs: Studies in Graphic Narratives* 2, no. 1 (2011): 7.

13. See Benoît Glaude's impressive cartography of the transnational circulation of *Mr Vieux Bois*: Benoît Glaude, "Circulation transnationale des *Amours de Mr Vieux Bois* de Rodolphe Töpffer," *Les Cahiers du GRIT* 3 (2016): 9–31.

14. Rodolphe Töpffer, "Notice sur la contrefaçon de *L'Histoire de M. Jabot*," in *M. Töpffer invente la bande dessinée*, ed. Thierry Groensteen (Brussels: Les Impressions Nouvelles, 2014), 222.

15. For a fleshed-out analysis of the reflexive mediality of the anthology, see Alexander Starre, "American Comics Anthologies: Mediality – Canonization – Transnationalism," in *Transnational American Studies*, ed. Udo J. Hebel (Heidelberg: Winter, 2012), 541–60.

16. See Chapter 3 for the fleshed-out analysis of this example.

17. Art Spiegelman, *In the Shadow of No Towers* (New York: Pantheon Books, 2004).

18. See Hillary L. Chute, "Temporality and Seriality in Spiegelman's *In the Shadow of No Towers*," *American Periodicals* 17, no. 2 (2007): 228–44; Michelle Ann Abate, "Art Spiegelman's *In the Shadow of No Towers* as Board Book: From the Matter of Materiality to the Way That Materiality Matters," *Jeunesse: Young People, Texts, Cultures* 7, no. 2 (2015): 40–64.

19. Henry Jenkins, "Archival, Ephemeral, and Residual: The Functions of Early Comics in Art Spiegelman's *In the Shadow of No Towers*," in *From Comic Strips to Graphic Novels: Contributions to the Theory and History of Graphic Narratives*, ed. Daniel Stein and Jan-Noël Thon (Berlin: De Gruyter, 2013), 301–22.

20. For a refreshing take on the memory debate, see David Berliner, *Losing Culture: Nostalgia, Heritage, and Our Accelerated Times* (New Brunswick, NJ: Rutgers University Press, 2020).

21. Bart Beaty, "The Recession and the American Comic Book Industry: From Inelastic Cultural Good to Economic Integration," *Popular Communication* 8, no. 3 (2010): 203–7; Shawna Kidman, *Comic Books Incorporated: How the Business of Comics Became the Business of Hollywood* (Oakland: University of California Press, 2019). As Benjamin Woo has recently argued, it is good to bear in mind that there is no "comic book industry" but a "range of different models in different formats and channels addressing different audiences"; Benjamin Woo, "Is There a Comic Book Industry?" *Media Industries Journal* 5, no. 1 (June 5, 2018), https://doi.org/10.3998/mij.15031809.0005.102.

22. For a brief overview of the interactions and exchanges between digital culture and graphic novels, see Benoît Crucifix and Björn-Olav Dozo, "E-Graphic Novels," in *The Cambridge History of the Graphic Novel*, ed. Jan Baetens, Hugo Frey, and Stephen E. Tabachnick (Cambridge: Cambridge University Press, 2018), 574–90. A thorough and ambitious history of web and digital comics in the U.S. remains a gap in comics studies, but one can find a remarkable model in Julien Baudry, *Cases·Pixels: Une histoire de la BD numérique en France* (Tours: Presses Universitaires François-Rabelais, 2018).

23. Baudry, *Cases·Pixels*, 23.

24. David A. Beronä, *Wordless Books: The Original Graphic Novels* (New York: Abrams, 2008).

25. Jared Gardner, *Projections: Comics and the History of Twenty-First-Century Storytelling* (Stanford, CA: Stanford University Press, 2012), chapter 1; Thierry Smolderen, *The Origins of Comics: From William Hogarth to Winsor McCay*, trans. Bart Beaty and Nick Nguyen (Jackson: University Press of Mississippi, 2014), chapter 8.

26. Sticking to references that have inflected my methodology and conceptual framework, see for instance Jan Baetens and Steven Surdiacourt, "European Graphic Narratives: Toward a Cultural and Mediological History," in *From Comic Strips to Graphic Novels: Contributions to the Theory and History of Graphic Narrative*, ed. Daniel Stein and Jan-Noël Thon (Berlin: De Gruyter, 2013), 347–62; Smolderen, *The Origins of Comics*; Philippe Marion, "La bande dessinée et ses identités culturelles. Paysages et frontières," in *Le Statut culturel de la bande dessinée: ambiguïtés et évolutions / The Cultural Standing of Comics: Ambiguities and Change*, ed. Maaheen Ahmed, Stéphanie Delneste, and Jean-Louis Tilleuil (Louvain-la-Neuve: Academia-L'Harmattan, 2016), 39–52; Sylvain Lesage, *L'Effet livre: métamorphoses de la bande dessinée* (Tours: Presses Universitaires François-Rabelais, 2019).

27. Smolderen, "A Chapter on Methodology," 2.

28. Thierry Smolderen, "Attraction, auteurisation, institutionnalisation. Notes pour une théorie historique des configurations éditoriales," in *La bande dessinée à la croisée des médias*, ed. Désirée Lorenz and Elsa Caboche (Tours: Presses Universitaires François-Rabelais, 2019), 162, my translation.

29. Jan Baetens, Hugo Frey, and Stephen E. Tabachnick, "Introduction," in *The Cambridge History of the Graphic Novel*, ed. Jan Baetens, Hugo Frey, and Stephen E. Tabachnick (New York: Cambridge University Press, 2018), 17.

30. Baetens and Frey, *The Graphic Novel*, 6.

31. Baetens, Frey, and Tabachnick, "Introduction," 2.

32. Paul Williams, *Dreaming the Graphic Novel: The Novelization of Comics* (New Brunswick, NJ: Rutgers University Press, 2020).

33. Catherine Labio, "What's in a Name? The Academic Study of Comics and the 'Graphic Novel,'" *Cinema Journal* 50, no. 3 (2011): 124. For a more recent but similar rejection of the term, see Marc Singer, *Breaking the Frame: Populism and Prestige in Comics Studies* (Austin: University of Texas Press, 2019), 18–21.

34. Christopher Pizzino, *Arresting Development: Comics at the Boundaries of Literature* (Austin: University of Texas Press, 2016), 3.

35. Ibid., 45.

36. Spiegelman, *In the Shadow of No Towers*, n.p.

37. See Pizzino's analysis of the "injury to the eye" motif used in Ed Brubaker and Sean Phillips' *Criminal* series; Christopher Pizzino, "Comics History and the Question of Delinquency: The Case of Criminal," in *Comics Memory: Archives and Styles*, ed. Maaheen Ahmed and Benoît Crucifix (New York: Palgrave, 2018), 169–70.

38. Pizzino, *Arresting Development*, 69.

39. Baetens and Frey, *The Graphic Novel*, 19.

40. See Greice Schneider, *What Happens When Nothing Happens: Boredom and Everyday Life in Contemporary Comics* (Leuven: Leuven University Press, 2016).

41. On the methodological bias and blindness that comes in some graphic novel studies, see Bart Beaty, "Some Classics," in *The Cambridge Companion to the Graphic Novel*, ed. Stephen E. Tabachnick, Cambridge Companions to Literature (Cambridge: Cambridge University Press, 2017), 175–91.
42. Baetens and Frey, *The Graphic Novel*, 21.
43. Williams, *Dreaming the Graphic Novel*, 25.
44. Ibid., 25.
45. Will Straw, "Systems of Articulation, Logics of Change: Communities and Scenes in Popular Music," *Cultural Studies* 5, no. 3 (1991): 374.
46. Benoît Berthou, ed., "La bande dessinée: un 'art sans mémoire'?" *Comicalités*, 2011, https://journals.openedition.org/comicalites/198; Maaheen Ahmed and Benoît Crucifix, eds., *Comics Memory: Archives and Styles* (New York: Palgrave, 2018).
47. Charles Hatfield, *Alternative Comics: An Emerging Literature* (Jackson: University Press of Mississippi, 2005), 20–31.
48. Eric Hoffman and Dominick Grace, eds., *Seth: Conversations* (Jackson: University Press of Mississippi, 2015), 148.
49. Beaty and Woo, *The Greatest Comic Book of All Time*, 1–4.
50. On women creators in the graphic novel, see the foundational work of Hillary L. Chute, *Graphic Women: Life Narrative and Contemporary Comics* (New York: Columbia University Press, 2010); and more recently Tahneer Oksman and Seamus O'Malley, eds., *The Comics of Julie Doucet and Gabrielle Bell: A Place inside Yourself* (Jackson: University Press of Mississippi, 2019).
51. Daniel Worden, "The Shameful Art: McSweeney's Quarterly Concern, Comics, and the Politics of Affect," *Modern Fiction Studies* 52, no. 4 (2006): 893.
52. Trina Robbins and Catherine Yronwode, *Women and the Comics* (New York: Eclipse, 1985); Trina Robbins, *A Century of Women Cartoonists* (Northampton, MA: Kitchen Sink Press, 1993); Trina Robbins, *From Girls to Grrrlz: A History of Women's Comics from Teens to Zines* (San Francisco, CA: Chronicle Books, 1999).
53. Trina Robbins, *Nell Brinkley and the New Woman in the Early 20th Century* (Jefferson, NC: McFarland, 2001).
54. Maaheen Ahmed, "Loving Comics in *Neil the Horse Comics and Stories*," *Comicalités*, History and influence of bedephilia (April 1, 2021): 10, https://journals.openedition.org/comicalites/6300.
55. Ibid., 15.
56. Other areas of popular visual production have taken on such approaches early on, see Cheryl Buckley, "Made in Patriarchy: Toward a Feminist Analysis of Women and Design," *Design Issues* 3, no. 2 (1986): 3–14.
57. Margaret Galvan and Leah Misemer, "Introduction: The Counterpublics of Underground Comics," *Inks: The Journal of the Comics Studies Society* 3, no. 1 (2019): 1.
58. Daniel Worden, "Introduction: R. Crumb in Comics History," in *The Comics of R. Crumb: Underground in the Art Museum*, ed. Daniel Worden (Jackson: University Press of Mississippi, 2021), 12.

59. Margaret Galvan, "Archiving Wimmen: Collectives, Networks, and Comix," *Australian Feminist Studies* 32, no. 91–92 (2017): 23.

60. There would be several initiatives to continue the project of a feminist comics anthology in the 1990s; see Rachel R. Miller, "When Feminism Went to Market: Issues in Feminist Anthology Comics of the 1980s and '90s," in *The Oxford Handbook of Comic Book Studies*, ed. Frederick Luis Aldama (Oxford: Oxford University Press, 2019), 419–36.

61. See for instance the common erasure of Mouly's editorial role in *RAW*, as exposed by Jeet Heer, *In Love with Art: Françoise Mouly's Adventures in Comics with Art Spiegelman* (Toronto: Coach House Books, 2013); Colin Beineke, "Assembling Comics: The House Style and Legacy of RAW Books and Graphics" (PhD thesis, University of Missouri, 2017).

62. Rebecca Ann Wanzo, *The Content of Our Caricature: African American Comic Art and Political Belonging* (New York: New York University Press, 2020), 2.

63. Ibid., 22.

64. Baetens and Frey, *The Graphic Novel*, 232.

65. Seth, "Afterword," in *Graphic Witness: Four Wordless Graphic Novels*, ed. George A. Walker (Buffalo, NY: Firefly Books, 2007), 416.

66. Heer, "Inventing Cartooning Ancestors," 4. I come back to this point and analyze Ware's *Walt & Skeezix* reprints at length in Chapter 3.

67. Jorge Luis Borges, "Kafka and His Precursors," in *The Total Library: Non Fiction 1922–1986*, trans. Ester Allen, Suzanne Jill Levine, and Eliot Weinberger (London: Penguin, 1999), 365.

68. Heer, "Inventing Cartooning Ancestors," 5.

69. On "narrative memory" in Marvel productions, see Jean-Matthieu Méon, "Sons and Grandsons of Origins: Narrative Memory in Mainstream Superhero Publishing," in *Comics Memory: Archives and Styles*, ed. Maaheen Ahmed and Benoît Crucifix (New York: Palgrave, 2019), 189–210.

70. Beaty and Woo, *The Greatest Comic Book of All Time*, 15.

71. Following "a tripartite story for the graphic novel of sites of anticipation, emergence, and dominance" in Baetens, Frey, and Tabachnick, "Introduction," 3.

72. Beaty and Woo, *The Greatest Comic Book of All Time*, 140–41.

73. Jan Baetens and Ben De Bruyn, "Éloge de la canonisation," *LHT Fabula*, May 2014, §29, www.fabula.org/lht/12/mdrn.html.

74. John Guillory, "Monuments and Documents: Panofsky on the Object of Study in the Humanities," *History of Humanities* 1, no. 1 (2016): 22, 27. I return to this question in Chapter 3.

75. Brian Cremins, *Captain Marvel and the Art of Nostalgia* (Jackson: University Press of Mississippi, 2016), 151.

76. Stuart Hall, "Constituting an Archive," *Third Text* 15, no. 54 (2001): 89.

77. Pizzino, *Arresting Development*.

78. Hall, "Constituting an Archive," 89.

79. Ibid., 91.

80. The "archival turn" was largely sustained by two landmark publications in critical theory: Michel Foucault, *The Archeology of Knowledge*, trans. A. M. Sheridan Smith, Collection Tel 354 (New York: Pantheon Books, 1972); Jacques Derrida, *Archive Fever: A Freudian Impression*, trans. Eric Prenowitz (Chicago, IL: University of Chicago Press, 1995).

81. For a few landmark publications in these various fields, see among many others Robin Earle Kelsey, *Archive Style: Photographs & Illustrations for U.S. Surveys, 1850–1890* (Berkeley: University of California Press, 2007); Giovanna Fossati, *From Grain to Pixel: The Archival Life of Film in Transition* (Amsterdam: Amsterdam University Press, 2009); Catherine Russell, *Archiveology: Walter Benjamin and Archival Film Practices* (Durham, NC: Duke University Press, 2018); Hal Foster, "An Archival Impulse," *October* 110, Fall (2004): 3–22; Ernst Van Alphen, *Staging the Archive: Art and Photography in the Age of New Media* (London: Reaktion Books, 2014); Gabriella Giannachi, *Archive Everything: Mapping the Everyday* (Cambridge, MA: MIT Press, 2016); Lorraine Daston, ed., *Science in the Archives: Pasts, Presents, Futures* (Chicago, IL: University of Chicago Press, 2017).

82. Ann Laura Stoler, *Along the Archival Grain: Epistemic Anxieties and Colonial Common Sense* (Princeton, NJ: Princeton University Press, 2009), 44–45.

83. Kate Eichhorn, *The Archival Turn in Feminism: Outrage in Order* (Philadelphia, PA: Temple University Press, 2014), 4.

84. For an early reflection from within archival sciences, see Eric Ketelaar, "Tacit Narratives: The Meanings of Archives," *Archival Science* 1, no. 2 (2001): 131–41. For a good example in cinema studies, see Fossati, *From Grain to Pixel*.

85. Abigail De Kosnik, *Rogue Archives: Digital Cultural Memory and Media Fandom* (Cambridge, MA: MIT Press, 2016), 274–75. See also Wolfgang Ernst, *Digital Memory and the Archive*, ed. Jussi Parikka (Minneapolis: University of Minnesota Press, 2013); Ina Blom, Trond Lundemo, and Eivind Røssaak, eds., *Memory in Motion: Archives, Technology, and the Social* (Amsterdam: Amsterdam University Press, 2017).

86. De Kosnik, *Rogue Archives*, 4.

87. Ibid., 4.

88. Thierry Groensteen, *La bande dessinée: un objet culturel non identifié* (Angoulême: L'An 2, 2006), 67.

89. Ibid., 67.

90. This largely builds on the collaborative reflection in Ahmed and Crucifix, *Comics Memory*.

91. Gardner, *Projections*, 150.

92. Ibid., 177. The parallel rests on Lev Manovich's influential notion of "database logic" as a "symbolic form" of new media, distinct from traditional narrative; see Lev Manovich, *The Language of New Media* (Cambridge, MA: MIT Press, 2001), 225. It is furthermore useful to note that it finds echoes in two different articles that draw a similar parallel between the importance of collector culture in comics and the formal fragmentation of comics; see Thierry Groensteen, "Le Plaisir de la bande dessinée," *Neuvième Art* 2 (1997): 14–21; Matteo Stefanelli, "La bande dessinée, expérience 'archivable'.

La mémoire en bédé, entre dispositifs de lecture et stratégies culturelles," *Cinergie* 4 (2010): 114–19.

93. Gardner, *Projections*, 177–88.

94. Ibid., 150.

95. Speaking of gestures enables a focus on a pragmatic dimension and emphasizes the active role of all those involved in the transmission process; in this, I adopt the notion from the theoretical concept of "discursive gesture" elaborated in LTTR 13, "Figures de l'énonciation: les gestes discursifs du savoir," in *Figures en discours: au cœur des textes*, ed. Amir Biglari and Geneviève Salvan (Louvain-la-Neuve: Academia/L'Harmattan, 2016), 95–96. On "transmission through gestures" and "transmission of gestures," see also Sophie Aymes and Marie-Odile Bernez, eds., "Gestures and Transmissions," *Interfaces* 40 (2018), https://preo.u-bourgogne.fr/interfaces/index.php?id=598.

96. David Berliner, "Anthropologie et transmission," *Terrain* 55 (2010): 14.

97. I am aware of the negative connotations that might come with the term "appropriation" in an Anglophone context, but, out of a lack of proper synonyms, I want to stick by the more neutral definition of the term that has become common in French-language cultural history, where it is used to designate "a social history of usages and interpretations, caught in their fundamental determinations and inscribed in the specific practices that produce them"; see Roger Chartier, *Au bord de la falaise: L'histoire entre certitudes et inquiétudes* (Paris: Albin Michel, 2009), 83, my translation. A key work in establishing appropriation as a cultural-historical concept to describe readers' and consumers' practices is of course Michel de Certeau, *The Practice of Everyday Life* (Berkeley: University of California Press, 2013).

98. This book thus builds on the "material turn" in comics studies; see Sylvain Lesage and Bounthavy Suvilay, "Introduction thématique: pour un tournant matériel des études sur la bande dessinée," *Comicalités*, December 21, 2019, http://journals.openedition.org/comicalites/3692. For a recent take on comics as "things" and "stuff," see Henry Jenkins, *Comics and Stuff* (New York: New York University Press, 2020).

99. Aaron Kashtan, *Between Pen and Pixel: Comics, Materiality, and the Book of the Future* (Columbus: Ohio State University Press, 2018).

100. Franck Leibovici, *des opérations d'écriture qui ne disent pas leur nom* (Paris: Questions théoriques, 2020).

101. Julien Baudry, Xavier Hébert, and Kevin Roger, "Hériter, imiter," in *Style(s) de (la) bande dessinée*, ed. Benoît Berthou and Jacques Dürrenmatt (Paris: Garnier, 2019), 53, my translation.

102. See the examples of Osamu Tezuka and of Hergé's clear line fleshed out in Baudry, Hébert, and Roger, "Hériter, imiter."

103. For a fascinating reflection on the uses and appropriations of existing images in historiographic nonfiction comics, more attuned to the genetic dimension of creative production and what happens on the drawing board than to the circulation and transmission of comics themselves, see Adrien Genoudet, *Dessiner l'histoire: Pour une histoire visuelle* (Paris: Le Manuscrit, 2015).

CHAPTER 1 COLLECTING

1. Hoffman and Grace, eds., *Seth*, 175.

2. Ibid., 175.

3. Gardner, *Projections*, 176.

4. Ibid., 172.

5. Jenkins, *Comics and Stuff*, 117.

6. Starre, "American Comics Anthologies," 550.

7. Dominique Kalifa, "L'ère de la culture-marchandise," *Revue d'histoire du XIXe siècle* 19 (1999): 7–14.

8. See for instance the "patchy" case of Marvel's history of archiving its own materials, described in Darren Wershler and Kalervo A. Sinervo, "Marvel and the Form of Motion Comics," in *Make Ours Marvel: Media Convergence and a Comics Universe*, ed. Matt Yockey (Austin: University of Texas Press, 2017), 187–206.

9. Darren Wershler, "Digital Comics, Circulation, and the Importance of Being Eric Sluis," *Cinema Journal* 50, no. 3 (2011): 127.

10. Aleida Assmann, "Canon and Archive," in *A Companion to Cultural Memory Studies*, ed. Astrid Erll and Ansgar Nünning (Berlin/New York: De Gruyter, 2010), 334–37.

11. Frank Kelleter, "Five Ways of Looking at Popular Seriality," in *Media of Serial Narrative*, ed. Frank Kelleter (Columbus: Ohio State University Press, 2017), 7–34; Matthieu Letourneux, *Fictions à la chaîne: littératures sérielles et culture médiatique* (Paris: Seuil, 2017).

12. Mel Gibson, *Remembered Reading: Memory, Comics and Post-War Constructions of British Girlhood* (Leuven: Leuven University Press, 2015), 189.

13. Benjamin Woo, "An Age-Old Problem: Problematics of Comic Book Historiography," *International Journal of Comic Art* 10, no. 1 (2008): 268–79; Jean-Paul Gabilliet, *Of Comics and Men: A Cultural History of American Comic Books*, trans. Bart Beaty and Nick Nguyen (Jackson: University Press of Mississippi, 2010), 293–306; Bart Beaty, *Comics versus Art* (Toronto: Toronto University Press, 2012), 71–99.

14. Beaty, *Comics versus Art*, 153.

15. Matthew Pustz, *Comic Book Culture: Fanboys and True Believers* (Jackson: University Press of Mississippi, 1999); Lincoln Geraghty, *Cult Collectors: Nostalgia, Fandom and Collecting Popular Culture* (London: Routledge, 2014); Benjamin Woo, "The Android's Dungeon: Comic-Bookstores, Cultural Spaces, and the Social Practices of Audiences," *Journal of Graphic Novels & Comics* 2, no. 2 (2011): 125–36.

16. Gibson, *Remembered Reading*, 21–22.

17. Margaret Galvan, "Archiving Grassroots Comics: The Radicality of Networks and Lesbian Community," *Archive Journal*, November 2015, www.archivejournal.net/essays/archiving-grassroots-comics-the-radicality-of-networks-and-lesbian-community/, last accessed October 22, 2022.

18. Hatfield, *Alternative Comics*, ix.

19. For a more nuanced version of that origin story and notably its connections to wider printing and distribution networks, including the Print Mint shop, see Jean-Paul Gabilliet, *R. Crumb* (Bordeaux: Presses Universitaires de Bordeaux, 2012), 64–72.

20. Corey K. Creekmur, "Multiculturalism Meets the Counterculture: Representing Racial Difference in Robert Crumb's Underground Comix," in *Representing Multiculturalism in Comics and Graphic Novels*, ed. Carolene Ayaka and Ian Hague (London: Routledge, 2015), 26.

21. Robert Boyd, "Shary Flenniken," *The Comics Journal* 146 (1991): 62.

22. Bill Blackbeard, "Articles of the Association of the San Francisco Academy of Comic Art," Box 4, San Francisco Academy of Comic Art (SFACA) collection, Billy Ireland Cartoon Library & Museum, Ohio State University, Columbus.

23. Jenny E. Robb, "Bill Blackbeard: The Collector Who Rescued the Comics," *Journal of American Culture* 32, no. 3 (2009): 247; Bill Blackbeard, "The Four Color Paper Trail: A Look Back," *International Journal of Comic Art* 5, no. 2 (2003): 205–15. Nonprofit status also meant that donations to the SFACA were tax-deductible; see the correspondence letters in Bill Blackbeard's scrapbook in the SFACA collection, Billy Ireland Cartoon Library & Museum.

24. Dylan Williams, "An Interview with Bill Blackbeard," *Destroy All Comics* 3 (1995): 20.

25. It is part of a longer story since the archival interest in comics at the Ohio State University Libraries was kindled by the comic strip artist Milton Caniff's successive donations to his alma mater as of 1974 (and which would make the institution a logical home for the SFACA collection), and the further development of comics scholarship around the collection spearheaded by in-house curator Lucy Shelton Caswell. See Jenny E. Robb, "The Librarians and Archivists," in *The Secret Origins of Comics Studies*, ed. Matthew J. Smith and Randy Duncan (New York: Routledge, 2017), 71–88.

26. As Jenny Robb underlines, Blackbeard fits into the identity formation of the "heroic collector," "rescuing the materials from certain destruction"; Robb, "Bill Blackbeard," 251.

27. David Lowenthal, *The Past Is a Foreign Country – Revisited* (Cambridge: Cambridge University Press, 2013); Caitlin DeSilvey, *Curated Decay: Heritage Beyond Saving* (Minneapolis: University of Minnesota Press, 2017).

28. Judith E. Schlanger, *Présence des œuvres perdues* (Paris: Hermann, 2010), 207.

29. Nicholson Baker, *Double Fold: Libraries and the Assault on Paper* (New York: Random House, 2001), 8.

30. Robb, "Bill Blackbeard," 250.

31. For a further discussion of this convergence, see Chapter 3.

32. Lisa Gitelman, *Paper Knowledge: Toward a Media History of Documents* (Durham, NC: Duke University Press, 2014), 110.

33. Ibid., 92–93.

34. The phrase "heritage overload" is borrowed from David Lowenthal, *The Heritage Crusade and the Spoils of History* (Cambridge: Cambridge University Press, 2010), 12. See also Pierre Nora, "Between Memory and History: Les Lieux de Mémoire," *Representations* 26 (1989): 13–14.

35. Miles Ogborn, "Archives," in *Patterned Ground: Entanglements of Nature and Culture*, ed. Stephan Harrison, Steve Pile, and Nigel J. Thrift (London: Reaktion Books, 2004), 240.

36. Williams, "An Interview with Bill Blackbeard," 20.

37. Jonathan Auerbach and Lisa Gitelman, "Microfilm, Containment, and the Cold War," *American Literary History* 19, no. 3 (2007): 745–68; Michael Faciejew, "Une bibliothèque portative: le microfilm et son architecture," trans. Jean-François Caro, *Transbordeur photographie* 3 (2019): 48–59.

38. Arlette Farge, *The Allure of the Archives*, trans. Thomas Scott-Railton and Natalie Zemon Davis (New Haven, CT: Yale University Press, 2013).

39. Coulton Waugh, *The Comics* (reprint of the 1947 original; Jackson: University Press of Mississippi, 1991), 16.

40. Gardner, *Projections*, chapter 5.

41. N. Katherine Hayles, *How We Became Posthuman: Virtual Bodies in Cybernetics, Literature, and Informatics* (Chicago, IL: University of Chicago Press, 1999), 4. This remains present in some archivists' response to Baker's *Double Fold*, which questions his fetishizing of the printed newspaper as sheer aesthetics: "Pretty pictures in pretty bindings are pretty nice, but they are pretty much immaterial to most historians"; James M. O'Toole, "Do Not Fold, Spindle, or Mutilate," *The American Archivist* 64, no. 2 (2001): 388.

42. Roger Chartier, "Languages, Books, and Reading from the Printed Word to the Digital Text," *Critical Inquiry* 31, no. 1 (2004): 147–49.

43. Auerbach and Gitelman, "Microfilm, Containment, and the Cold War," 749. On the relationship between libraries and copy shops in campus areas, see Kate Eichhorn, "Breach of Copy/Rights: The University Copy District as Abject Zone," *Public Culture* 18, no. 3 (2006): 551–71.

44. Blackbeard, "The Four Color Paper Trail," 213.

45. Ellen Gruber Garvey, *Writing with Scissors: American Scrapbooks from the Civil War to the Harlem Renaissance* (Oxford: Oxford University Press, 2013).

46. See Blackbeard, "The Four Color Paper Trail." The language itself shows how much Blackbeard understood his work as a kind of "counter-institution," partly mimicking the structures of bureaucracy that he was vehemently criticizing at the same time; on amateurdom as counter-institution, see Gitelman, *Paper Knowledge*, 149.

47. See the descriptions of Blackbeard's curatorial choices by the OSU archivist who processed, cataloged, and organized the material: Amy McCrory, "Archiving Newspaper Comic Strips: The San Francisco Academy of Comic Art Collection," *Archival Issues* 27, no. 2 (2002): 137–50. On the *Nancy* exception, see Paul Karasik and Mark Newgarden, *How to Read Nancy: The Elements of Comics in Three Easy Panels* (Seattle, WA: Fantagraphics Books, 2017), 23.

48. Williams, "An Interview with Bill Blackbeard," 31.

49. Reproduction rights, use policies, and processing fees of institutional libraries might also be prohibitive and in some cases lead publishing houses to work with a network of private collectors; see Tracy Hurren, "The Golden Age of Reprints: An Analysis of Classic Comics in a Contemporary Industry" (MA thesis, Simon Fraser University, 2011), 19.

50. Spiegelman, *Co-Mix*.

51. Bill Blackbeard and Martin Williams, eds., *The Smithsonian Collection of Newspaper Comics* (Washington, DC/New York: Smithsonian Institution Press/Harry N. Abrams, Inc., 1977).

52. On the distribution of the anthology, see Williams, "An Interview with Bill Blackbeard," 25. The book sold 14,011 copies between October 1978 and April 1979, with record numbers for mailing orders (13,099); these sales would ensure an interesting additional revenue for the editors; Bill Blackbeard, "Articles of the Association of the San Francisco Academy of Comic Art," Box 23, SFACA collection.

53. Blackbeard and Williams, *The Smithsonian Collection of Newspaper Comics*, 18.

54. Garrett Price, *White Boy in Skull Valley* (Palo Alto, CA: Sunday Press Books, 2015).

55. Dan Nadel, ed., "Bill Blackbeard: Tributes," *The Comics Journal* (April 25, 2011), www.tcj.com/bill-blackbeard-tributes/, last accessed October 22, 2022.

56. Heer, "Inventing Cartooning Ancestors," 7.

57. The quoted lines are taken from the anthology's annotated index, see Blackbeard and Williams, *The Smithsonian Collection of Newspaper Comics*, 328.

58. Heer, "Inventing Cartooning Ancestors," 7–8.

59. Thomas A. Bredehoft, "Comics Architecture, Multidimensionality, and Time: Chris Ware's Jimmy Corrigan: The Smartest Kid on Earth," *Modern Fiction Studies* 52, no. 4 (2006): 869–90; José Manuel Trabado, *Antes de la novela gráfica. Clásicos del cómic en la prensa norteamericana* (Madrid: Cátedra, 2012), 61–74; Thierry Groensteen, "La Cage de Martin Vaughn-James et ses avatars contemporains," in *L'Engendrement des images en bande dessinée*, ed. Henri Garric (Tours: Presses Universitaires François-Rabelais, 2013), 99–113.

60. For a close analysis of the visual and narrative strategies used by Seth to effect a sense of nostalgia, see Giorgio Busi Rizzi, "Portrait of the Artist as a Nostalgic: Seth's It's a Good Life, If You Don't Weaken," in *Comics Memory: Archives and Styles*, ed. Maaheen Ahmed and Benoît Crucifix (New York: Palgrave, 2018), 15–35.

61. Marjorie Garber, "Over the Influence," *Critical Inquiry* 42, no. 4 (2016): 748.

62. Blackbeard and Williams, *The Smithsonian Collection of Newspaper Comics*, 13.

63. In the French context, a similar figure would be Francis Lacassin, whose memoir is revealing for those issues; see Francis Lacassin, *Mémoires. Sur les chemins qui marchent* (Monaco: Editions du Rocher, 2006).

64. Robert Darnton, "The Great Book Massacre," *New York Review of Books*, April 26, 2001.

65. Spiegelman, *In the Shadow of No Towers*, 15.

66. Jenkins, "Archival, Ephemeral, and Residual," 314–18.

67. Spiegelman, *In the Shadow of No Towers*, 15.

68. Patrick M. Bray, "Aesthetics in the Shadow of No Towers: Reading Virilio in the Twenty-First Century," *Yale French Studies* 114 (2008): 15.

69. For a fascinatingly close look at the history of so-called Ben Day dots, see the series of blog posts on the topic written by Guy Lawley at legionofandy.com/category/ben-day/, last accessed October 22, 2022.

70. Chute, "Temporality and Seriality in Spiegelman's *In the Shadow of No Towers*," 240.

71. Benoît Crucifix, "Sunday Comics Reloaded – An Interview with Peter Maresca," *du9, l'autre Bande Dessinée*, March 2016. www.du9.org/en/entretien/sunday-comics-reloaded-an-interview-with-peter-maresca/, last accessed October 22, 2022.

72. Katherine Hayles indeed reminds us that digitality is now found everywhere in the twenty-first-century chain of book production; N. Katherine Hayles, *Electronic*

Literature: New Horizons for the Literary (Notre Dame, IN: University of Notre Dame Press, 2008), 159.

73. Alan Moore and Eddie Campbell, *From Hell* (Marietta, GA: Top Shelf, 1999); Eddie Campbell, *Alec: The Years Have Pants* (Marietta, GA: Top Shelf, 2009).

74. Eddie Campbell, *The Goat Getters: Jack Johnson, the Fight of the Century, and How a Bunch of Raucous Cartoonists Reinvented Comics* (San Diego, CA/Columbus: IDW/Ohio State University Press, 2018), 11.

75. Ibid., 53–54. On the rigidity of Blackbeard's definition of comics, see also Beaty, *Comics versus Art*, 27–28.

76. In this, Campbell clearly extends the propositions made by Smolderen, *The Origins of Comics*; Smolderen, "A Chapter on Methodology."

77. Campbell, *The Goat Getters*, 12.

78. Ibid., 75 and 280–81.

79. Ibid., 11.

80. Kashtan, *Between Pen and Pixel*, 95.

81. Lesage and Suvilay, "Introduction thématique," §33.

82. François Brunet, *La Photographie: histoire et contre-histoire* (Paris: Presses Universitaires de France, 2017), 361.

CHAPTER 2 CURATING

1. Art Spiegelman, *MetaMaus*, ed. Hillary Chute (New York: Pantheon Books, 2011), 105.

2. Lev Manovich, "The Practice of Everyday (Media) Life: From Mass Consumption to Mass Cultural Production?" *Critical Inquiry* 35, no. 2 (2009): 319–31.

3. David Balzer, *Curationism: How Curating Took Over the Art World – And Everything Else* (Toronto: Coach House Books, 2014), 121.

4. Simon Reynolds, *Retromania: Pop Culture's Addiction to Its Own Past* (London: Faber and Faber, 2011); Jim Collins, *Bring on the Books for Everybody: How Literary Culture Became Popular Culture* (Durham, NC: Duke University Press, 2010); M. J. Robinson, *Television on Demand: Curatorial Culture and the Transformation of TV* (London: Bloomsbury, 2017).

5. Erin La Cour and Rik Spanjers, "Ingratiation, Appropriation, Rebellion: Comics' Sociability in the Milieux of Art and Literature," *Image [&] Narrative* 17, no. 4 (2016): 1.

6. See in particular the chapter on Robert Crumb in Beaty and Woo, *The Greatest Comic Book of All Time*, chapter 3.

7. Jan Baetens, "Stories and Storytelling in the Era of Graphic Narrative," in *Stories*, ed. Ian Christie and Annie van den Oever (Amsterdam: Amsterdam University Press, 2018), 33; Beaty, *Comics versus Art*.

8. Jean-Paul Gabilliet, "Reading Facsimile Reproductions of Original Artwork: The Comics Fan as Connoisseur," *Image [&] Narrative* 17, no. 4 (2016): 16–25.

9. Beaty and Woo, *The Greatest Comic Book of All Time*, 37.

10. Beaty, *Comics versus Art*, 13.

11. Baetens and Frey, *The Graphic Novel*, 225.

12. Kim Munson, "Forming a Visual Canon: Comics in Museums," in *The Secret Origins of Comics Studies*, ed. Matthew J. Smith and Randy Duncan (New York: Routledge, 2017), 226–39.

13. Anna Brzyski, "Introduction: Canons and Art History," in *Partisan Canons*, ed. Anna Brzyski (Durham, NC: Duke University Press, 2007), 3.

14. John Carlin, Paul Karasik, and Brian Walker, eds., *Masters of American Comics* (Los Angeles, CA/New Haven, CT: Hammer Museum/Yale University Press, 2005).

15. Beaty, *Comics versus Art*, 198.

16. Jean-Matthieu Méon, "Fragmenter, matérialiser. Prises en charge de la matérialité de la bande dessinée par l'exposition," *Comicalités*, December 21, 2019, §1, http://journals .openedition.org/comicalites/3711, last accessed October 22, 2022.

17. Jeet Heer quoted in Munson, "Forming a Visual Canon."

18. Spiegelman, *MetaMaus*, 105.

19. Alvin Buenaventura, ed., *The Art of Daniel Clowes: Modern Cartoonist* (Seattle, WA: Fantagraphics Books, 2012); Spiegelman, *Co-Mix*.

20. Beaty, *Comics versus Art*.

21. Jenkins, "Archival, Ephemeral, and Residual," 306.

22. Beaty and Woo, *The Greatest Comic Book of All Time*.

23. Ibid., 94–95.

24. Jean-Matthieu Méon, "Comics Exhibitions in Contemporary France: Diversity and Symbolic Ambivalence," *International Journal of Comic Art* 17, no. 1 (2015): 454.

25. Assmann, "Canon and Archive," 98.

26. Ibid., 106.

27. Ibid., 101.

28. Hans Ulrich Obrist, *Ways of Curating* (London: Penguin, 2014); Balzer, *Curationism*; Paul O'Neill, "The Curatorial Turn: From Practice to Discourse," in *Issues in Curating Contemporary Art and Performance*, ed. Judith Rugg and Michèle Sedgwick (Bristol: Intellect, 2007), 13–28.

29. Hubert Damisch, *L'Amour m'expose* (Geneva: Klincksieck, 2007).

30. For a survey of the "artist-curator" in the art world, see Julie Bawin, *L'Artiste commissaire: entre posture critique, jeu créatif et valeur ajoutée* (Paris: Editions des Archives Contemporaines, 2014).

31. Art Spiegelman, "Le Musée privé d'Art Spiegelman," *Cité internationale de la bande dessinée*, April 2014, www.citebd.org/spip.php?article3385, accessed October 22, 2022.

32. The *Co-Mix* retrospective of Spiegelman's own work was organized separately, managed by different organizers and curators. It took place in the exhibition space of the Vaisseau Mœbius, facing the CIBDI across the Charente river.

33. Interview with Thierry Groensteen, January 23, 2017, Angoulême.

34. Florian Moine, "Construire la légitimité culturelle du Neuvième Art: Le musée de la bande dessinée d'Angoulême," *Belphégor* 17, no. 1 (2019): 1–13.

35. Florian Moine, "Bande dessinée et patrimoine. Histoire du Musée de la bande dessinée d'Angoulême (1983–2010)" (unpublished MA thesis, Université Paris 1 Panthéon-Sorbonne, 2013), 141–42.

36. Thierry Groensteen, *La Bande dessinée: son histoire et ses maîtres* (Paris/Angoulême: Skira Flammarion/Cité internationale de la bande dessinée et de l'image, 2009).

37. Interview with Thierry Groensteen, January 23, 2017, Angoulême.

38. Groensteen, *La Bande dessinée: son histoire et ses maîtres.*

39. The breadth of choice from the CIBDI's archive was further constrained by the strict conservation policy they abide by, which entails that each item that is displayed for three months needs to "rest" in the archive for three years.

40. Robb, "Bill Blackbeard."

41. The canonical position that these cartoonists occupy in fan histories of comics still guides the editorial line of patrimonial collections such as IDW's Library of American Comics.

42. Art Spiegelman and Chip Kidd, *Jack Cole and Plastic Man: Forms Stretched to Their Limits* (San Francisco, CA: Chronicle Books, 2001).

43. John Benson, David Kasakove, and Art Spiegelman, "An Examination of 'Master Race,'" *Squa Tront* 6 (1975).

44. Art Spiegelman, "Commix: An Idiosyncratic Historical and Aesthetic Overview," *Print* 42, no. 6 (1988): 61–96.

45. Art Spiegelman, *Comix, Graphics, Essays & Scraps. From Maus to Now to MAUS to Now* (New York: Raw Books/Sellerio, 1998), 78.

46. Ibid.

47. Beaty and Woo, *The Greatest Comic Book of All Time*, 94–95.

48. Alfred Bergdoll and Art Spiegelman, "Art Spiegelman," in *Art Spiegelman: Conversations*, ed. Joseph Witek (Jackson: University Press of Mississippi, 2007), 17.

49. The videos were shot, directed, and edited by the Canadian comics scholar Jacques Samson (Lux Pictoria, Montreal).

50. Simon Grennan, "Misrecognizing Misrecognition: The Capacity to Influence in the Milieux of Comics and Fine Art," *Image [&] Narrative* 17, no. 4 (2016): 5–15.

51. Jenkins, "Archival, Ephemeral, and Residual," 304.

52. George Gene Gustines, "'Master Race' Original Art Sells for $600,000," *The New York Times*, November 16, 2018, www.nytimes.com/2018/11/16/arts/master-race-comic-book-sold.html, last accessed October 22, 2022.

53. David Filipi and Jenny E. Robb, "'Through the Eyes of the Cartoonist.' Gallery Guide to *Eye of the Cartoonist: Daniel Clowes's Selections from Comics History* and *Modern Cartoonist: The Art of Daniel Clowes*" (Wexner Center for the Arts, 2014).

54. Svetlana Alpers, "The Museum as a Way of Seeing," in *Exhibiting Cultures: The Poetics and Politics of Museum Display*, ed. Steven Lavine (Washington, DC: Smithsonian Institution Press, 1991), 27.

55. Christian Rosset, "Tenir le mur," *Neuvième Art* 15 (2009): 166–75.

56. W. J. T. Mitchell and Art Spiegelman, "Public Conversation: What the %$#! Happened to Comics?" *Critical Inquiry* 40, no. 3 (2014): 20–35.

57. Email correspondence with Daniel Clowes, September 12, 2016.

58. Beaty and Woo, *The Greatest Comic Book of All Time*, 23.

59. Daniel Clowes, "Introduction," in *Nancy Is Happy*, ed. Ernie Bushmiller (Seattle, WA: Fantagraphics Books, 2012), n.p.

60. Daniel Clowes, *Ice Haven* (New York: Pantheon Books, 2005).

61. Daniel Clowes, "Modern Cartoonist," *Eightball* 18 (1997): insert.

62. Pizzino, *Arresting Development*, 4.

63. Clowes, *Ice Haven*; Daniel Clowes, *Wilson* (New York: Pantheon Books, 2010).

64. Judith Schlanger, *Le neuf, le différent et le déjà-là: une exploration de l'influence* (Paris: Hermann, 2014), 209.

CHAPTER 3 REPRINTING

1. Ian Gordon, *Ben Katchor: Conversations* (Jackson: University Press of Mississippi, 2018), 124.

2. Ann Rigney, "Portable Monuments: Literature, Cultural Memory, and the Case of Jeanie Deans," *Poetics Today* 25, no. 2 (June 1, 2004): 361–96.

3. Seth, "Creating a Personal Vernacular Canadian Design Style," *Devil's Artisan* 69 (2011): 39.

4. Here a true *lieu de mémoire* in the sense of Pierre Nora; see "Between Memory and History: Les Lieux de Mémoire." It is important to signal that Seth's relationship to Canadian identity stays far from reactionary nationalist ideologies and is perhaps best described as open and "quietly Canadian"; see Daniel Marrone, *Forging the Past: Seth and the Art of Memory* (Jackson: University Press of Mississippi, 2016), 163.

5. Erwin Panofsky, "The History of Art as a Humanistic Discipline," in *Meaning in the Visual Arts: Papers in and on Art History* (Garden City, NY: Doubleday Anchor Books, 1955), 1–26.

6. Guillory, "Monuments and Documents," 27.

7. Ibid., 25.

8. Beaty and Woo, *The Greatest Comic Book of All Time*, 92.

9. Daniel Stein, "'Mummified Objects': Superhero Comics in the Digital Age," *Journal of Graphic Novels and Comics* 7, no. 3 (2016): 283–92.

10. Marie-Ève Thérenty, "Pour une poétique historique du support," *Romantisme* 143 (2009): 109–15. For a thorough book history approach to comics, see Lesage, *L'Effet livre*.

11. Following studies of diverse reprints such as Jan Baetens, "La livraison versus le livre: Une réédition singulière de *Terry et les Pirates*," *Espressione e Contenuto* 7, no. 13 (2013): 23–38.

12. Emmanuël Souchier, "Formes et pouvoirs de l'énonciation éditoriale," *Communication et langages* 154, no. 1 (2007): 26.

13. See for instance Robert C. Harvey, "Reprint Revolution," *The Comics Journal* 153 (1992): 121–25.

14. See, although in an art-historical context, Bruno Latour and Adam Lowe, "The Migration of the Aura or How to Explore the Original through Its Facsimiles," in

Switching Codes. Thinking Through Digital Technology in the Humanities and the Arts, ed. Thomas Bartscherer (Chicago, IL: University of Chicago Press, 2011), 275–97.

15. Jules Feiffer, *The Great Comic Book Heroes* (New York: Dial Press, 1965).

16. Hugo Frey and Jan Baetens, "Comics Culture and Roy Lichtenstein Revisited: Analysing a Forgotten 'Feedback Loop,'" *Art History* 42, no. 1 (2019): 141.

17. Ibid.

18. Sylvain Lesage, *Publier la bande dessinée: les éditeurs franco-belges et l'album, 1950–1990* (Villeurbanne: Presses de l'Enssib, 2018), 225.

19. Jared Gardner, "Before the Underground: Jay Lynch, Art Spiegelman, Skip Williamson and the Fanzine Culture of the Early 1960s," *Inks: The Journal of the Comics Studies Society* 1, no. 1 (2017): 75–84. An account of Gelman's position at Topps can be found in essays written by ex-workers: Bhob Stewart, "Bubbling Over," *Blab!* 3 (1988): 20–35; Art Spiegelman, "Wacky Days," in *Wacky Packages*, ed. Charles Kochman (New York: Abrams, 2008).

20. See Woody Gelman, "A Nostalgic Vignette" (on T. S. Sullivant and Milt Gross), *Help!* 23 (1965): 32–35.

21. Art Spiegelman, ed., "Noble Efforts," *Nostalgia Comics* 1 (1970): 30–35. The selection includes early strips by George McManus, Ken Kling, Carl Ed, Gene Byrnes, and Billy DeBeck.

22. Art Spiegelman and Bill Griffith, "The Arcade Archives," *Arcade* 1, no. 4 (1975): 41–44.

23. For a perfect example of the importance of studying magazines in the history of American comics, which still remain largely unmapped, see Nicolas Labarre, *Heavy Metal, l'autre Métal Hurlant* (Bordeaux: Presses Universitaires de Bordeaux, 2017).

24. One of the first reprints of *Flash Gordon* in France, published by Serg in 1968, is directly based on the Nostalgia Press reprint of 1967, borrowing its layout and design. Gelman is also frequently cited in the various reprint experiments of newspaper comics done by the Amsterdam-based underground Real Free Press.

25. Gabilliet, *Of Comics and Men*, 304.

26. On the peritextual uses of the graphic novel label in the 1970s, see Jean-Matthieu Méon, "Introduire le graphic novel, une ambition circonscrite: les premiers usages nord-américains de l'étiquette et leur péritexte," *Revue française d'études américaines* 151 (2017): 176–93.

27. Williams, *Dreaming the Graphic Novel*, 21.

28. Campbell, *Alec*, 243.

29. Hatfield, *Alternative Comics*, 21. On the history of specialized comic book shops, see also Dan Gearino, *Comic Shop: The Retail Mavericks Who Gave Us a New Geek Culture* (Athens: Swallow Press/Ohio University Press, 2017).

30. Will Straw, "Embedded Memories," in *Residual Media*, ed. Charles R. Acland (Minneapolis: University of Minnesota Press, 2007), 5.

31. Hatfield, *Alternative Comics*, 24.

32. Pustz, *Comic Book Culture*.

33. First in 1973 and 1974, in magazine collaborations with James Warren, then as comic books from 1977 to 1992.

34. For a comparison with the Franco-Belgian situation in the 1970s, where small publishing stores played a key role in constituting comics as heritage, see Lesage, *Publier la bande dessinée*, 240–70.

35. Gibson, *Remembered Reading*, 194.

36. Beaty, "The Recession and the American Comic Book Industry."

37. A good example is the progress-oriented periodization of comics history in terms of "age"; see Woo, "An Age-Old Problem."

38. The phrase is borrowed from an essay about Michel Deligne's vintage comics shop, one of the first establishments to retail old comics in 1970s Brussels; Philippe Capart, "Store Memory," in *Comics Memory: Archives and Styles*, ed. Maaheen Ahmed and Benoît Crucifix (New York: Palgrave, 2018), 277–80.

39. Beaty, "The Recession and the American Comic Book Industry," 204.

40. Fantagraphics is distributed by W.W. Norton and Drawn & Quarterly by Macmillan (USA) and Raincoast Books (Canada). See Hatfield's update of his argument: Charles Hatfield, "Do Independent Comics Still Exist in US and Canada?" in *La bande dessinée en dissidence alternative, indépendance, auto-édition [Comics in Dissent: Alternative, Independence, Self-Publishing]*, ed. Christophe Dony, Tanguy Habrand, and Gert Meesters (Liège: Presses Universitaires de Liège, 2014), 59–77. On the marketing strategy of Drawn & Quarterly, see Bart Beaty, "Chris Oliveros, Drawn and Quarterly, and the Expanded Definition of the Graphic Novel," in *The Cambridge History of the Graphic Novel*, ed. Jan Baetens, Hugo Frey, and Stephen E. Tabachnick (Cambridge: Cambridge University Press, 2018), 426–42.

41. Hatfield, *Alternative Comics*, 162.

42. For an original extension of this argument, see Pizzino, *Arresting Development*.

43. See the catalog listing included in Tom Spurgeon and Michael Dean, eds., *We Told You So: Comics as Art* (Seattle, WA: Fantagraphics Books, 2016).

44. Spurgeon and Dean, 473–91.

45. Sales numbers from Brian Hibbs, "Tilting at Windmills: Looking at BookScan, 2004," *The Beat*, February 2005, www.comicsbeat.com/tilting-at-windmills-archive/tilting-at-windmills-looking-at-bookscan-2004/, last accessed October 22, 2022.

46. It is thus a "mediasphere" in which agents have become key players in what gets adapted – and thus also in terms of reprints; see Simone Murray, *The Adaptation Industry: The Cultural Economy of Contemporary Literary Adaptation* (New York: Routledge, 2012), chapter 2. For a survey of the role of different intermediaries in comics publishing, see Jean-Matthieu Méon, "Logiques et pratiques de l'intermédiation dans l'édition de bande dessinée en France," in *La culture et ses intermédiaires*, ed. Laurent Jeanpierre and Olivier Roueff (Paris: Éditions des archives contemporaines, 2014). Given the orientation of alternative comics publishers toward the literary market, literary agents have started to play an increasingly important role in comics publishing (see the New York-based literary agency Am-Book, for instance).

47. Chris Anderson, *The Long Tail: Why the Future of Business Is Selling Less of More* (New York: Hyperion, 2006). On reprints in the 2000s book business, see Alain Vaillant, "L'édition

des textes du passé: enjeu théorique et marché éditorial en l'an 2000," *Littérature* 124 (2001): 98–108.

48. Hatfield, *Alternative Comics*, 154.

49. For an insightful account of the practical issues involved in marketing reprint series, see Tracy Hurren's MA thesis, based on interviews with Peggy Burns and Chris Oliveros; Hurren, "The Golden Age of Reprints," 21–23.

50. To give just one example: Fantagraphics only got around to publishing three volumes in its projected "complete dailies" series of Ernie Bushmiller's *Nancy*.

51. An agenda explicitly articulated in the house's internal history; see Spurgeon and Dean, *We Told You So*.

52. Björn-Olav Dozo, "De la logique de guerre à la patrimonialisation. Faire catalogue en faisant collection," in *L'Association. Une utopie éditoriale et esthétique*, ed. ACME (Brussels: Les Impressions Nouvelles, 2011), 37–57. "Patrimoine" can also be seen as an additional "discursive weapon" according to Bart Beaty, "The Concept of 'Patrimoine' in Contemporary Franco-Belgian Comics Production," in *History and Politics in French-Language Comics and Graphic Novels*, ed. Mark McKinney (Jackson: University Press of Mississippi, 2008), 69–93.

53. Beaty, "Chris Oliveros, Drawn and Quarterly, and the Expanded Definition of the Graphic Novel," 438.

54. Hoffman and Grace, *Seth*, 173.

55. James F. English, *The Economy of Prestige: Prizes, Awards, and the Circulation of Cultural Value* (Cambridge, MA: Harvard University Press, 2005).

56. Heer, "Inventing Cartooning Ancestors," 5.

57. By the 2000s, the format of the alternative comic book had pretty much disappeared; see Hatfield, "Do Independent Comics Still Exist in US and Canada?" Graphic novel creators have, accordingly, found alternative ways to segment and serialize their works; see Benoît Crucifix, "From Loose to Boxed Fragments and Back Again. Seriality and Archive in Chris Ware's *Building Stories*," *Journal of Graphic Novels and Comics* 9, no. 1 (2018): 3–22; Raphaël Baroni, "Le chapitrage dans le roman graphique américain et la bande dessinée européenne: une segmentation précaire," *Cahiers de Narratologie* 34 (2018), https://doi.org/10.4000/narratologie.8594, last accessed October 22, 2022.

58. Baetens and Frey, *The Graphic Novel*, 155.

59. Côme Martin, "Les Livres-mondes de Chris Ware, ou la tentation de l'homogène," *Formules* 17 (2013): 69–88. On the notion of perigraphy, see Jan Baetens and Pascal Lefèvre, *Pour une lecture moderne de la bande dessinée* (Brussels: Centre belge de la bande dessinée, 1993); chapter translated into English as "The Work and Its Surround," in Ann Miller and Bart Beaty, eds., *French Comics Theory Reader* (Leuven: Leuven University Press, 2014), 191–200. For an updated take on the paratext of graphic novels (where the notion of "perigraphy" is no longer maintained, however), see Baetens and Frey, *The Graphic Novel*, 153–56. I have retained the use of perigraphy to strengthen the visual and graphic dimension, whenever most relevant.

60. Baetens and Frey, *The Graphic Novel*, 157–61. See also Gene Kannenberg Jr., "The Comics of Chris Ware: Text, Image, and Visual Narrative Strategies," in *The Language*

of Comics: Word and Image, ed. Robin Varnum and Christina T. Gibbons (Jackson: University Press of Mississippi, 2001), 174–97.

61. Emma Tinker, "Manuscript in Print: The Materiality of Alternative Comics," *Literature Compass* 4, no. 4 (2007): 1169–82.

62. Benoît Peeters, *Lire la bande dessinée* (Paris: Flammarion, 2003), 155–57.

63. Collins, *Bring on the Books for Everybody*; Alexander Starre, *Metamedia: American Book Fictions and Literary Print Culture after Digitization* (Iowa City: University of Iowa Press, 2015).

64. Spiegelman and Kidd, *Jack Cole and Plastic Man*.

65. Chip Kidd, ed., *Peanuts: The Art of Charles M. Schulz* (New York: Pantheon Books, 2001).

66. Baetens and Frey, *The Graphic Novel*, 200. For a general (albeit slightly dated) overview of Chip Kidd's career with an emphasis on his book covers, see Véronique Vienne, *Chip Kidd* (London: Laurence King, 2003).

67. In this sense, it fits within the larger panel of issues dressed up in Jan Baetens, "Adaptation: A Writerly Strategy?" in *Comics and Adaptation*, ed. Benoît Mitaine, David Roche, and Isabelle Schmitt-Pitiot, trans. Aarnoud Rommens (Jackson: University Press of Mississippi, 2018), 31–46.

68. Michel Foucault, "What Is an Author?" in *The Foucault Reader*, ed. Paul Rabinow (New York: Pantheon Books, 1984), 101–20.

69. Seth, "Creating a Personal Vernacular Canadian Design Style," 7.

70. Dorothy Parker, *The Portable Dorothy Parker*, ed. Marion Meade (London: Penguin, 2006); Stephen Leacock, *Sunshine Sketches of a Little Town* (New York: Skyhorse, 2013).

71. See the interviews in Hoffman and Grace, *Seth*.

72. Seth, "John Stanley's Teen Trilogy: Exposing Forgotten Comics History," *The Comics Journal* 238 (2001): 39–51.

73. Beaty, *Comics versus Art*.

74. Hoffman and Grace, *Seth*, 141. Perhaps as a result of this criticism, Fantagraphics would adopt a much more colorful cover design for the paperback editions of the *Complete Peanuts*.

75. Designers are indeed part of his large crowd of "invisible workers" that compose the comics world; see Casey Brienza and Paddy Johnston, eds., *Cultures of Comics Work* (New York: Palgrave Macmillan, 2016).

76. Hoffman and Grace, *Seth*, 143.

77. Baetens and Frey, *The Graphic Novel*, 221.

78. Jared Gardner and Ian Gordon, eds., *The Comics of Charles Schulz: The Good Grief of Modern Life* (Jackson: University Press of Mississippi, 2017).

79. Beaty, *Comics versus Art*, 93.

80. See the Peanuts Studio blog: www.peanutsstudio.com/about, last accessed October 22, 2022.

81. Charles Hatfield, "Redrawing the Comic-Strip Child: Charles M. Schulz's as Cross-Writing," in *The Oxford Handbook of Children's Literature*, ed. Lynne Vallonne and Julia Mickenberg (Oxford: Oxford University Press, 2011), 178.

82. On the collaboration between Gary Groth, Seth, and Jean Schulz and her associates, see Spurgeon and Dean, *We Told You So*, 486–91. On the mourning work implicated by postmortem copyright terms (with its attendant dangers of deriving toward "legal mummification and undeath"), see Paul K. Saint-Amour, *The Copywrights: Intellectual Property and the Literary Imagination* (Ithaca, NY: Cornell University Press, 2003), 202–15.

83. Beaty, *Comics versus Art*, 95.

84. Seth, "Creating a Personal Vernacular Canadian Design Style," 33.

85. Hatfield, "Redrawing the Comic-Strip Child," 171.

86. Schneider, *What Happens When Nothing Happens*.

87. Candida Rifkind, "The Biotopographies of Seth's *George Sprott (1894–1975)*," in *Material Cultures in Canada*, ed. Thomas Allen and Jennifer Blair (Waterloo, ONT: Wilfrid Laurier University Press, 2015), 226.

88. Three volumes published by Fantagraphics so far, starting in 2013.

89. "I want this series to appear as if it was of King's own devising; I think this sensibility applies more readily to King's work than to Herriman's. Besides, I'd never presume to pass off a mark of my hand as one of George Herriman's. I think King, however, who used countless assistants, wouldn't mind in the least; his concern was for readability and story, I believe"; Ware quoted in Ivan Brunetti, ed., *An Anthology of Graphic Fiction, Cartoons, & True Stories* (New Haven, CT: Yale University Press, 2006), 238.

90. See Philip Nel, "Crockett Johnson and the Purple Crayon: A Life in Art," *Comic Art* 5 (2004): 8.

91. Hatfield, "Redrawing the Comic-Strip Child," 171.

92. Futura is a key example of the new typography elaborated in the interwar period in Germany: Renner taught at two technical schools in Munich where he collaborated with Jan Tschichold, whose principles about *Neue Typographie* would mark a key moment, advocating for a new approach to book design that was further commanded by his commitment to crafting cheap, accessible objects; see Robin Kinross, *Modern Typography: An Essay in Critical History* (London: Hyphen Press, 1992), 114–28.

93. "Spotting blacks" is cartoonist slang for the distribution of solid black areas; see Karasik and Newgarden, *How to Read Nancy*, 130–31.

94. These elements might seem like nit-picking details, but as soon as one chips at them, the whole graphic edifice falls to the ground, as appears by looking at the reworked cover for the French translation of the volume by Actes Sud/L'An 2 in 2015: it dropped the Futura for the title for Gill Sans and changed the color to a subdued brown tint, losing both the continuity between text and image, between graphic and typographic styles, as well as the connection to the historical reprints.

95. Dan Nadel, ed., *Art Out of Time: Unknown Comics Visionaries, 1900–1969* (New York: Abrams, 2006).

96. Gardner, *Projections*, 42.

97. Daniel Stein and Lukas Etter, "Long-Length Serials in the Golden Age of Comic Strips: Production and Reception," in *The Cambridge History of the Graphic Novel*, ed. Jan Baetens, Hugo Frey, and Stephen E. Tabachnick (Cambridge: Cambridge University Press, 2018), 47.

98. Gardner, *Projections*, 42–45.

99. Jared Gardner, "A History of the Narrative Comic Strip," in *From Comic Strips to Graphic Novels: Contributions to the Theory and History of the Graphic Narrative*, ed. Daniel Stein and Jean-Noël Thon (New York/Berlin: De Gruyter, 2013), 245–46. See also Waugh, *The Comics*, chapter 7; Robert C. Harvey, *The Art of the Funnies: An Aesthetic History* (Jackson: University Press of Mississippi, 1994), chapter 4. For a detailed examination of the "serial pleasures" and active engagement with audiences that these strips created, through a close look at *The Gumps*, see Gardner, *Projections*, chapter 2.

100. The phrase is borrowed from Michael Warner, *Publics and Counterpublics* (New York: Zone Books, 2010), quoted in Will Straw, "Circulation," in *A Companion to Critical and Cultural Theory*, ed. Imre Szeman, Sarah Blacker, and Justin Sully (Chichester: Wiley, 2017), 429.

101. Mediagenic is a concept coined by Philippe Marion; see Philippe Marion, "Narratologie médiatique et médiagénie des récits," *Recherches en communication* 7 (1997): 61–88; André Gaudreault and Philippe Marion, *The End of Cinema? A Medium in Crisis in the Digital Age*, Film and Culture series (New York: Columbia University Press, 2015), 169–79.

102. For an overview of the merchandising and King's involvement, see Chris Ware, "Skeezix for Sale: A Semi-Comprehensive Catalog of the Merchandise of Gasoline Alley," in *Walt & Skeezix: 1925 & 1926*, by Frank King, ed. Jeet Heer, Chris Oliveros, and Chris Ware (Montreal: Drawn & Quarterly, 2007), 24–61. Ware notes the ambiguities of serializing a strip whose characters grow old with their readers (and hence often outgrow the merchandised dolls and toys).

103. Frank King, *Skeezix and Uncle Walt* (New York: Reilly & Lee, 1924). Save for one exception as the *Chicago Tribune* itself issued in 1929 a collection of early automobile gags from the early years of *Gasoline Alley*, allegedly as a way of targeting an adult male readership (by contrast with the children readers that the novelizations of Reilly & Lee were aimed at). By comparison, the few publishers doing collections of comic strips, such as Cupples & Leons or Landfield-Kupfer, reprinted some continuity strips such as *The Gumps* or *Mutt and Jeff.*

104. Promotional address for WGN Radio in 1924, reproduced in Frank King, *Walt & Skeezix: 1923 & 1924*, ed. Jeet Heer, Chris Oliveros, and Chris Ware (Montreal: Drawn & Quarterly, 2006), ixx.

105. Drawn & Quarterly's experiment with that anthological format would last only three years, with three volumes (numbered 3 to 5), but it undoubtedly helped the publisher along its path from periodical comic book to graphic novel publishers, with the company signing its *Selling Graphic Novels in the Book Trade: A Drawn & Quarterly Manifesto* in 2003. See Sean Rogers and Jeet Heer, "A History of Drawn & Quarterly," in *Drawn and Quarterly: Twenty-Five Years of Contemporary Cartooning, Comics, and Graphic Novels*, ed. Tom Devlin et al. (Montreal: Drawn & Quarterly, 2016), 26–29.

106. Chris Ware had already explored this technique in an experimental short story, where the visual narrative is a pastiche of 1930s superhero comic books; Chris Ware, "I Guess," *RAW* 2, no. 3 (1991).

107. Chris Ware, "Frank King," in *Drawn and Quarterly*, vol. 3 (Montreal: Drawn & Quarterly, 2000).

108. Benjamin Widiss, "Autobiography with Two Heads: Quimby the Mouse," in *The Comics of Chris Ware: Drawing Is a Way of Thinking*, ed. David M. Ball and Martha B. Kuhlman (Jackson: University Press of Mississippi, 2010), 168.

109. Jeet Heer, "Introduction," in *Walt & Skeezix: 1921 & 1922*, by Frank King, ed. Jeet Heer, Chris Oliveros, and Chris Ware (Montreal: Drawn & Quarterly, 2006), 9.

110. Bart Beaty, *Unpopular Culture: Transforming the European Comic Book in the 1990s* (Toronto: University of Toronto Press, 2007).

111. Heer, "Introduction," 43.

112. On this form, see Isaac Cates, "The Diary Comic," in *Graphic Subjects: Critical Essays on Autobiography and Graphic Novels*, ed. Michael A. Chaney (Madison: University of Wisconsin Press, 2011), 209–26.

113. Heer, "Inventing Cartooning Ancestors," 10.

114. Gilbert Seldes, *The Seven Lively Arts* (New York: Harper & Brothers, 1924); Gilbert Seldes, "The 'Vulgar' Comic Strip," in *A Comics Studies Reader*, ed. Jeet Heer and Kent Worcester (Jackson: University Press of Mississippi, 2009), 49.

115. Schneider, *What Happens When Nothing Happens*.

116. Eddie Campbell and Dirk Deppey, "The Eddie Campbell Interview," *The Comics Journal* (2006), 83.

117. Stein and Etter, "Long-Length Serials in the Golden Age of Comic Strips: Production and Reception," 55.

118. Baetens and Frey, *The Graphic Novel*, 232.

CHAPTER 4 FORGING

1. Hoffman and Grace, *Seth*, 175.

2. Schlanger, *Présence des œuvres perdues*, 111, my translation.

3. Dylan Horrocks, *Hicksville* (Toronto: Black Eye Comics, 1998).

4. Sonny Liew, *The Art of Charlie Chan Hock Chye* (Singapore: Epigram Books, 2015).

5. Charissa Yong, "NAC Pulled Grant from Comic as It 'Potentially Undermines the Authority of the Government,'" *The Straits Times*, June 3, 2015. It should nevertheless be noted that the book was also well-received in Singapore and that the author also received other forms of state support that were not jeopardized by the content of the book.

6. Smolderen, *The Origins of Comics*, 129.

7. Ibid., 56.

8. Ibid., 129.

9. Spiegelman, *MetaMaus*, 189.

10. Jan Baetens and Charlotte Pylyser, "Comics and Time," in *The Routledge Companion to Comics*, ed. Frank Bramlett, Roy T. Cook, and Aaron Meskin (London: Routledge, 2016), 308.

11. Will Elder, Bernard Krigstein, and Harvey Kurtzman, "Bringing Back Father!" *Mad* 17 (1954).

12. Umberto Eco, "The Myth of Superman," trans. Nathalie Chilton, *Diacritics* 2, no. 1 (1972): 19.

13. Earle Doud and Wallace Wood, "The Yellowed Kids Department: If Comic Strip Characters were as Old as Their Strips," *Mad* 72 (1962): 26.

14. Marshall McLuhan, *Understanding Media: Extensions of Man* (New York: McGraw-Hill, 1964), 166.

15. This idea also played out within mainstream comics, with the development of "revisionary" superhero narratives such as Frank Miller's fifty-five-year-old Batman in *The Dark Knight Returns* (DC, 1986); see Geoff Klock, "The Revisionary Superhero Narrative," in *The Superhero Reader*, ed. Charles Hatfield, Jeet Heer, and Kent Worcester (Jackson: University Press of Mississippi, 2013), 116–35. For a historical overview of boredom and the everyday in alternative comics, see Schneider, *What Happens When Nothing Happens*, chapter 2.

16. Hillary L. Chute, *Disaster Drawn: Visual Witness, Comics, and Documentary Form* (Cambridge, MA: Belknap Press, 2016), 96–97.

17. Elder quoted in Bill Schelly, *Harvey Kurtzman, The Man Who Created Mad and Revolutionized Humor in America: A Biography* (Seattle, WA: Fantagraphics Books, 2015), 261.

18. W. J. T. Mitchell and Art Spiegelman, "Public Conversation: What the %$#! Happened to Comics?" *Critical Inquiry* 40, no. 3 (2014): 22. For a reading of Spiegelman's thoughts on "chicken fat" relating to questions of cultural status, see Pizzino, *Arresting Development*, 123.

19. Maggie Gray similarly describes chicken fat from an intertextual perspective, particularly in the way *Mad* influenced Alan Moore's work; see Maggie Gray, *Alan Moore, out from the Underground: Cartooning, Performance, and Dissent* (New York: Palgrave Macmillan, 2017), 164.

20. Daniel Clowes, "A Mozart of Zaniness," in *Will Elder: The Mad Playboy of Art*, ed. Gary Groth and Greg Sadowski (Seattle, WA: Fantagraphics Books, 2003), 2.

21. Baetens and Frey, *The Graphic Novel*, 19.

22. Clowes, *Ice Haven*.

23. Emil Ferris, *My Favorite Thing Is Monsters* (Seattle, WA: Fantagraphics Books, 2017).

24. Rachel Miller, "Keep Out, or Else: Girls' Diaries in Comics," *Public Books*, May 4, 2018, www.publicbooks.org/keep-out-or-else-girls-diaries-in-comics/, last accessed October 22, 2022.

25. Seth, *It's a Good Life, If You Don't Weaken* (Montreal: Drawn & Quarterly, 1996); Seth, *The G.N.B Double C: The Great Northern Brotherhood of Canadian Cartoonists* (Montreal: Drawn and Quarterly, 2011).

26. Marrone, *Forging the Past*; Dominick Grace, "An Alternative History of Canadian Cartoonists," *International Journal of Comic Art* 17, no. 2 (2015): 133–61; Dominick Grace, "Seth's It's a Good Life, If You Don't Weaken as Anti-Nostalgia," in *The Canadian Alternative: Cartoonists, Comics, and Graphic Novels*, ed. Dominick Grace and

Eric Hoffman (Jackson: University Press of Mississippi, 2017), 150–61; Hoffman and Grace, *Seth.*

27. Baetens and Frey, *The Graphic Novel,* 141.

28. Letter from James Kochalka to Seth, reproduced in the letters column of *Palookaville* 6 (Montreal: Drawn & Quarterly, 1994).

29. For an insightful look at the way Seth portrays himself in relationship to his peers, in the construction of a "Toronto School" of comics, see Bart Beaty, "Selective Mutual Reinforcement in the Comics of Chester Brown, Joe Matt, and Seth," in *Graphic Subjects: Critical Essays on Autobiography and Graphic Novels,* ed. Michael A. Chaney (Madison: University of Wisconsin Press, 2011), 247–51.

30. Following the argument advanced by Linda Hutcheon, *A Poetics of Postmodernism: History, Theory, Fiction* (New York: Routledge, 1988).

31. Marrone, *Forging the Past,* 165.

32. Grace, "Seth's *It's a Good Life, If You Don't Weaken* as Anti-Nostalgia."

33. For a comprehensive overview of nostalgia debates, especially as they relate to comics, see Giorgio Busi Rizzi, "Always at Home in the Past: Exploring Nostalgia in the Graphic Novel" (PhD thesis, University of Bologna and KU Leuven, 2018). For a more general media perspective on nostalgia, see Katharina Niemeyer, ed., *Media and Nostalgia: Yearning for the Past, Present and Future* (New York: Palgrave Macmillan, 2014).

34. Busi Rizzi, "Portrait of the Artist as a Nostalgic."

35. Richard Dyer, *Pastiche* (New York: Routledge, 2007), 4.

36. Busi Rizzi, "Portrait of the Artist as a Nostalgic," 33.

37. Cole Closser, *Little Tommy Lost: Book One* (Toronto: Koyama Press, 2013).

38. Andrei Molotiu, "Art Comics," in *The Routledge Companion to Comics,* ed. Frank Bramlett, Roy T. Cook, and Aaron Meskin (London: Routledge, 2016), 119–27. The convergence of comics, zines, pop culture, and contemporary art in the Koyama Press is for instance evident in its ties with the Toronto-based Wowee Zonk collective, which mixes comics, illustration, and painting in the continuity of other, older collectives such as the Hairy Who or Fort Thunder. It can be recognized in the context of "lowbrow art" or "pervasive art," favoring an intermedial exchange between comics, art, and popular culture, finely detailed in Beaty, *Comics versus Art,* chapter 6.

39. Several Koyama cartoonists have contributed to online comics platforms such as Vice and the Nib. Social media platforms such as Tumblr, Twitter, and Instagram are also increasingly used for serializing webcomics (with an interesting impact on form: DeForge's *Leaving Richard's Valley* used a regular four-panel grid that adapts well to the constrained image display options of social media such as Instagram and Twitter).

40. For a compelling reading of DeForge's visual style, see Shiamin Kwa, "Comics at the Surface: Michael DeForge's Ant Colony," *Word & Image* 32, no. 4 (2016): 340–59.

41. Brett Camper, "Retro Reflexivity: La Mulana, an 8-Bit Period Piece," in *The Video Game Theory Reader 2,* ed. Bernard Perron and Mark J. P. Wolf (London/New York: Routledge, 2009), 169–95. The concept of remediation comes from Jay David Bolter and Richard Grusin, *Remediation: Understanding New Media* (Cambridge, MA: MIT Press, 2000).

42. Camper, "Retro Reflexivity," 186.

43. Baetens and Frey, *The Graphic Novel*, 6.
44. Bolter and Grusin, *Remediation*.
45. Irina O. Rajewsky, "Intermediality, Intertextuality, and Remediation: A Literary Perspective on Intermediality," *Intermédialités* 6 (2005): 54.
46. It is thus necessary to note the republican convictions of Harold Gray, who often tried to intervene in the political debates of his time through Little Orphan Annie; which does not prevent a more progressive reading of the series, as it features a female character with considerable agency over her own situation; see Pamela Robertson Wojcik, "Little Orphan Annie as Streetwalker," in *Picturing Childhood: Youth in Transnational Comics*, ed. Mark Heimerman and Brittany Tullis (Austin: University of Texas Press, 2017), 13–29.
47. Simon Grennan, "Demonstrating Discours: Two Comic Strip Projects in Self-Constraint," *Studies in Comics* 2, no. 2 (January 5, 2012): 299.
48. Olivier Schrauwen, *My Boy* (Antwerp: Bries, 2006); Gert Meesters, "Les significations du style graphique: *Mon fiston* d'Olivier Schrauwen et *Faire semblant c'est mentir* de Dominique Goblet," *Textyles* 36/37 (2010): 215–33.
49. Gardner, *Projections*, 46–47. See also Jennifer Hayward, *Consuming Pleasures: Active Audiences and Serial Fictions from Dickens to Soap Opera* (Lexington: University Press of Kentucky, 2009), chapter 2.
50. Blurb by Tony Millionaire, hand-lettered by Closser, on the back cover of Closser, *Little Tommy Lost: Book One*.
51. Dominik Schrey, "Analogue Nostalgia and the Aesthetics of the Digital," in *Media and Nostalgia: Yearning for the Past, Present and Future*, ed. Katharina Niemeyer (New York: Palgrave Macmillan, 2014), 27–38.
52. Laura U. Marks, *Touch: Sensuous Theory and Multisensory Media* (Minneapolis: Minnesota University Press, 2002), 152.
53. Nadel, *Art Out of Time*.
54. Jean-Matthieu Méon, "Tisser d'autres liens? Pratiques éditoriales et discours critique de l'éditeur PictureBox: indépendance et champ de la bande dessinée," in *La bande dessinée en dissidence alternative, indépendance, auto-édition [Comics in Dissent: Alternative, Independence, Self-Publishing]*, ed. Christophe Dony, Tanguy Habrand, and Gert Meesters (Liège: Presses Universitaires de Liège, 2014), 84.
55. Frank Santoro, "Herriman Riff," *The Comics Journal* (January 7, 2016), www.tcj.com/herriman-riff/, last accessed October 22, 2022; Campbell, *The Goat Getters*.

CHAPTER 5 SWIPING

1. Mitchell and Spiegelman, "Comics as Media."
2. Todd Hignite, *In the Studio: Visits with Contemporary Cartoonists* (New Haven, CT: Yale University Press, 2006), 106.
3. Garvey, *Writing with Scissors*. On clippings as a means of compensating for the lack of comic strip reprints, see Gardner, "A History of the Narrative Comic Strip," 249.

4. The practice is not unique to comics artists naturally; other visual artists have extensively drawn from their scrapbooks and comics clippings, such as Chicago Imagist Ray Yoshida and outsider artist Henry Darger.

5. Michael Chabon, *The Amazing Adventures of Kavalier and Clay* (New York: Random House, 2000), 7–8.

6. As Burns demonstrated in his public talk at the Columbus College of Art and Design on October 15, 2016 during the Cartoon Crossroads Columbus festival.

7. See johnnytwentythree.tumblr.com, last accessed October 22, 2022; Charles Burns, *Close Your Eyes* (Marseille: Le Denier Cri, 2001); Charles Burns, *Swipe File* (Philadelphia, PA: Common Press, 2008); Charles Burns, *Love Nest* (Bordeaux: Cornélius, 2016).

8. Darcy Sullivan, "Charles Burns," *The Comics Journal* (1992): 52.

9. Beaty and Woo, *The Greatest Comic Book of All Time*, 5.

10. Diana Taylor, *The Archive and the Repertoire: Performing Cultural Memory in the Americas* (Durham, NC: Duke University Press, 2003).

11. On medium-specificity and transmediality, see also Jan Baetens, "Between Adaptation, Intermediality and Cultural Series: The Example of the Photonovel," *Artnodes* 18 (2016): 47–55.

12. Swiping, read as a form of remix, could arguably address some of the blind spots of remix studies, which tend to privilege digital culture and emphasize remix as resistance on the part of users (rather than producers). See Margie Borschke, *This Is Not a Remix: Piracy, Authenticity and Popular Music* (New York: Bloomsbury Academic, 2017).

13. Philippe Marion, *Traces en cases: travail graphique, figuration narrative et participation du lecteur* (Louvain-la-Neuve: Academia, 1993), 35. For a critical introduction to the concept, see Jan Baetens, "Revealing Traces: A New Theory of Graphic Enunciation," in *The Language of Comics: Word and Image*, ed. Robin Varnum and Christina T. Gibbons (Jackson: University Press of Mississippi, 2001), 145–55.

14. Jared Gardner, "Storylines," *SubStance* 40, no. 1 (2011): 65.

15. Lukas Etter, "Visible Hand? Subjectivity and Its Stylistic Markers in Graphic Narratives," in *Subjectivity Across Media: Interdisciplinary and Transmedial Perspectives*, ed. Maike Sarah Reinerth and Jan-Noël Thon (New York: Routledge, 2017), 92–110. The "second hand" phrase is borrowed from Antoine Compagnon, *La Seconde Main, ou, Le Travail de la citation* (Paris: Seuil, 1979).

16. Gardner, "Storylines," 66.

17. Charles Hatfield, *Hand of Fire: The Comics Art of Jack Kirby* (Jackson: University Press of Mississippi, 2012), 49.

18. Feiffer, *The Great Comic Book Heroes*, 38–41. More recently, Feiffer also wrote about his early swipes in a memoir: Jules Feiffer, *Backing into Forward: A Memoir* (Chicago, IL: University of Chicago Press, 2012), 9–12.

19. Simon Grennan, *A Theory of Narrative Drawing* (New York: Palgrave, 2017), 68–69.

20. Baetens, "Revealing Traces," 152.

21. Gérard Genette, *Palimpsests: Literature in the Second Degree*, trans. Channa Newman and Claude Doubinsky (Lincoln: University of Nebraska Press, 1997).

22. Harold Bloom, *The Anxiety of Influence: A Theory of Poetry* (Oxford: Oxford University Press, 1973); Jonathan Lethem, "The Ecstasy of Influence: A Plagiarism," *Harper's Magazine*, February 2007.

23. François Brunet, ed., *Circulation* (Chicago, IL: Terra Foundation for American Art, 2017). For an introduction to the concept of intericonicity, see Mathilde Arrivé, "L'intelligence des images – l'intericonicité, enjeux et méthodes," *E-rea* 13, no. 1 (2015), http://erea.revues.org/4620, last accessed October 22, 2022. And in the same issue, see also Nicolas Labarre, Laura Perna, and Errol Rivera, "The Circulation of Icons in Planetary – Pictures, Popular Culture and Materiality," *E-Rea* 13, no. 1 (2015), https://doi.org/10.4000/erea.4557, last accessed October 22, 2022.

24. Jussi Parikka, "Copy," in *Software Studies*, ed. Matthew Fuller (Cambridge, MA: MIT Press, 2008), 73. Parikka notes how these "copy routines" have been largely overlooked in media studies in favor of a stronger focus on copyright issues and remixing.

25. Benoît Peeters, "Between Writing and Image: A Scriptwriter's Way of Working," *European Comic Art* 3, no. 1 (2010): 113.

26. On this "inefficient" temporal economy of comics making, see Jared Gardner, "Time Under Siege," in *The Comics of Joe Sacco: Journalism in a Visual World*, ed. Daniel Worden (Jackson: University Press of Mississippi, 2016), 21–22.

27. For a more extensive explication of comics making and creative labor, see Brienza and Johnston, *Cultures of Comics Work*.

28. Wallace Wood quoted by his assistant Larry Hama in Larry Hama, "Old Ink, New Ink," in *Against the Grain: MAD Artist Wallace Wood*, ed. Bhob Steward (Raleigh, NC: TwoMorrows Publishing, 2003), 195.

29. Email correspondence with J. David Spurlock, director of the Wallace Wood Estate, July 27, 2021.

30. The fascination for the autodidact and the "self-made" cartoonist has to be nuanced, though. Despite the dearth of dedicated tracks for cartooning or comics in technical or art institutions, cartoonists regularly followed at least some form of artistic training, from correspondence courses to commercial illustration or fine art programs; see Gabilliet, *Of Comics and Men*, 159–60; Jessica Kohn, *Dessiner des petits mickeys. Une histoire sociale de la BD en France et en Belgique (1945–1968)* (Paris: Éditions de la Sorbonne, 2022).

31. Will Eisner, *The Dreamer* (Princeton, WI: Kitchen Sink Press, 1986).

32. Joseph Witek, "If a Way to the Better There Be: Excellence, Mere Competence, and the Worst Comics Ever Made," *Image [&] Narrative* 17, no. 4 (2016): 32.

33. Kidman, *Comic Books Incorporated*, 102.

34. See for instance the emblematic case of *Detective Comics* v. *Bruns Publications* (1939). In the fierce competition of the 1940s, publishers would rely on any possible transgressions, often simultaneously claiming copyright infringement (at the level of the "expression") or unfair competition (at the level of the "idea"). On the copyrightability of visual characters and side-by-side image comparisons, featuring an example of a "swipe file" comparing clipped-out panels from *Action Comics* and *Wonder Comics*, see Kidman, *Comic Books Incorporated*, 20–24.

35. Printers' Ink. "The Persistent 'Swipe' Evil," *Printers' Ink: A Journal of Advertisers* 71, no. 11 (1910): 32.

36. Bernard Joubert, *Polyepoxy: la case la plus copiée* (Brussels: Fondation Paul Cuvelier, 2016). By including a fold-out of the original panel from Paul Cuvelier and Jean Van Hamme's *Epoxy* (Paris: Losfeld, 1968), the booklet somewhat tends to inscribe this network of swipes within something of a binary original/copy model. Joubert's essay, however, does point out that the proliferating logic of this image and its exact genealogy (how a Belgian comic became a repeated swipe in the Italian studios) is complex and hard to unearth.

37. Beaty, *Comics versus Art*, 75. Forensic denotes a level of engagement and scrutiny but here differs from the narrative-oriented concept of "forensic fandom" put forward by Jason Mittell, *Complex TV: The Poetics of Contemporary Television Storytelling* (New York: New York University Press, 2015).

38. See for instance Charles N. Landon, "Collecting a Morgue," in *The Landon Course of Cartooning 1* (Cleveland, OH: Landon School, 1914); Clare Briggs, *How to Draw Cartoons* (New York/London: Harper & Brothers, 1926), 40.

39. Garvey, *Writing with Scissors*, 21.

40. Feiffer, *The Great Comic Book Heroes*, 38–41. Feiffer also recently recalled his early swipes in *Backing into Forward*, 9–12.

41. Feiffer, *The Great Comic Book Heroes*, 38.

42. Ibid., 39–41.

43. Gardner, *Projections*, 73.

44. Garvey, *Writing with Scissors*, 21.

45. De Certeau, *The Practice of Everyday Life*, 174. For its use in the context of fan studies, see Henry Jenkins, *Textual Poachers: Television Fans and Participatory Culture*, Revised (London: Routledge, 2013).

46. Fredric Wertham, *The World of Fanzines: A Special Form of Communication* (Carbondale: Southern Illinois University Press, 1973), 109.

47. Robert Boyd, "Swipe File," *The Comics Journal* 140 (1991): 28.

48. See for instance the Facebook group "Comics Swipes," managed by cartoonist and publisher Craig Yoe.

49. See Doug Singsen, "Critical Perspectives on Mainstream, Groundlevel, and Alternative Comics in *The Comics Journal*, 1977 to 1996," *Journal of Graphic Novels and Comics* 8, no. 2 (2017): 156–72.

50. Ted White, "It All Boils Down to the Editor," *The Comics Journal* 83 (1983): 31–36.

51. Hatfield, *Hand of Fire*, 9.

52. Mark Burbey, "The Trouble with Keith Giffen," *The Comics Journal* 105 (1986): 9–14.

53. Thom Powers, "Muñoz vs. Giffen: Plagiarism or Influence?," *The Comics Journal* 118 (1987): 19–20; Dan Parmenter, "To Swipe or Not to Swipe," *The Comics Journal* 109 (1986): 35; Ernie Colon, "Sticking Up for Giffen," *The Comics Journal* 116 (1987): 42–43.

54. Powers, "Muñoz vs. Giffen," 20.

55. Originally published as José Muñoz and Carlos Sampayo, "Pour quelques dessins ...,"
    trans. Dominique Grange *(À suivre)* 159 (1991). Translated into English in José Muñoz
    and Carlos Sampayo, *Alack Sinner: The Age of Disenchantment* (San Diego, CA: IDW,
    2017), 89–106.

56. On the narrative and poetic structure of *Alack Sinner*, see Erwin Dejasse, "La Musique
    silencieuse de José Muñoz et Carlos Sampayo: déconstruction des normes et lecture
    émotionnelle" (PhD thesis, University of Liège, 2015), 188.

57. Muñoz and Sampayo, *Alack Sinner*, 90.

58. See Giffen's arguments quoted in Powers, "Muñoz vs. Giffen."

59. Muñoz and Sampayo, *Alack Sinner*, 100.

60. I analyze this short story at some more length; see Benoît Crucifix, "Retour à l'imit-
    ateur: à propos d'un récit de Muñoz et Sampayo," in *(À suivre): archives d'une revue culte*,
    ed. Gert Meesters and Sylvain Lesage (Tours: Presses Universitaires François-Rabelais,
    2018), 319–21.

61. Saint-Amour, *The Copywrights*, 164.

62. The court condemned *Air Pirates* for copyright infringement because of the substantial
    amount of actual copies. For a full account of this legal feud, see Bob Levin, *The Pirates
    and the Mouse: Disney's War against the Counterculture* (Seattle, WA: Fantagraphics Books,
    2003).

63. It is, of course, a more complicated story: the case of Jack Kirby precisely highlights
    these tensions between "personal" graphic style and issues of ownership and copyright.
    In a different context, the style established by Osamu Tezuka would become so present
    and hegemonic that it quickly defied any attempts to police its further appropriation,
    but also because the emphasis put on authorial styles has been less strong in manga
    culture; see Baudry, Hébert, and Roger, "Hériter, imiter," 55–76.

64. Baetens and Frey, *The Graphic Novel*, 135.

65. For a detailed discussion of the context for this piece, see Williams, *Dreaming the Graphic
    Novel*, 32.

66. Baetens and Frey, *The Graphic Novel*, 135–36.

67. Ibid., 100.

68. For an excellent analysis of the contrast that this page stages, see Schneider, *What
    Happens When Nothing Happens*, 15–17.

69. Daniel Clowes Archive, University of Chicago Library, box 9, folder 4.

70. On the *ressentiment* of alternative comics toward the art world, including a reading of
    Clowes's other satire "Art School Confidential," see Beaty, *Comics versus Art*, 52–55.

71. Quoted in Beaty, ibid., 58.

72. Frey and Baetens, "Comics Culture and Roy Lichtenstein Revisited," 151.

73. Sullivan, "Charles Burns," 85.

74. Charles Burns, "Introduction," in *The Best American Comics 2009*, ed. Charles Burns
    (New York: Houghton Mifflin Harcourt, 2009), xii.

75. Ibid., xiii.

76. As collected in Charles Burns, *Free Shit* (Marseille: Le Denier Cri, 2016).

77. Pizzino, *Arresting Development*, 48–49.

78. Ibid., 141.

79. Eric Maigret, "Bande dessinée et postlégitimité," in *La bande dessinée: une médiaculture*, Collection "Médiacultures" (Paris: Armand Colin, 2012), 130–48.

80. Burns's small-press publishers often put out his books with a larger print run than their conventional practices, but restricting the volume to a manageable amount for their operation (labor, storage, distribution). There is some level of "organized scarcity" (for the lack of a better term) in that Burns's books frequently sell out their initial print run but are rarely reissued.

81. Pizzino, *Arresting Development*, 149–51.

82. Ibid., 48.

83. Taylor, *The Archive and the Repertoire*, 20. For an overview of the relationship between archive and repertoire in the digital age, see also De Kosnik, *Rogue Archives*, 63–71.

84. Charles Burns, "Johnny 23: Random Images from the Hinterland," Tumblr Blog, 2019, johnnytwentythree.tumblr.com, last accessed October 22, 2022.

85. Burns, *Swipe File*; Burns, *Close Your Eyes*; Burns, *Love Nest*.

86. Burns, *Close Your Eyes*, 3.

87. Ibid., 127.

88. On the widespread use of swipe files in romance comics, see John Benson, *Confessions, Romances, Secrets, and Temptations: Archer St. John and the St. John Romance Comics* (Seattle, WA: Fantagraphics Books, 2007), 17–18.

89. Laura Mulvey, *Death 24x a Second: Stillness and the Moving Image* (London: Reaktion Books, 2006), 171.

90. Thierry Groensteen, *The System of Comics*, trans. Nick Nguyen and Bart Beaty (Jackson: University Press of Mississippi, 2009), 17.

91. Burns, *Swipe File*.

92. Referring to the description of Chester Gould's graphic style in Waugh, *The Comics*, 216.

93. Pizzino, *Arresting Development*, 142.

94. I am extremely thankful to Rich Dannys for sharing his digging works into romance comics looking for Charles Burns's swipes, and particularly identifying the "Marked Woman" story as a source for *Love Nest*.

95. For an in-depth analysis of "devices of permeability" and cringing visual motifs of gaps, cracks, and contamination in Burns's work, see Jean-Paul Gabilliet, "Sutures génériques et fêlures intérieures chez Charles Burns," *Sillages Critiques* 28 (May 1, 2020), https://doi.org/10.4000/sillagescritiques.9579, last accessed October 22, 2022.

96. See Jan Baetens, "From Black & White to Color and Back: What Does It Mean (Not) to Use Color?" *College Literature* 38, no. 3 (2011): 111–28.

97. Charles Burns, "And I Pressed My Hand against His Face, Feeling His Thick Massive Lips, And . . .," *RAW* 1, no. 3 (1981). Burns calls it an "abstract piece" in his interview with Hillary L. Chute, ed., *Outside the Box: Interviews with Contemporary Cartoonists* (Chicago, IL: University of Chicago Press, 2014), 41.

98. Pizzino, *Arresting Development*, 139.

99. Charles Burns, *Last Look* (New York: Pantheon Books, 2016); first published by Pantheon as three separate volumes, *X'ed Out* (2010), *The Hive* (2012), and *Sugar Skull* (2014).

100. Referring to Thierry Groensteen's concept of braiding to designate infra-narrative, nonlinear networks of interconnected images; see Groensteen, *The System of Comics*, 146–48.

101. For a close-reading of this performance, see Jan Baetens, "La poésie n'est pas le slam: Charles Burns," in *À voix haute. Poésie et lecture publique* (Brussels: Les Impressions Nouvelles, 2016), 155–60.

102. Rajewsky, "Intermediality, Intertextuality, and Remediation," 52–53.

103. William S. Burroughs and Brion Gysin, *The Third Mind* (New York: Viking Press, 1978), 29–31.

104. Rajewsky, "Intermediality, Intertextuality, and Remediation," 54.

105. Xavier Guilbert, "The Inner Worlds of Charles Burns," *du9*, July 2016, www.du9.org /en/entretien/the-inner-worlds-of-charles-burns/, last accessed October 22, 2022.

106. On the way Burns's rigid layout allows him to experiment with narration, see Jan Baetens and Hugo Frey, "'Layouting' for the Plot: Charles Burns and the Clear Line Revisited," *Journal of Graphic Novels and Comics* 8, no. 2 (2017): 193–202. See also Philippe Maupeu's reading of *Last Look* in terms of montage: Philippe Maupeu, "Montage et hantise chez Charles Burns (ToXic, La Ruche, Calavera)," *Textimage* 6 (2016), http://revue-textimage.com/conferencier/06_montage_demontage_re montage/maupeu1.html, last accessed October 22, 2022.

107. I elaborate on the idea of "dispersed serialization" in an article on Ware's *Building Stories*, "From Loose to Boxed Fragments and Back Again."

108. Charles Burns, "Cut Up. Random Fragments, 1977–1979," in *2W Box Set Y* (Geneva: B. ü.l.b., 2011); Charles Burns, *Johnny 23* (Marseille: Le Dernier Cri, 2011); Charles Burns, *Vortex* (Bordeaux: Cornélius, 2016).

109. Charles Burns, *The Hive* (New York: Pantheon Books, 2012), n.p.

110. Jan Baetens and Hugo Frey, "Modernizing Tintin: From Myth to New Stylizations," in *The Comics of Hergé: When the Lines Are Not So Clear*, ed. Joe Sutliff Sanders, Critical Approaches to Comics Artists (Jackson: University Press of Mississippi, 2016), 111.

111. Ibid., 109.

112. Burns, *The Hive*.

113. Ibid.

114. Maupeu, "Montage et hantise chez Charles Burns," 5.

115. Ken Parille, "Secret Loves: A Short History of Two Panels in Charles Burns's The Hive," *The Comics Journal* (November 26, 2012), www.tcj.com/secret-loves-a-short-history-of-two-panels-in-charles-burnss-the-hive/, last accessed October 22, 2022.

116. Taylor, *The Archive and the Repertoire*, 20.

117. Gardner, "Storylines," 66.

118. Groensteen, "Le Plaisir de la bande dessinée." The article echoes debates of the time around the notion of the "memorable panel" that, in the Francophone context, operates in a way similar to the "swipe" in US comics fan cultures. For a further

discussion of the memorable panel, its theoretical context, and its use in contemporary *bande dessinée*, see Benoît Crucifix, "Rethinking the 'Memorable Panel' from Pierre Sterckx to Olivier Josso Hamel," *European Comic Art* 10, no. 2 (2017): 24–47.

119. Gardner, *Projections*, 177.
120. Borschke, *This Is Not a Remix*, 57.

CHAPTER 6 UNDRAWING

1. "In 1998, Zou Luoyang, chief-editor of the risographed art zine *Rude*, controversially declared: 'The future of comics is in the trash can'"; citation from the collection curated for the online alternative archive Monoskop by Ilan Manouach, "Conceptual Comics [CoCo]" (April 28, 2019), https://monoskop.org/Conceptual_comics, last accessed October 22, 2022. The entry is devoted to the fictive Luoyang's *Rude*, a non-archival zine disseminated in landfills and a reflection on the "energizing potential of trash" in the comics industry.

2. Wendy Hui Kyong Chun, "The Enduring Ephemeral, or the Future Is a Memory," *Critical Inquiry* 35, no. 1 (2008): 148–71.

3. De Kosnik, *Rogue Archives*, 3.

4. Ibid., 4.

5. Williams, "An Interview with Bill Blackbeard," 15.

6. Gardner, *Projections*, 173. On the database as symbolic form, see Manovich, *The Language of New Media*. On the interplay between database and narrative, see N. Katherine Hayles, "Narrative and Database: Natural Symbionts," *PMLA* 122, no. 5 (2007): 1603–8.

7. Ilan Manouach, "The Library," *Futures of Comics* website (n.d.), https://futuresofcomics .org/guests/library, last accessed October 22, 2022.

8. Kenneth Goldsmith, *Uncreative Writing: Managing Language in the Digital Age* (New York: Columbia University Press, 2011), 1.

9. This chapter expands on a previous text that put forward the idea of "undrawing"; see Benoît Crucifix, "Drawing, Redrawing, and Undrawing," in *The Oxford Handbook of Comic Book Studies*, ed. Frederick Luis Aldama (Oxford: Oxford University Press, 2019).

10. Witek, "If a Way to the Better There Be."

11. Andrea Juno, "Chris Ware," in *Dangerous Drawings: Interviews with Comix & Graphix Artists* (New York: Juno Books, 1997), 41.

12. Art Spiegelman, "The Malpractice Suite," *Arcade* 6 (1976): 12–13.

13. Simone Castaldi, "'The Inexhaustible Surface of Things': Stefano Tamburini's Comic Book Work," *European Comic Art* 13, no. 1 (2020): 82–85.

14. We can indeed find a copy of a *Frigidaire* issue with Tamburini's "Snake Agent" in the Françoise Mouly and Art Spiegelman collection, Billy Ireland Cartoon Library & Museum.

15. Mark Newgarden, "Love's Savage Fury," *RAW*, 1986.

16. Robert Sikoryak, "Good Ol' Gregor Brown," *RAW* 2, no. 2 (1990).

17. Robert Sikoryak, *Masterpiece Comics* (Montreal: Drawn & Quarterly, 2009).

18. Following his description on the Drawn & Quarterly page of his latest graphic novel; see R. Sikoryak, *The Unquotable Trump*, https://drawnandquarterly.com/unquotable-trump, last accessed October 22, 2022.

19. R. Sikoryak, *Terms and Conditions: The Graphic Novel* (Montreal: Drawn & Quarterly, 2017).

20. Manovich, "The Practice of Everyday (Media) Life," 319.

21. Redrawn page available at: https://redrawncomics.tumblr.com/, last accessed October 22, 2022. See also Kannenberg's analysis of different mash-ups on online platforms such as DeviantArt; Gene Kannenberg Jr., "Chips Off the Ol' Blockhead: Evidence of Influence in Peanuts Parodies," in *The Comics of Charles Schulz: The Good Grief of Modern Life*, ed. Jared Gardner and Ian Gordon (Jackson: University Press of Mississippi, 2017), 197–212.

22. Kevin Huizenga, *The Half Men* (Saint Louis, MO: Self-published, 2013).

23. While maintaining the possibility for a reading that ignores both genres, as pointed out in Nicolas Labarre, *Understanding Genres in Comics* (Cham: Palgrave, 2020), 5.

24. In 2017, Huizenga sold some original drawings from his *Kona* version in order to raise funds to support Sam Glanzman's medical operations.

25. Another example would be Ron Regé, Jr., *Diana* (Echo Park, LA: Self-published, 2013), an extensive redrawing, in his own graphic style, of the origin story of *Wonder Woman* as it was published in William Moulton Marston and H. G. Peter's newspaper comic strips in 1945–46.

26. Derik Badman, *Badman's Cave* (Ambler, PA: Self-published, 1948).

27. Simon Grennan, Roger Sabin, and Julian Waite, *Marie Duval: Maverick Victorian Cartoonist* (Manchester: Manchester University Press, 2020).

28. Simon Grennan, *Drawing in Drag by Marie Duval* (London: Book Works, 2018).

29. Grennan, *A Theory of Narrative Drawing*.

30. Mark Laliberte, *BrickBrickBrick* (Toronto: BookThug, 2010).

31. Marjorie Perloff, *Unoriginal Genius: Poetry by Other Means in the New Century* (Chicago, IL: University of Chicago Press, 2012).

32. Email correspondence with Mark Laliberte, February 2018.

33. Think, for instance, of the drive to identify Carl Barks, "the good duck artist," thanks to his "distinct visual signature"; Beaty, *Comics versus Art*, 80.

34. Kalervo A. Sinervo, "Pirates and Publishers: Comics Scanning and the Audience Function," in *The Comics World: Comic Books, Graphic Novels, and Their Publics*, ed. Benjamin Woo and Jeremy Stoll (Jackson: University Press of Mississippi, 2021), 217.

35. I here expand on a previous account of Manouach's work in the light of "post-comics"; see Benoît Crucifix, "A Chamber of Echo: On the Post-Comics of Ilan Manouach," in *Post-Comics: Beyond Comics, Illustration and the Graphic Novel*, ed. Sébastien Conard (Ghent: KASK/Het Balanseer, 2020), 77–86.

36. Ilan Manouach, *Riki fermier* (Brussels: La Cinquième Couche, 2015).

37. Ilan Manouach, *Katz* (Brussels: La Cinquième Couche, 2011); Ilan Manouach, *MetaKatz* (Brussels: La Cinquième Couche, 2013).

38. Pedro Moura, "Les Schtroumpfs Noirs," *du9 – l'autre bande dessinée*, April 2014, https://www.du9.org/en/chronique/les-schtroumpfs-noirs-2/, last accessed October 22, 2022.

39. Ilan Manouach, *Compendium of Franco-Belgian Comics* (Brussels: La Cinquième Couche, 2018).

40. Ilan Manouach, *Blanco* (Brussels: La Cinquième Couche, 2018).

41. Jean-Christophe Menu, *Plates-bandes* (Paris: l'Association, 2005).

42. N. Katherine Hayles and Jessica Pressman, eds., *Comparative Textual Media: Transforming the Humanities in the Postprint Era* (Minneapolis: University of Minnesota Press, 2013).

43. Ilan Manouach, *The Cubicle Island* (Brussels: La Cinquième Couche, 2019), 4.

44. Gitelman, *Paper Knowledge*, 104–6.

45. Jonathan Crary, *24/7: Late Capitalism and the Ends of Sleep* (London: Verso, 2014).

46. Ilan Manouach, *Peanuts Minus Schulz: Distributed Labor as a Compositional Practice* (Paris: Jean Boîte éditions, 2021), 28.

47. De Kosnik, *Rogue Archives*, 87.

48. Manouach, "Conceptual Comics."

CONCLUSION

1. Paul Williams and Jim Woodring, "Interview: Jim Woodring," in *The Rise of the American Comics Artist: Creators and Contexts*, ed. Paul Williams and James Lyons (Jackson: University Press of Mississippi, 2010), 131.

2. See Sascha Bru, "The Genealogy-Complex: History Beyond the Avant-Garde Myth of Originality," *Filozofski Vestnik* 35, no. 2 (2014): 18.

3. Compagnon, *La Seconde Main*, 29.

4. Guillaume Mazeau, *Histoire* (Paris: Anamosa, 2020), 82.

5. Singer, *Breaking the Frame*.

6. James Elkins, "An Introduction to the Visual as Argument," in *Theorizing Visual Studies: Writing Through the Discipline*, ed. James Elkins et al. (New York: Routledge, 2013), 26.

7. Margaret Galvan, "'The Lesbian Norman Rockwell': Alison Bechdel and Queer Grassroots Networks," *American Literature* 90, no. 2 (2018): 409.

8. Lisa Gitelman, *Always Already New: Media, History, and the Data of Culture* (Cambridge, MA: MIT Press, 2006), 21.

References

Abate, Michelle Ann. "Art Spiegelman's *In the Shadow of No Towers* as Board Book: From the Matter of Materiality to the Way That Materiality Matters." *Jeunesse: Young People, Texts, Cultures* 7, no. 2 (2015): 40–64.

Ahmed, Maaheen. "Comics and Authorship: An Introduction." *Authorship* 6, no. 2 (2017): 1–13.

"Loving Comics in Neil the Horse Comics and Stories." *Comicalités*, History and influence of bedephilia (April 1, 2021). https://journals.openedition.org/comicalites/6300, last accessed October 22, 2022.

Ahmed, Maaheen, and Benoît Crucifix, eds. *Comics Memory: Archives and Styles.* New York: Palgrave, 2018.

Alpers, Svetlana. "The Museum as a Way of Seeing." In *Exhibiting Cultures: The Poetics and Politics of Museum Display*, edited by Steven Lavine, 25–32. Washington, DC: Smithsonian Institution Press, 1991.

Anderson, Chris. *The Long Tail: Why the Future of Business Is Selling Less of More.* New York: Hyperion, 2006.

Arrivé, Mathilde. "L'intelligence des images – l'intericonicité, enjeux et méthodes." *E-rea* 13, no. 1 (2015). http://erea.revues.org/4620, last accessed October 22, 2022.

Assmann, Aleida. "Canon and Archive." In *A Companion to Cultural Memory Studies*, edited by Astrid Erll and Ansgar Nünning, 334–37. Berlin/New York: De Gruyter, 2010.

Auerbach, Jonathan, and Lisa Gitelman. "Microfilm, Containment, and the Cold War." *American Literary History* 19, no. 3 (2007): 745–68.

Aymes, Sophie, and Marie-Odile Bernez, eds. "Gestures and Transmissions." *Interfaces* 40 (2018). https://preo.u-bourgogne.fr/interfaces/index.php?id=598, last accessed October 22, 2022.

Badman, Derik. *Badman's Cave.* Ambler, PA: Self-published, 1948.

Baetens, Jan. "Adaptation: A Writerly Strategy?" In *Comics and Adaptation*, edited by Benoît Mitaine, David Roche, and Isabelle Schmitt-Pitiot, translated by Aarnoud Rommens, 31–46. Jackson: University Press of Mississippi, 2018.

"Between Adaptation, Intermediality and Cultural Series: The Example of the Photonovel." *Artnodes* 18 (2016): 47–55.

"From Black & White to Color and Back: What Does It Mean (Not) to Use Color?" *College Literature* 38, no. 3 (2011): 111–28.

"La livraison versus le livre: Une réédition singulière de *Terry et les Pirates*." *Espressione e Contenuto* 7, no. 13 (2013): 23–38.

"La poésie n'est pas le slam: Charles Burns." In *À voix haute. Poésie et lecture publique*, 155–60. Brussels: Les Impressions Nouvelles, 2016.

"Revealing Traces: A New Theory of Graphic Enunciation." In *The Language of Comics: Word and Image*, edited by Robin Varnum and Christina T. Gibbons, 145–55. Jackson: University Press of Mississippi, 2001.

"Stories and Storytelling in the Era of Graphic Narrative." In *Stories*, edited by Ian Christie and Annie van den Oever, 27–43. Amsterdam: Amsterdam University Press, 2018.

Baetens, Jan, and Ben De Bruyn. "Éloge de la canonisation." *LHT Fabula*, May 2014. www.fabula.org/lht/12/mdrn.html, last accessed October 22, 2022.

Baetens, Jan, and Hugo Frey. "'Layouting' for the Plot: Charles Burns and the Clear Line Revisited." *Journal of Graphic Novels and Comics* 8, no. 2 (2017): 193–202.

"Modernizing Tintin: From Myth to New Stylizations." In *The Comics of Hergé: When the Lines Are Not So Clear*, edited by Joe Sutliff Sanders, 98–112. Critical Approaches to Comics Artists. Jackson: University Press of Mississippi, 2016.

The Graphic Novel: An Introduction. New York: Cambridge University Press, 2015.

Baetens, Jan, Hugo Frey, and Stephen E. Tabachnick. "Introduction." In *The Cambridge History of the Graphic Novel*, edited by Jan Baetens, Hugo Frey, and Stephen E. Tabachnick, 1–18. New York: Cambridge University Press, 2018.

Baetens, Jan, and Pascal Lefèvre. *Pour une lecture moderne de la bande dessinée*. Brussels: Centre belge de la bande dessinée, 1993.

Baetens, Jan, and Charlotte Pylyser. "Comics and Time." In *The Routledge Companion to Comics*, edited by Frank Bramlett, Roy T. Cook, and Aaron Meskin, 303–10. London: Routledge, 2016.

Baetens, Jan, and Steven Surdiacourt. "European Graphic Narratives: Toward a Cultural and Mediological History." In *From Comic Strips to Graphic Novels: Contributions to the Theory and History of Graphic Narrative*, edited by Daniel Stein and Jan-Noël Thon, 347–62. Berlin: De Gruyter, 2013.

Baker, Nicholson. *Double Fold: Libraries and the Assault on Paper*. New York: Random House, 2001.

Balzer, David. *Curationism: How Curating Took Over the Art World – And Everything Else*. Toronto: Coach House Books, 2014.

Baroni, Raphaël. "Le chapitrage dans le roman graphique américain et la bande dessinée européenne: une segmentation précaire." *Cahiers de Narratologie* 34 (2018). https://doi.org/10.4000/narratologie.8594, last accessed October 22, 2022.

Baudry, Julien. *Cases-Pixels: Une histoire de la BD numérique en France*. Tours: Presses Universitaires François-Rabelais, 2018.

Baudry, Julien, Xavier Hébert, and Kevin Roger. "Hériter, imiter." In *Style(s) de (la) bande dessinée*, edited by Benoît Berthou and Jacques Dürrenmatt, 53–111. Paris: Garnier, 2019.

Bawin, Julie. *L'Artiste commissaire: entre posture critique, jeu créatif et valeur ajoutée.* Paris: Editions des Archives Contemporaines, 2014.

Beaty, Bart. "Chris Oliveros, Drawn and Quarterly, and the Expanded Definition of the Graphic Novel." In *The Cambridge History of the Graphic Novel,* edited by Jan Baetens, Hugo Frey, and Stephen E. Tabachnick, 426–42. Cambridge: Cambridge University Press, 2018.

Comics versus Art. Toronto: Toronto University Press, 2012.

"Selective Mutual Reinforcement in the Comics of Chester Brown, Joe Matt, and Seth." In *Graphic Subjects: Critical Essays on Autobiography and Graphic Novels,* edited by Michael A. Chaney, 247–51. Madison: University of Wisconsin Press, 2011.

"Some Classics." In *The Cambridge Companion to the Graphic Novel,* edited by Stephen E. Tabachnick, 175–91. Cambridge Companions to Literature. Cambridge: Cambridge University Press, 2017.

"The Concept of 'Patrimoine' in Contemporary Franco-Belgian Comics Production." In *History and Politics in French-Language Comics and Graphic Novels,* edited by Mark McKinney, 69–93. Jackson: University Press of Mississippi, 2008.

"The Recession and the American Comic Book Industry: From Inelastic Cultural Good to Economic Integration." *Popular Communication* 8, no. 3 (2010): 203–7.

Unpopular Culture: Transforming the European Comic Book in the 1990s. Toronto: University of Toronto Press, 2007.

Beaty, Bart, and Benjamin Woo. *The Greatest Comic Book of All Time: Symbolic Capital and the Field of American Comic Books.* New York: Palgrave Macmillan, 2016.

Beineke, Colin. "Assembling Comics: The House Style and Legacy of RAW Books and Graphics." PhD thesis, University of Missouri, 2017.

Benson, John. *Confessions, Romances, Secrets, and Temptations: Archer St. John and the St. John Romance Comics.* Seattle, WA: Fantagraphics Books, 2007.

Benson, John, David Kasakove, and Art Spiegelman. "An Examination of 'Master Race.'" *Squa Tront* 6 (1975).

Bergdoll, Alfred, and Art Spiegelman. "Art Spiegelman." In *Art Spiegelman: Conversations,* edited by Joseph Witek, 3–19. Jackson: University Press of Mississippi, 2007.

Berliner, David. "Anthropologie et transmission." *Terrain* 55 (2010): 4–19.

Losing Culture: Nostalgia, Heritage, and Our Accelerated Times. New Brunswick, NJ: Rutgers University Press, 2020.

Beronä, David A. *Wordless Books: The Original Graphic Novels.* New York: Abrams, 2008.

Berthou, Benoît, ed. "La bande dessinée: un 'art sans mémoire'?" *Comicalités,* 2011. https://journals.openedition.org/comicalites/198, last accessed October 22, 2022.

Blackbeard, Bill. "Articles of the Association of the San Francisco Academy of Comic Art," Boxes 4 and 23. San Francisco Academy of Comic Art (SFACA) collection, Billy Ireland Cartoon Library & Museum, Ohio State University, Columbus.

"The Four Color Paper Trail: A Look Back." *International Journal of Comic Art* 5, no. 2 (2003): 205–15.

Blackbeard, Bill, and Martin Williams, eds. *The Smithsonian Collection of Newspaper Comics.* Washington, DC/New York: Smithsonian Institution Press/Harry N. Abrams, 1977.

Blom, Ina, Trond Lundemo, and Eivind Røssaak, eds. *Memory in Motion: Archives, Technology, and the Social.* Amsterdam: Amsterdam University Press, 2017.

Bloom, Harold. *The Anxiety of Influence: A Theory of Poetry.* Oxford: Oxford University Press, 1973.

Bolter, Jay David, and Richard Grusin. *Remediation: Understanding New Media.* Cambridge, MA: MIT Press, 2000.

Borges, Jorge Luis. "Kafka and His Precursors." In *The Total Library: Non Fiction 1922-1986,* translated by Ester Allen, Suzanne Jill Levine, and Eliot Weinberger. London: Penguin, 1999.

Borschke, Margie. *This Is Not a Remix: Piracy, Authenticity and Popular Music.* New York: Bloomsbury Academic, 2017.

Boyd, Robert. "Shary Flenniken." *Comics Journal* 146 (1991): 55–85.

"Swipe File." *The Comics Journal* 140 (1991): 28.

Bray, Patrick M. "Aesthetics in the Shadow of No Towers: Reading Virilio in the Twenty-First Century." *Yale French Studies* 114 (2008): 4–17.

Bredehoft, Thomas A. "Comics Architecture, Multidimensionality, and Time: Chris Ware's *Jimmy Corrigan: The Smartest Kid on Earth.*" *Modern Fiction Studies* 52, no. 4 (2006): 869–90.

Brienza, Casey, and Paddy Johnston, eds. *Cultures of Comics Work.* New York: Palgrave Macmillan, 2016.

Briggs, Clare. *How to Draw Cartoons.* New York/London: Harper & Brothers, 1926.

Bru, Sascha. "The Genealogy-Complex: History Beyond the Avant-Garde Myth of Originality." *Filozofski Vestnik* 35, no. 2 (2014): 13–28.

Brunet, François, ed. *Circulation.* Chicago, IL: Terra Foundation for American Art, 2017.

La Photographie: histoire et contre-histoire. Paris: Presses Universitaires de France, 2017.

Brunetti, Ivan, ed. *An Anthology of Graphic Fiction, Cartoons, & True Stories.* New Haven, CT: Yale University Press, 2006.

Brzyski, Anna. "Introduction: Canons and Art History." In *Partisan Canons,* edited by Anna Brzyski, 1–25. Durham, NC: Duke University Press, 2007.

Buckley, Cheryl. "Made in Patriarchy: Toward a Feminist Analysis of Women and Design." *Design Issues* 3, no. 2 (1986): 3–14.

Buenaventura, Alvin, ed. *The Art of Daniel Clowes: Modern Cartoonist.* Seattle, WA: Fantagraphics Books, 2012.

Burbey, Mark. "The Trouble with Keith Giffen." *The Comics Journal* 105 (1986): 9–14.

Burns, Charles. "And I Pressed My Hand against His Face, Feeling His Thick Massive Lips, And ..." *RAW* 1, no. 3 (1981).

Close Your Eyes. Marseille: Le Denier Cri, 2001.

"Cut Up. Random Fragments, 1977–1979." In *2W Box Set Y.* Geneva: B.ü.l.b., 2011.

Free Shit. Marseille: Le Denier Cri, 2016.

"Introduction." In *The Best American Comics 2009*, edited by Charles Burns. New York: Houghton Mifflin Harcourt, 2009.

Johnny 23. Marseille: Le Dernier Cri, 2011.

"Johnny 23: Random Images from the Hinterland." Tumblr Blog, 2019. john nytwentythree.tumblr.com, last accessed October 22, 2022.

Last Look. New York: Pantheon Books, 2016.

Love Nest. Bordeaux: Cornélius, 2016.

Swipe File. Philadelphia, PA: Common Press, 2008.

The Hive. New York: Pantheon Books, 2012.

Vortex. Bordeaux: Cornélius, 2016.

Burroughs, William S., and Brion Gysin. *The Third Mind.* New York: Viking Press, 1978.

Busi Rizzi, Giorgio. "Always at Home in the Past: Exploring Nostalgia in the Graphic Novel." PhD thesis, University of Bologna and KU Leuven, 2018.

"Portrait of the Artist as a Nostalgic: Seth's It's a Good Life, If You Don't Weaken." In *Comics Memory: Archives and Styles*, edited by Maaheen Ahmed and Benoît Crucifix, 15–35. New York: Palgrave, 2018.

Campbell, Eddie. *Alec: The Years Have Pants.* Marietta, GA: Top Shelf, 2009.

The Goat Getters: Jack Johnson, the Fight of the Century, and How a Bunch of Raucous Cartoonists Reinvented Comics. San Diego, CA/Columbus: IDW/Ohio State University Press, 2018.

Campbell, Eddie, and Dirk Deppey. "The Eddie Campbell Interview." *The Comics Journal* (2006).

Camper, Brett. "Retro Reflexivity: *La Mulana*, an 8-Bit Period Piece." In *The Video Game Theory Reader 2*, edited by Bernard Perron and Mark J. P. Wolf, 169–95. London/New York: Routledge, 2009.

Capart, Philippe. "Store Memory." In *Comics Memory: Archives and Styles*, edited by Maaheen Ahmed and Benoît Crucifix, 277–80. New York: Palgrave, 2018.

Carlin, John, Paul Karasik, and Brian Walker, eds. *Masters of American Comics.* Los Angeles, CA/New Haven, CT: Hammer Museum/Yale University Press, 2005.

Castaldi, Simone. "'The Inexhaustible Surface of Things': Stefano Tamburini's Comic Book Work." *European Comic Art* 13, no. 1 (2020): 70–94.

Cates, Isaac. "The Diary Comic." In *Graphic Subjects: Critical Essays on Autobiography and Graphic Novels*, edited by Michael A. Chaney, 209–26. Madison: University of Wisconsin Press, 2011.

Chabon, Michael. *The Amazing Adventures of Kavalier and Clay.* New York: Random House, 2000.

Chartier, Roger. *Au bord de la falaise: L'histoire entre certitudes et inquiétudes.* Paris: Albin Michel, 2009.

"Languages, Books, and Reading from the Printed Word to the Digital Text." *Critical Inquiry* 31, no. 1 (2004): 133–52.

Chun, Wendy Hui Kyong. "The Enduring Ephemeral, or the Future Is a Memory." *Critical Inquiry* 35, no. 1 (2008): 148–71.

Chute, Hillary L. *Disaster Drawn: Visual Witness, Comics, and Documentary Form.* Cambridge, MA: Belknap Press, 2016.

Graphic Women: Life Narrative and Contemporary Comics. New York: Columbia University Press, 2010.

ed. *Outside the Box: Interviews with Contemporary Cartoonists.* Chicago, IL: University of Chicago Press, 2014.

"Temporality and Seriality in Spiegelman's *In the Shadow of No Towers.*" *American Periodicals* 17, no. 2 (2007): 228–44.

Closser, Cole. *Little Tommy Lost: Book One.* Toronto: Koyama Press, 2013.

Clowes, Daniel. "A Mozart of Zaniness." In *Will Elder: The Mad Playboy of Art,* edited by Gary Groth and Greg Sadowski, 1–3. Seattle, WA: Fantagraphics Books, 2003.

Ice Haven. New York: Pantheon Books, 2005.

"Introduction." In *Nancy Is Happy,* edited by Ernie Bushmiller. Seattle, WA: Fantagraphics Books, 2012.

"Modern Cartoonist." *Eightball* 18 (1997): insert.

Wilson. New York: Pantheon Books, 2010.

Collins, Jim. *Bring on the Books for Everybody: How Literary Culture Became Popular Culture.* Durham, NC: Duke University Press, 2010.

Colon, Ernie. "Sticking Up for Giffen." *The Comics Journal* 116 (1987): 42–43.

Compagnon, Antoine. *La Seconde Main, ou, Le Travail de la citation.* Paris: Seuil, 1979.

Crary, Jonathan. *24/7: Late Capitalism and the Ends of Sleep.* London: Verso, 2014.

Creekmur, Corey K. "Multiculturalism Meets the Counterculture: Representing Racial Difference in Robert Crumb's Underground Comix." In *Representing Multiculturalism in Comics and Graphic Novels,* edited by Carolene Ayaka and Ian Hague, 19–33. London: Routledge, 2015.

Cremins, Brian. *Captain Marvel and the Art of Nostalgia.* Jackson: University Press of Mississippi, 2016.

Crucifix, Benoît. "A Chamber of Echo: On the Post-Comics of Ilan Manouach." In *Post-Comics: Beyond Comics, Illustration and the Graphic Novel,* edited by Sébastien Conard, 77–86. Ghent: KASK/Het Balanseer, 2020.

"Drawing, Redrawing, and Undrawing." In *The Oxford Handbook of Comic Book Studies,* edited by Frederick Luis Aldama. Oxford: Oxford University Press, 2019.

"From Loose to Boxed Fragments and Back Again. Seriality and Archive in Chris Ware's *Building Stories.*" *Journal of Graphic Novels and Comics* 9, no. 1 (2018): 3–22.

"Rethinking the 'Memorable Panel' from Pierre Sterckx to Olivier Josso Hamel." *European Comic Art* 10, no. 2 (2017): 24–47.

"Retour à l'imitateur: à propos d'un récit de Muñoz et Sampayo." In (*À suivre*): *archives d'une revue culte,* edited by Gert Meesters and Sylvain Lesage, 319–21. Tours: Presses Universitaires François-Rabelais, 2018.

"Sunday Comics Reloaded – An Interview with Peter Maresca." *Du9, l'autre Bande Dessinée,* March 2016. www.du9.org/en/entretien/sunday-comics-reloaded-an-interview-with-peter-maresca/, last accessed October 22, 2022.

Crucifix, Benoît, and Björn-Olav Dozo. "E-Graphic Novels." In *The Cambridge History of the Graphic Novel*, edited by Jan Baetens, Hugo Frey, and Stephen E. Tabachnick, 574–90. Cambridge: Cambridge University Press, 2018.

Cuvelier, Paul, and Jean Van Hamme. *Epoxy*. Paris: Losfeld, 1968.

Damisch, Hubert. *L'Amour m'expose*. Geneva: Klincksieck, 2007.

Darnton, Robert. "The Great Book Massacre." *New York Review of Books*, April 26, 2001.

Daston, Lorraine, ed. *Science in the Archives: Pasts, Presents, Futures*. Chicago, IL: University of Chicago Press, 2017.

De Certeau, Michel. *The Practice of Everyday Life*. Berkeley: University of California Press, 2013.

Dejasse, Erwin. "La Musique silencieuse de José Muñoz et Carlos Sampayo: déconstruction des normes et lecture émotionnelle." PhD thesis, University of Liège, 2015.

De Kosnik, Abigail. *Rogue Archives: Digital Cultural Memory and Media Fandom*. Cambridge, MA: MIT Press, 2016.

Derrida, Jacques. *Archive Fever: A Freudian Impression*, translated by Eric Prenowitz. Chicago, IL: University of Chicago Press, 1995.

DeSilvey, Caitlin. *Curated Decay: Heritage Beyond Saving*. Minneapolis: University of Minnesota Press, 2017.

Doud, Earle, and Wallace Wood, "The Yellowed Kids Department: If Comic Strip Characters were as Old as Their Strips." *Mad* 72 (1962): 26.

Dozo, Björn-Olav. "De la logique de guerre à la patrimonialisation. Faire catalogue en faisant collection." In *L'Association. Une utopie éditoriale et esthétique*, edited by ACME, 37–57. Brussels: Les Impressions Nouvelles, 2011.

Dyer, Richard. *Pastiche*. New York: Routledge, 2007.

Eco, Umberto. "The Myth of Superman," translated by Nathalie Chilton. *Diacritics* 2, no. 1 (1972): 14–22.

Eichhorn, Kate. "Breach of Copy/Rights: The University Copy District as Abject Zone." *Public Culture* 18, no. 3 (2006): 551–71.

The Archival Turn in Feminism: Outrage in Order. Philadelphia, PA: Temple University Press, 2014.

Eisner, Will. *The Dreamer*. Princeton, WI: Kitchen Sink Press, 1986.

Elder, Will, Bernard Krigstein, and Harvey Kurtzman, "Bringing Back Father!" *Mad* 17 (1954).

Elkins, James. "An Introduction to the Visual as Argument." In *Theorizing Visual Studies: Writing Through the Discipline*, edited by James Elkins, Kristi McGuire, Maureen Burns, Alicia Chester, and Joel Kuennen, 25–60. New York: Routledge, 2013.

English, James F. *The Economy of Prestige: Prizes, Awards, and the Circulation of Cultural Value*. Cambridge, MA: Harvard University Press, 2005.

Erll, Astrid. "Generation in Literary History: Three Constellations of Generationality, Genealogy, and Memory." *New Literary History* 45, no. 3 (2014): 385–409.

Ernst, Wolfgang. *Digital Memory and the Archive*, edited by Jussi Parikka. Minneapolis: University of Minnesota Press, 2013.

Etter, Lukas. "Visible Hand? Subjectivity and Its Stylistic Markers in Graphic Narratives." In *Subjectivity Across Media: Interdisciplinary and Transmedial Perspectives*, edited by Maike Sarah Reinerth and Jan-Noël Thon, 92–110. New York: Routledge, 2017.

Faciejew, Michael. "Une bibliothèque portative: le microfilm et son architecture," translated by Jean-François Caro. *Transbordeur photographie* 3 (2019): 48–59.

Farge, Arlette. *The Allure of the Archives*, translated by Thomas Scott-Railton and Natalie Zemon Davis. New Haven, CT: Yale University Press, 2013.

Feiffer, Jules. *Backing into Forward: A Memoir*. Chicago, IL: University of Chicago Press, 2012.

The Great Comic Book Heroes. New York: Dial Press, 1965.

Ferris, Emil. *My Favorite Thing Is Monsters*. Seattle, WA: Fantagraphics Books, 2017.

Filipi, David, and Jenny E. Robb. "'Through the Eyes of the Cartoonist.' Gallery Guide to Eye of the Cartoonist: Daniel Clowes's Selections from Comics History and Modern Cartoonist: The Art of Daniel Clowes." Wexner Center for the Arts, 2014.

Fossati, Giovanna. *From Grain to Pixel: The Archival Life of Film in Transition*. Amsterdam: Amsterdam University Press, 2009.

Foster, Hal. "An Archival Impulse." *October* 110, Fall (2004): 3–22.

Foucault, Michel. *The Archeology of Knowledge*, translated by A. M. Sheridan Smith. Collection Tel 354. New York: Pantheon Books, 1972.

"What Is an Author?" In *The Foucault Reader*, edited by Paul Rabinow, 101–20. New York: Pantheon Books, 1984.

Frey, Hugo, and Jan Baetens. "Comics Culture and Roy Lichtenstein Revisited: Analysing a Forgotten 'Feedback Loop.'" *Art History* 42, no. 1 (2019): 126–52.

Gabilliet, Jean-Paul. *Of Comics and Men: A Cultural History of American Comic Books*, translated by Bart Beaty and Nick Nguyen. Jackson: University Press of Mississippi, 2010.

R. Crumb. Bordeaux: Presses Universitaires de Bordeaux, 2012.

"Reading Facsimile Reproductions of Original Artwork: The Comics Fan as Connoisseur." *Image [&] Narrative* 17, no. 4 (2016): 16–25.

"Sutures génériques et fêlures intérieures chez Charles Burns," *Sillages Critiques* 28 (May 1, 2020). https://doi.org/10.4000/sillagescritiques.9579, last accessed October 22, 2022.

Galvan, Margaret. "Archiving Grassroots Comics: The Radicality of Networks and Lesbian Community." *Archive Journal*, November 2015. www.archivejournal.net/essays/archiving-grassroots-comics-the-radicality-of-networks-and-lesbian-community/, last accessed October 22, 2022.

"Archiving Wimmen: Collectives, Networks, and Comix." *Australian Feminist Studies* 32, no. 91–92 (2017): 22–40.

"'The Lesbian Norman Rockwell': Alison Bechdel and Queer Grassroots Networks." *American Literature* 90, no. 2 (2018): 407–38.

Galvan, Margaret, and Leah Misemer. "Introduction: The Counterpublics of Underground Comics." *Inks: The Journal of the Comics Studies Society* 3, no. 1 (2019): 1–5.

Garber, Marjorie. "Over the Influence." *Critical Inquiry* 42, no. 4 (2016): 731–59.

Gardner, Jared. "A History of the Narrative Comic Strip." In *From Comic Strips to Graphic Novels: Contributions to the Theory and History of the Graphic Narrative,* edited by Daniel Stein and Jean-Noël Thon, 241–53. New York/Berlin: De Gruyter, 2013.

"Before the Underground: Jay Lynch, Art Spiegelman, Skip Williamson and the Fanzine Culture of the Early 1960s." *Inks: The Journal of the Comics Studies Society* 1, no. 1 (2017): 75–84.

Projections: Comics and the History of Twenty-First-Century Storytelling. Stanford, CA: Stanford University Press, 2012.

"Storylines." *SubStance* 40, no. 1 (2011): 53–69.

"Time Under Siege." In *The Comics of Joe Sacco: Journalism in a Visual World,* edited by Daniel Worden, 21–38. Jackson: University Press of Mississippi, 2016.

Gardner, Jared, and Ian Gordon, eds. *The Comics of Charles Schulz: The Good Grief of Modern Life.* Jackson: University Press of Mississippi, 2017.

Garvey, Ellen Gruber. *Writing with Scissors: American Scrapbooks from the Civil War to the Harlem Renaissance.* Oxford: Oxford University Press, 2013.

Gaudreault, André, and Philippe Marion. *The End of Cinema? A Medium in Crisis in the Digital Age.* Film and Culture. New York: Columbia University Press, 2015.

Gearino, Dan. *Comic Shop: The Retail Mavericks Who Gave Us a New Geek Culture.* Athens: Swallow Press/Ohio University Press, 2017.

Gelman, Woody. "A Nostalgic Vignette." *Help!* 23 (1965): 32–35.

Genette, Gérard. *Palimpsests: Literature in the Second Degree,* translated by Channa Newman and Claude Doubinsky. Lincoln: University of Nebraska Press, 1997.

Genoudet, Adrien. *Dessiner l'histoire: Pour une histoire visuelle.* Paris: Le Manuscrit, 2015.

Geraghty, Lincoln. *Cult Collectors: Nostalgia, Fandom and Collecting Popular Culture.* London: Routledge, 2014.

Giannachi, Gabriella. *Archive Everything: Mapping the Everyday.* Cambridge, MA: MIT Press, 2016.

Gibson, Mel. *Remembered Reading: Memory, Comics and Post-War Constructions of British Girlhood.* Leuven: Leuven University Press, 2015.

Gitelman, Lisa. *Always Already New: Media, History, and the Data of Culture.* Cambridge, MA: MIT Press, 2006.

Paper Knowledge: Toward a Media History of Documents. Durham, NC: Duke University Press, 2014.

Glaude, Benoît. "Circulation transnationale des *Amours de Mr Vieux Bois* de Rodolphe Töpffer." *Les Cahiers du GRIT* 3 (2016): 9–31.

Goldsmith, Kenneth. *Uncreative Writing: Managing Language in the Digital Age.* New York: Columbia University Press, 2011.

Gordon, Ian. *Ben Katchor: Conversations.* Jackson: University Press of Mississippi, 2018.

Grace, Dominick. "An Alternative History of Canadian Cartoonists." *International Journal of Comic Art* 17, no. 2 (2015): 133–61.

"Seth's *It's a Good Life, If You Don't Weaken* as Anti-Nostalgia." In *The Canadian Alternative: Cartoonists, Comics, and Graphic Novels,* edited by Dominick Grace and Eric Hoffman, 150–61. Jackson: University Press of Mississippi, 2017.

Gray, Maggie. *Alan Moore, out from the Underground: Cartooning, Performance, and Dissent.* New York: Palgrave Macmillan, 2017.

Grennan, Simon. *A Theory of Narrative Drawing.* New York: Palgrave, 2017.

——— "Demonstrating *Discours*: Two Comic Strip Projects in Self-Constraint." *Studies in Comics* 2, no. 2 (January 5, 2012): 295–316.

——— *Drawing in Drag by Marie Duval.* London: Book Works, 2018.

——— "Misrecognizing Misrecognition: The Capacity to Influence in the Milieux of Comics and Fine Art." *Image [&] Narrative* 17, no. 4 (2016): 5–15.

Grennan, Simon, Roger Sabin, and Julian Waite. *Marie Duval: Maverick Victorian Cartoonist.* Manchester: Manchester University Press, 2020.

Groensteen, Thierry. *La Bande dessinée: son histoire et ses maîtres.* Paris/Angoulême: Skira Flammarion/Cité internationale de la bande dessinée et de l'image, 2009.

——— *La bande dessinée: un objet culturel non identifié.* Angoulême: L'An 2, 2006.

——— "*La Cage* de Martin Vaughn-James et ses avatars contemporains." In *L'Engendrement des images en bande dessinée,* edited by Henri Garric, 99–113. Tours: Presses Universitaires François-Rabelais, 2013.

——— "Le Plaisir de la bande dessinée." *Neuvième Art* 2 (1997): 14–21.

——— *The System of Comics,* translated by Nick Nguyen and Bart Beaty. Jackson: University Press of Mississippi, 2009.

Guilbert, Xavier. "The Inner Worlds of Charles Burns." *Du9 – l'autre Bande Dessinée,* July 2016. www.du9.org/en/entretien/the-inner-worlds-of-charles-burns/, last accessed October 22, 2022.

Guillory, John. "Monuments and Documents: Panofsky on the Object of Study in the Humanities." *History of Humanities* 1, no. 1 (2016): 9–30.

Gustines, George Gene. "'Master Race' Original Art Sells for $600,000." *The New York Times,* November 16, 2018. www.nytimes.com/2018/11/16/arts/master-race-comic-book-sold.html, last accessed October 22, 2022.

Hall, Stuart. "Constituting an Archive." *Third Text* 15, no. 54 (2001): 89–92.

Hama, Larry. "Old Ink, New Ink." In *Against the Grain: MAD Artist Wallace Wood,* edited by Bhob Steward, 195. Raleigh, NC: TwoMorrows Publishing, 2003.

Harvey, Robert C. "Reprint Revolution." *The Comics Journal* 153 (1992): 121–25.

——— *The Art of the Funnies: An Aesthetic History.* Jackson: University Press of Mississippi, 1994.

Hatfield, Charles. *Alternative Comics: An Emerging Literature.* Jackson: University Press of Mississippi, 2005.

——— "Do Independent Comics Still Exist in US and Canada?" In *La bande dessinée en dissidence alternative, indépendance, auto-édition / Comics in dissent: alternative, independence, self-publishing,* edited by Christophe Dony, Tanguy Habrand, and Gert Meesters, 59–77. Liège: Presses Universitaires de Liège, 2014.

——— *Hand of Fire: The Comics Art of Jack Kirby.* Jackson: University Press of Mississippi, 2012.

——— "Redrawing the Comic-Strip Child: Charles M. Schulz's as Cross-Writing." In *The Oxford Handbook of Children's Literature,* edited by Lynne Vallonne and Julia Mickenberg, 168–86. Oxford: Oxford University Press, 2011.

Hayles, N. Katherine. *Electronic Literature: New Horizons for the Literary.* Notre Dame, IN: University of Notre Dame Press, 2008.

How We Became Posthuman: Virtual Bodies in Cybernetics, Literature, and Informatics. Chicago, IL: University of Chicago Press, 1999.

"Narrative and Database: Natural Symbionts." *PMLA* 122, no. 5 (2007): 1603–8.

Hayles, N. Katherine, and Jessica Pressman, eds. *Comparative Textual Media: Transforming the Humanities in the Postprint Era.* Minneapolis: University of Minnesota Press, 2013.

Hayward, Jennifer. *Consuming Pleasures: Active Audiences and Serial Fictions from Dickens to Soap Opera.* Lexington: University Press of Kentucky, 2009.

Heer, Jeet. *In Love with Art: Françoise Mouly's Adventures in Comics with Art Spiegelman.* Toronto: Coach House Books, 2013.

"Introduction." In *Walt & Skeezix: 1921 & 1922*, by Frank King, edited by Jeet Heer, Chris Oliveros, and Chris Ware, 7–43. Montreal: Drawn & Quarterly, 2006.

"Inventing Cartooning Ancestors: Ware and the Comics Canon." In *The Comics of Chris Ware: Drawing Is a Way of Thinking*, edited by David M. Ball and Martha B. Kuhlman, 3–13. Jackson: University Press of Mississippi, 2010.

Hibbs, Brian. "Tilting at Windmills: Looking at BookScan, 2004." *The Beat*, February 2005. www.comicsbeat.com/tilting-at-windmills-archive/tilting-at-windmills-looking-at-bookscan–2004/, last accessed October 22, 2022.

Hignite, Todd. *In the Studio: Visits with Contemporary Cartoonists.* New Haven, CT: Yale University Press, 2006.

Hoffman, Eric, and Dominick Grace, eds. *Seth: Conversations.* Jackson: University Press of Mississippi, 2015.

Horrocks, Dylan. *Hicksville.* Toronto: Black Eye Comics, 1998.

Huizenga, Kevin. *The Half Men.* Saint Louis, MO: Self-published, 2013.

Hurren, Tracy. "The Golden Age of Reprints: An Analysis of Classic Comics in a Contemporary Industry." MA thesis, Simon Fraser University, 2011.

Hutcheon, Linda. *A Poetics of Postmodernism: History, Theory, Fiction.* New York: Routledge, 1988.

Jenkins, Henry. "Archival, Ephemeral, and Residual: The Functions of Early Comics in Art Spiegelman's *In the Shadow of No Towers*." In *From Comic Strips to Graphic Novels: Contributions to the Theory and History of Graphic Narratives*, edited by Daniel Stein and Jan-Noël Thon, 301–22. Berlin: De Gruyter, 2013.

Comics and Stuff. New York: New York University Press, 2020.

Textual Poachers: Television Fans and Participatory Culture. Revised. London: Routledge, 2013.

Joubert, Bernard. *Polyepoxy: la case la plus copiée.* Brussels: Fondation Paul Cuvelier, 2016.

Juno, Andrea. "Chris Ware." In *Dangerous Drawings: Interviews with Comix & Graphix Artists*, 32–53. New York: Juno Books, 1997.

Kalifa, Dominique. "L'ère de la culture-marchandise." *Revue d'histoire du XIXe siècle* 19 (1999): 7–14.

Kannenberg, Gene, Jr. "Chips Off the Ol' Blockhead: Evidence of Influence in Peanuts Parodies." In *The Comics of Charles Schulz: The Good Grief of Modern Life*, edited by Jared Gardner and Ian Gordon, 197–212. Jackson: University Press of Mississippi, 2017.

"The Comics of Chris Ware: Text, Image, and Visual Narrative Strategies." In *The Language of Comics: Word and Image*, edited by Robin Varnum and Christina T. Gibbons, 174–97. Jackson: University Press of Mississippi, 2001.

Karasik, Paul, and Mark Newgarden. *How to Read Nancy: The Elements of Comics in Three Easy Panels*. Seattle, WA: Fantagraphics Books, 2017.

Kashtan, Aaron. *Between Pen and Pixel: Comics, Materiality, and the Book of the Future*. Columbus: Ohio State University Press, 2018.

Kelleter, Frank. "Five Ways of Looking at Popular Seriality." In *Media of Serial Narrative*, edited by Frank Kelleter, 7–34. Columbus: Ohio State University Press, 2017.

Kelsey, Robin Earle. *Archive Style: Photographs & Illustrations for U.S. Surveys, 1850–1890*. Berkeley: University of California Press, 2007.

Ketelaar, Eric. "Tacit Narratives: The Meanings of Archives." *Archival Science* 1, no. 2 (2001): 131–41.

Kidd, Chip, ed. *Peanuts: The Art of Charles M. Schulz*. New York: Pantheon Books, 2001.

Kidman, Shawna. *Comic Books Incorporated: How the Business of Comics Became the Business of Hollywood*. Oakland: University of California Press, 2019.

King, Frank. *Skeezix and Uncle Walt*. New York: Reilly & Lee, 1924.

Walt & Skeezix: 1923 & 1924. Edited by Jeet Heer, Chris Oliveros, and Chris Ware. Montreal: Drawn & Quarterly, 2006.

Kinross, Robin. *Modern Typography: An Essay in Critical History*. London: Hyphen Press, 1992.

Klock, Geoff. "The Revisionary Superhero Narrative." In *The Superhero Reader*, edited by Charles Hatfield, Jeet Heer, and Kent Worcester, 116–35. Jackson: University Press of Mississippi, 2013.

Kohn, Jessica. *Dessiner des petits mickeys. Une histoire sociale de la BD en France et en Belgique (1945–1968)*. Paris: Éditions de la Sorbonne, 2022.

Kunzle, David. *Father of the Comic Strip: Rodolphe Töpffer*. Jackson: University Press of Mississippi, 2007.

Kwa, Shiamin. "Comics at the Surface: Michael DeForge's *Ant Colony*." *Word & Image* 32, no. 4 (2016): 340–59.

Labarre, Nicolas. *Heavy Metal, l'autre Métal Hurlant*. Bordeaux: Presses Universitaires de Bordeaux, 2017.

Understanding Genres in Comics. Cham: Palgrave, 2020.

Labarre, Nicolas, Laura Perna, and Errol Rivera. "The Circulation of Icons in *Planetary* – Pictures, Popular Culture and Materiality." *E-Rea* 13, no. 1 (2015). https://doi.org/10.4000/erea.4557, last accessed October 22, 2022.

Labio, Catherine. "What's in a Name? The Academic Study of Comics and the 'Graphic Novel.'" *Cinema Journal* 50, no. 3 (2011): 123–26.

Lacassin, Francis. *Mémoires. Sur les chemins qui marchent*. Monaco: Editions du Rocher, 2006.

La Cour, Erin, and Rik Spanjers. "Ingratiation, Appropriation, Rebellion: Comics' Sociability in the Milieux of Art and Literature." *Image [&] Narrative* 17, no. 4 (2016): 1–4.

Laliberte, Mark. *BrickBrickBrick.* Toronto: BookThug, 2010.

Landon, Charles N. "Collecting a Morgue." In *The Landon Course of Cartooning 1.* Cleveland, OH: Landon School, 1914.

Latour, Bruno, and Adam Lowe. "The Migration of the Aura or How to Explore the Original through Its Facsimiles." In *Switching Codes. Thinking Through Digital Technology in the Humanities and the Arts,* edited by Thomas Bartscherer, 275–97. Chicago, IL: University of Chicago Press, 2011.

Lawley, Guy. "Ben Day Dots: 1950s and 60s – the 'Silver Age' of Comics." April 6–7, 2021. legionofandy.com/category/ben-day/, last accessed October 22, 2022.

Leacock, Stephen. *Sunshine Sketches of a Little Town.* New York: Skyhorse, 2013.

Lefèvre, Pascal, and Charles Dierick, eds. *Forging a New Medium: The Comic Strip in the Nineteenth Century.* Brussels: VUB University Press, 1998.

Leibovici, Franck. *des opérations d'écriture qui ne disent pas leur nom.* Paris: Questions théoriques, 2020.

Lesage, Sylvain. *L'Effet livre: métamorphoses de la bande dessinée.* Tours: Presses Universitaires François-Rabelais, 2019.

Publier la bande dessinée: les éditeurs franco-belges et l'album, 1950-1990. Villeurbanne: Presses de l'Enssib, 2018.

Lesage, Sylvain, and Bounthavy Suvilay. "Introduction thématique: pour un tournant matériel des études sur la bande dessinée." *Comicalités,* December 21, 2019. http://journals.openedition.org/comicalites/3692, last accessed October 22, 2022.

Lethem, Jonathan. "The Ecstasy of Influence: A Plagiarism." *Harper's Magazine,* February 2007.

Letourneux, Matthieu. *Fictions à la chaîne: littératures sérielles et culture médiatique.* Paris: Seuil, 2017.

Levin, Bob. *The Pirates and the Mouse: Disney's War against the Counterculture.* Seattle, WA: Fantagraphics Books, 2003.

Liew, Sonny. *The Art of Charlie Chan Hock Chye.* Singapore: Epigram Books, 2015.

Lowenthal, David. *The Heritage Crusade and the Spoils of History.* Cambridge: Cambridge University Press, 2010.

The Past Is a Foreign Country – Revisited. Cambridge: Cambridge University Press, 2013.

LTTR 13. "Figures de l'énonciation: les gestes discursifs du savoir." In *Figures en discours: au cœur des textes,* edited by Amir Biglari and Geneviève Salvan, 93–116. Louvain-la-Neuve: Academia/L'Harmattan, 2016.

Maigret, Eric. "Bande dessinée et postlégitimité." In *La bande dessinée: une médiaculture,* 130–48. Collection "Médiacultures." Paris: Armand Colin, 2012.

Manouach, Ilan. *Blanco* (Brussels: La Cinquième Couche, 2018).

Compendium of Franco-Belgian Comics. Brussels: La Cinquième Couche, 2018.

"Conceptual Comics," April 28, 2019. https://monoskop.org/Conceptual_comics, last accessed October 22, 2022.

Katz. Brussels: La Cinquième Couche, 2011.

MetaKatz. Brussels: La Cinquième Couche, 2013.

Peanuts Minus Schulz: Distributed Labor as a Compositional Practice. Paris: Jean Boîte éditions, 2021.

Riki fermier. Brussels: La Cinquième Couche, 2015.

The Cubicle Island. Brussels: La Cinquième Couche, 2019.

"The Library," *Futures of Comics* website, n.d. https://futuresofcomics.org/gu ests/library, last accessed October 22, 2022.

Manovich, Lev. *The Language of New Media.* Cambridge, MA: MIT Press, 2001.

"The Practice of Everyday (Media) Life: From Mass Consumption to Mass Cultural Production?" *Critical Inquiry* 35, no. 2 (2009): 319–31.

Marion, Philippe. "La bande dessinée et ses identités culturelles. Paysages et frontières." In *Le Statut culturel de la bande dessinée: ambiguïtés et évolutions / The Cultural Standing of Comics: Ambiguities and Change,* edited by Maaheen Ahmed, Stéphanie Delneste, and Jean-Louis Tilleuil, 39–52. Louvain-la-Neuve: Academia-L'Harmattan, 2016.

"Narratologie médiatique et médiagénie des récits." *Recherches en communication* 7 (1997): 61–88.

Traces en cases: travail graphique, figuration narrative et participation du lecteur. Louvain-la-Neuve: Academia, 1993.

Marks, Laura U. *Touch: Sensuous Theory and Multisensory Media.* Minneapolis: Minnesota University Press, 2002.

Marrone, Daniel. *Forging the Past: Seth and the Art of Memory.* Jackson: University Press of Mississippi, 2016.

Martin, Côme. "Les Livres-mondes de Chris Ware, ou la tentation de l'homogène." *Formules* 17 (2013): 69–88.

Maupeu, Philippe. "Montage et hantise chez Charles Burns (*ToXic, La Ruche, Calavera*)." *Textimage* 6 (2016). http://revue-textimage.com/conferencier/06_ montage_demontage_remontage/maupeu1.html, last accessed October 22, 2022.

Mazeau, Guillaume. *Histoire.* Paris: Anamosa, 2020.

McCrory, Amy. "Archiving Newspaper Comic Strips: The San Francisco Academy of Comic Art Collection." *Archival Issues* 27, no. 2 (2002): 137–50.

McGrath, Charles. "Not Funnies." *The New York Times Magazine,* July 11, 2004.

McLuhan, Marshall. *Understanding Media: Extensions of Man.* New York: McGraw-Hill, 1964.

Meesters, Gert. "Les significations du style graphique: *Mon fiston* d'Olivier Schrauwen et *Faire semblant c'est mentir* de Dominique Goblet." *Textyles* 36/37 (2010): 215–33.

Menu, Jean-Christophe. *Plates-bandes.* Paris: l'Association, 2005.

Méon, Jean-Matthieu. "Comics Exhibitions in Contemporary France: Diversity and Symbolic Ambivalence." *International Journal of Comic Art* 17, no. 1 (2015): 446–64.

"Fragmenter, matérialiser. Prises en charge de la matérialité de la bande dessinée par l'exposition." *Comicalités,* December 21, 2019. http://journals .openedition.org/comicalites/3711, last accessed October 22, 2022.

"Introduire le graphic novel, une ambition circonscrite: les premiers usages nord-américains de l'étiquette et leur péritexte." *Revue française d'études américaines* 151 (2017): 176–93.

"Logiques et pratiques de l'intermédiation dans l'édition de bande dessinée en France." In *La culture et ses intermédiaires,* edited by

Laurent Jeanpierre and Olivier Roueff. Paris: Éditions des archives contemporaines, 2014.

"Sons and Grandsons of Origins: Narrative Memory in Mainstream Superhero Publishing." In *Comics Memory: Archives and Styles*, edited by Maaheen Ahmed and Benoît Crucifix, 189–210. New York: Palgrave, 2019.

"Tisser d'autres liens? Pratiques éditoriales et discours critique de l'éditeur PictureBox: indépendance et champ de la bande dessinée." In *La bande dessinée en dissidence alternative, indépendance, auto-édition / Comics in dissent: alternative, independence, self-publishing*, edited by Christophe Dony, Tanguy Habrand, and Gert Meesters, 79–92. Liège: Presses Universitaires de Liège, 2014.

Miller, Ann, and Bart Beaty, eds. *French Comics Theory Reader*. Leuven: Leuven University Press, 2014.

Miller, Rachel R. "Keep Out, or Else: Girls' Diaries in Comics." *Public Books*, May 4, 2018. www.publicbooks.org/keep-out-or-else-girls-diaries-in-comics/, last accessed October 22, 2022.

"When Feminism Went to Market: Issues in Feminist Anthology Comics of the 1980s and '90s." In *The Oxford Handbook of Comic Book Studies*, edited by Frederick Luis Aldama, 419–36. Oxford: Oxford University Press, 2019.

Mitchell, W. J. T., and Art Spiegelman. "Public Conversation: What the %$#! Happened to Comics?" *Critical Inquiry* 40, no. 3 (2014): 20–35.

Mittell, Jason. *Complex TV: The Poetics of Contemporary Television Storytelling*. New York: New York University Press, 2015.

Moine, Florian. "Bande dessinée et patrimoine. Histoire du Musée de la bande dessinée d'Angoulême (1983–2010)." Unpublished MA thesis, Université Paris 1 Panthéon-Sorbonne, 2013.

"Construire la légitimité 26ulturelle du Neuvième Art: Le musée de la bande dessinée d'Angoulême." *Belphégor* 17, no. 1 (2019): 1–13.

Molotiu, Andrei. "Art Comics." In *The Routledge Companion to Comics*, edited by Frank Bramlett, Roy T. Cook, and Aaron Meskin, 119–27. London: Routledge, 2016.

Moore, Alan, and Eddie Campbell. *From Hell*. Marietta, GA: Top Shelf, 1999.

Moura, Pedro. "Les Schtroumpfs Noirs." *Du9 – l'autre bande dessinée*, April 2014. https://www.du9.org/en/chronique/les-schtroumpfs-noirs-2/.

Mulvey, Laura. *Death 24x a Second: Stillness and the Moving Image*. London: Reaktion Books, 2006.

Muñoz, José, and Carlos Sampayo. *Alack Sinner: The Age of Disenchantment*. San Diego, CA: IDW, 2017.

"Pour quelques dessins …," translated by Dominique Grange. (*À suivre*) 159 (S1991).

Munson, Kim. "Forming a Visual Canon: Comics in Museums." In *The Secret Origins of Comics Studies*, edited by Matthew J. Smith and Randy Duncan, 226–39. New York: Routledge, 2017.

Murray, Simone. *The Adaptation Industry: The Cultural Economy of Contemporary Literary Adaptation*. New York: Routledge, 2012.

Nadel, Dan, ed. *Art Out of Time: Unknown Comics Visionaries, 1900-1969*. New York: Abrams, 2006.

ed. "Bill Blackbeard: Tributes." *The Comics Journal* (April 25, 2011). www .tcj.com/bill-blackbeard-tributes/, last accessed October 22, 2022.

Nel, Philip. "Crockett Johnson and the Purple Crayon: A Life in Art." *Comic Art* 5 (2004): 2–18.

Newgarden, Mark. "Love's Savage Fury." *RAW*, 1986.

Niemeyer, Katharina, ed. *Media and Nostalgia: Yearning for the Past, Present and Future.* New York: Palgrave Macmillan, 2014.

Nora, Pierre. "Between Memory and History: Les Lieux de Mémoire." *Representations* 26 (1989): 7–24.

Obrist, Hans Ulrich. *Ways of Curating.* London: Penguin, 2014.

Ogborn, Miles. "Archives." In *Patterned Ground: Entanglements of Nature and Culture*, edited by Stephan Harrison, Steve Pile, and Nigel J. Thrift, 240–42. London: Reaktion Books, 2004.

Oksman, Tahneer, and Seamus O'Malley, eds. *The Comics of Julie Doucet and Gabrielle Bell: A Place inside Yourself.* Jackson: University Press of Mississippi, 2019.

O'Neill, Paul. "The Curatorial Turn: From Practice to Discourse." In *Issues in Curating Contemporary Art and Performance*, edited by Judith Rugg and Michèle Sedgwick, 13–28. Bristol: Intellect, 2007.

O'Toole, James M. "Do Not Fold, Spindle, or Mutilate." *The American Archivist* 64, no. 2 (2001): 385–93.

Panofsky, Erwin. "The History of Art as a Humanistic Discipline." In *Meaning in the Visual Arts: Papers in and on Art History*, 1–26. Garden City, NY: Doubleday Anchor Books, 1955.

Parikka, Jussi. "Copy." In *Software Studies*, edited by Matthew Fuller, 70–78. Cambridge, MA: MIT Press, 2008.

Parille, Ken. "Secret Loves: A Short History of Two Panels in Charles Burns's The Hive." *The Comics Journal* (November 26, 2012). www.tcj.com/secret-loves-a-sh ort-history-of-two-panels-in-charles-burnss-the-hive/, last accessed October 22, 2022.

Parker, Dorothy. *The Portable Dorothy Parker*, edited by Marion Meade. London: Penguin, 2006.

Parmenter, Dan. "To Swipe or Not to Swipe." *The Comics Journal* 109 (1986): 35.

Peeters, Benoît. "Between Writing and Image: A Scriptwriter's Way of Working." *European Comic Art* 3, no. 1 (2010): 105–15.

Lire la bande dessinée. Paris: Flammarion, 2003.

Perloff, Marjorie. *Unoriginal Genius: Poetry by Other Means in the New Century.* Chicago, IL: University of Chicago Press, 2012.

Pizzino, Christopher. *Arresting Development: Comics at the Boundaries of Literature.* Austin: University of Texas Press, 2016.

"Comics History and the Question of Delinquency: The Case of *Criminal.*" In *Comics Memory: Archives and Styles*, edited by Maaheen Ahmed and Benoît Crucifix, 165–85. New York: Palgrave, 2018.

Powers, Thom. "Muñoz vs. Giffen: Plagiarism or Influence?" *The Comics Journal* 118 (1987): 19–20.

Price, Garrett. *White Boy in Skull Valley.* Palo Alto, CA: Sunday Press Books, 2015.

Printers' Ink. "The Persistent 'Swipe' Evil." *Printers' Ink: A Journal of Advertisers* 71, no. 11 (1910).

Pustz, Matthew. *Comic Book Culture: Fanboys and True Believers*. Jackson: University Press of Mississippi, 1999.

Raeburn, Daniel K. *Chris Ware*. New Haven, CT: Yale University Press, 2004.

Rajewsky, Irina O. "Intermediality, Intertextuality, and Remediation: A Literary Perspective on Intermediality." *Intermédialités* 6 (2005): 43–64.

Regé, Jr., Ron. *Diana*. Echo Park, LA: Self-published, 2013.

Reynolds, Simon. *Retromania: Pop Culture's Addiction to Its Own Past*. London: Faber and Faber, 2011.

Rifkind, Candida. "The Biotopographies of Seth's *George Sprott (1894-1975)*." In *Material Cultures in Canada*, edited by Thomas Allen and Jennifer Blair. Waterloo, ONT: Wilfrid Laurier University Press, 2015.

Rigney, Ann. "Portable Monuments: Literature, Cultural Memory, and the Case of Jeanie Deans." *Poetics Today* 25, no. 2 (June 1, 2004): 361–96.

Robb, Jenny E. "Bill Blackbeard: The Collector Who Rescued the Comics." *Journal of American Culture* 32, no. 3 (2009): 244–56.

"The Librarians and Archivists." In *The Secret Origins of Comics Studies*, edited by Matthew J. Smith and Randy Duncan, 71–88. New York: Routledge, 2017.

Robbins, Trina. *A Century of Women Cartoonists*. Northampton, MA: Kitchen Sink Press, 1993.

From Girls to Grrrlz: A History of Women's Comics from Teens to Zines. San Francisco, CA: Chronicle Books, 1999.

Nell Brinkley and the New Woman in the Early 20th Century. Jefferson, NC: McFarland, 2001.

Robbins, Trina, and Catherine Yronwode. *Women and the Comics*. New York: Eclipse, 1985.

Robinson, M. J. *Television on Demand. Curatorial Culture and the Transformation of TV*. London: Bloomsbury, 2017.

Rogers, Sean, and Jeet Heer. "A History of Drawn & Quarterly." In *Drawn and Quarterly: Twenty-Five Years of Contemporary Cartooning, Comics, and Graphic Novels*, edited by Tom Devlin, Chris Oliveros, Peggy Burns, Tracy Hurren, and Julia Pohl-Miranda, 13–57. Montreal: Drawn & Quarterly, 2016.

Rosset, Christian. "Tenir le mur." *Neuvième Art* 15 (2009): 166–75.

Russell, Catherine. *Archiveology: Walter Benjamin and Archival Film Practices*. Durham, NC: Duke University Press, 2018.

Saint-Amour, Paul K. *The Copywrights: Intellectual Property and the Literary Imagination*. Ithaca, NY: Cornell University Press, 2003.

Santoro, Frank. "Herriman Riff." *The Comics Journal* (January 7, 2016). www.tcj.com/herriman-riff/, last accessed October 22, 2022.

Schelly, Bill. *Harvey Kurtzman, The Man Who Created* Mad *and Revolutionized Humor in America: A Biography*. Seattle, WA: Fantagraphics Books, 2015.

Schlanger, Judith. *Le neuf, le différent et le déjà-là: une exploration de l'influence*. Paris: Hermann, 2014.

Schlanger, Judith. *Présence des œuvres perdues*. Paris: Hermann, 2010.

Schneider, Greice. *What Happens When Nothing Happens: Boredom and Everyday Life in Contemporary Comics*. Leuven: Leuven University Press, 2016.

Schrauwen, Olivier. *My Boy*. Antwerp: Bries, 2006.

Schrey, Dominik. "Analogue Nostalgia and the Aesthetics of the Digital." In *Media and Nostalgia: Yearning for the Past, Present and Future*, edited by Katharina Niemeyer, 27–38. New York: Palgrave Macmillan, 2014.

Seldes, Gilbert. *The Seven Lively Arts*. New York: Harper & Brothers, 1924.

"The 'Vulgar' Comic Strip." In *A Comics Studies Reader*, edited by Jeet Heer and Kent Worcester, 46–52. Jackson: University Press of Mississippi, 2009.

Seth. "Afterword." In *Graphic Witness: Four Wordless Graphic Novels*, edited by George A. Walker, 415–16. Buffalo, NY: Firefly Books, 2007.

"Creating a Personal Vernacular Canadian Design Style." *Devil's Artisan* 69 (2011): 3–60.

It's a Good Life, If You Don't Weaken. Montreal: Drawn & Quarterly, 1996.

"John Stanley's Teen Trilogy: Exposing Forgotten Comics History." *The Comics Journal* 238 (2001): 39–51.

The G.N.B Double C: The Great Northern Brotherhood of Canadian Cartoonists. Montreal: Drawn and Quarterly, 2011.

Sikoryak, R. *Terms and Conditions: The Graphic Novel*. Montreal: Drawn & Quarterly, 2017.

The Unquotable Trump, https://drawnandquarterly.com/unquotable-trump, last accessed October 22, 2022.

Sikoryak, Robert. "Good Ol' Gregor Brown." *RAW* 2, no. 2 (1990).

Masterpiece Comics. Montreal: Drawn and Quarterly, 2009.

Sinervo, Kalervo A. "Pirates and Publishers: Comics Scanning and the Audience Function." In *The Comics World: Comic Books, Graphic Novels, and Their Publics*, edited by Benjamin Woo and Jeremy Stoll, 208–33. Jackson: University Press of Mississippi, 2021.

Singer, Marc. *Breaking the Frame: Populism and Prestige in Comics Studies*. Austin: University of Texas Press, 2019.

Singsen, Doug. "Critical Perspectives on Mainstream, Groundlevel, and Alternative Comics in *The Comics Journal*, 1977 to 1996." *Journal of Graphic Novels and Comics* 8, no. 2 (2017): 156–72.

Smolderen, Thierry. "A Chapter on Methodology." *SIGNs: Studies in Graphic Narratives* 2, no. 1 (2011): 1–23.

"Attraction, auteurisation, institutionnalisation. Notes pour une théorie historique des configurations éditoriales." In *La Bande Dessinée à la Croisée des Médias*, edited by Désirée Lorenz and Elsa Caboche, 160–70. Tours: Presses Universitaires François-Rabelais, 2019.

The Origins of Comics: From William Hogarth to Winsor McCay, translated by Bart Beaty and Nick Nguyen. Jackson: University Press of Mississippi, 2014.

Souchier, Emmanuël. "Formes et pouvoirs de l'énonciation éditoriale." *Communication et langages* 154, no. 1 (2007): 23–38.

Spiegelman, Art. *Co-Mix: A Retrospective of Comics, Graphics, and Scraps*. Montreal: Drawn & Quarterly, 2013.

Comix, Graphics, Essays & Scraps: From Maus to Now to MAUS to Now. New York: Raw Books/Sellerio, 1998.

"Commix: An Idiosyncratic Historical and Aesthetic Overview." *Print* 42, no. 6 (1988): 61–96.

In the Shadow of No Towers. New York: Pantheon Books, 2004.

"Le Musée privé d'Art Spiegelman," *Cité internationale de la bande dessinée*, April 2014. www.citebd.org/spip.php?article3385, last accessed October 22, 2022.

MetaMaus, edited by Hillary Chute. New York: Pantheon Books, 2011.

ed., "Noble Efforts," *Nostalgia Comics* 1 (1970): 30–35.

"The Malpractice Suite." *Arcade* 6 (1976): 12–13.

"Wacky Days." In *Wacky Packages*, edited by Charles Kochman. New York: Abrams, 2008.

Spiegelman, Art, and Bill Griffith, "The Arcade Archives," *Arcade* 1, no. 4 (1975): 41–44.

Spiegelman, Art, and Chip Kidd. *Jack Cole and Plastic Man: Forms Stretched to Their Limits*. San Francisco, CA: Chronicle Books, 2001.

Spurgeon, Tom, and Michael Dean, eds. *We Told You So: Comics as Art*. Seattle, WA: Fantagraphics Books, 2016.

Starre, Alexander. "American Comics Anthologies: Mediality – Canonization – Transnationalism." In *Transnational American Studies*, edited by Udo J. Hebel, 541–60. Heidelberg: Winter, 2012.

Metamedia: American Book Fictions and Literary Print Culture after Digitization. Iowa City: University of Iowa Press, 2015.

Stefanelli, Matteo. "La bande dessinée, expérience 'archivable'. La mémoire en bédé, entre dispositifs de lecture et stratégies culturelles." *Cinergie* 4 (2010): 114–19.

Stein, Daniel. "'Mummified Objects': Superhero Comics in the Digital Age." *Journal of Graphic Novels and Comics* 7, no. 3 (2016): 283–92.

Stein, Daniel, and Lukas Etter. "Long-Length Serials in the Golden Age of Comic Strips: Production and Reception." In *The Cambridge History of the Graphic Novel*, edited by Jan Baetens, Hugo Frey, and Stephen E. Tabachnick, 39–58. Cambridge: Cambridge University Press, 2018.

Stewart, Bhob. "Bubbling Over." *Blab!* 3 (1988): 20–35.

Stoler, Ann Laura. *Along the Archival Grain: Epistemic Anxieties and Colonial Common Sense*. Princeton, NJ: Princeton University Press, 2009.

Straw, Will. "Circulation." In *A Companion to Critical and Cultural Theory*, edited by Imre Szeman, Sarah Blacker, and Justin Sully, 423–33. Chichester: Wiley, 2017.

"Embedded Memories." In *Residual Media*, edited by Charles R. Acland, 3–15. Minneapolis: University of Minnesota Press, 2007.

"Systems of Articulation, Logics of Change: Communities and Scenes in Popular Music." *Cultural Studies* 5, no. 3 (1991): 368–88.

Sullivan, Darcy. "Charles Burns." *The Comics Journal* (1992).

Taylor, Diana. *The Archive and the Repertoire: Performing Cultural Memory in the Americas*. Durham, NC: Duke University Press, 2003.

Thérenty, Marie-Ève. "Pour une poétique historique du support." *Romantisme* 143 (2009): 109–15.

Tinker, Emma. "Manuscript in Print: The Materiality of Alternative Comics." *Literature Compass* 4, no. 4 (2007): 1169–82.

Töpffer, Rodolphe. "Notice sur la contrefaçon de *L'Histoire de M. Jabot*." In *M. Töpffer invente la bande dessinée*, edited by Thierry Groensteen, 221–22. Brussels: Les Impressions Nouvelles, 2014.

Trabado, José Manuel. *Antes de la novela gráfica. Clásicos del cómic en la prensa norteamericana.* Madrid: Cátedra, 2012.

Vaillant, Alain. "L'édition des textes du passé: enjeu théorique et marché éditorial en l'an 2000." *Littérature* 124 (2001): 98–108.

Van Alphen, Ernst. *Staging the Archive: Art and Photography in the Age of New Media.* London: Reaktion Books, 2014.

Vienne, Véronique. *Chip Kidd.* London: Laurence King, 2003.

Wanzo, Rebecca Ann. *The Content of Our Caricature: African American Comic Art and Political Belonging.* New York: New York University Press, 2020.

Ware, Chris. "Frank King." In *Drawn and Quarterly* 3. Montreal: Drawn & Quarterly, 2000.

"I Guess." *RAW* 2, no. 3 (1991).

ed. *McSweeney's Quarterly Concern, Issue Number 13.* San Francisco, CA: McSweeney's, 2004.

"Skeezix for Sale: A Semi-Comprehensive Catalog of the Merchandise of *Gasoline Alley.*" In *Walt & Skeezix: 1925 & 1926*, by Frank King, edited by Jeet Heer, Chris Oliveros, and Chris Ware, 24–61. Montreal: Drawn & Quarterly, 2007.

Warner, Michael. *Publics and Counterpublics.* New York: Zone Books, 2010.

Waugh, Coulton. *The Comics.* Reprint of the 1947 original. Jackson: University Press of Mississippi, 1991.

Wershler, Darren. "Digital Comics, Circulation, and the Importance of Being Eric Sluis." *Cinema Journal* 50, no. 3 (2011): 127–34.

Wershler, Darren, and Kalervo A. Sinervo. "Marvel and the Form of Motion Comics." In *Make Ours Marvel: Media Convergence and a Comics Universe*, edited by Matt Yockey, 187–206. Austin: University of Texas Press, 2017.

Wertham, Fredric. *The World of Fanzines: A Special Form of Communication.* Carbondale: Southern Illinois University Press, 1973.

White, Ted. "It All Boils Down to the Editor." *The Comics Journal* 83 (1983): 31–36.

Widiss, Benjamin. "Autobiography with Two Heads: *Quimby the Mouse.*" In *The Comics of Chris Ware: Drawing Is a Way of Thinking*, edited by David M. Ball and Martha B. Kuhlman, 159–73. Jackson: University Press of Mississippi, 2010.

Williams, Dylan. "An Interview with Bill Blackbeard." *Destroy All Comics* 3 (1995): 15–31.

Williams, Paul. *Dreaming the Graphic Novel: The Novelization of Comics.* New Brunswick, NJ: Rutgers University Press, 2020.

Williams, Paul, and Jim Woodring. "Interview: Jim Woodring." In *The Rise of the American Comics Artist: Creators and Contexts*, edited by Paul Williams and James Lyons, 124–32. Jackson: University Press of Mississippi, 2010.

Witek, Joseph. "If a Way to the Better There Be: Excellence, Mere Competence, and the Worst Comics Ever Made." *Image [&] Narrative* 17, no. 4 (2016): 26–42.

Wojcik, Pamela Robertson. "Little Orphan Annie as Streetwalker." In *Picturing Childhood: Youth in Transnational Comics*, edited by Mark Heimerman and Brittany Tullis, 13–29. Austin: University of Texas Press, 2017.

Woo, Benjamin. "An Age-Old Problem: Problematics of Comic Book Historiography." *International Journal of Comic Art* 10, no. 1 (2008): 268–79.

"Is There a Comic Book Industry?" *Media Industries Journal* 5, no. 1 (June 5, 2018). https://doi.org/10.3998/mij.15031809.0005.102, last accessed October 22, 2022.

"The Android's Dungeon: Comic-Bookstores, Cultural Spaces, and the Social Practices of Audiences." *Journal of Graphic Novels & Comics* 2, no. 2 (2011): 125–36.

Worden, Daniel. "Introduction: R. Crumb in Comics History." In *The Comics of R. Crumb: Underground in the Art Museum,* edited by Daniel Worden, 3–18. Jackson: University Press of Mississippi, 2021.

"The Shameful Art: *McSweeney's Quarterly Concern,* Comics, and the Politics of Affect." *Modern Fiction Studies* 52, no. 4 (2006): 892–917.

Yong, Charissa. "NAC Pulled Grant from Comic as It 'Potentially Undermines the Authority of the Government.'" *The Straits Times,* June 3, 2015.

Index

Ingram Content Group UK Ltd.
Milton Keynes UK
UKHW010656270723
425860UK00004B/9